Verse by Verse Commentary on the Book of

2 KINGS

Enduring Word Commentary Series
By David Guzik

*The grass withers, the flower fades,
but the word of our God stands forever.*
Isaiah 40:8

Commentary on 2 Kings

Copyright ©2018 by David Guzik

Printed in the United States of America or in the United Kingdom

Print Edition ISBN: 978-1-939466-44-0

Enduring Word

5662 Calle Real #184

Goleta, CA 93117

Electronic Mail: ewm@enduringword.com

Internet Home Page: www.enduringword.com

All rights reserved. No portion of this book may be reproduced in any form (except for quotations in reviews) without the written permission of the publisher.

Scripture references, unless noted, are from the New King James Version of the Bible, copyright ©1979, 1980, 1982, Thomas Nelson, Inc., Publisher.

Contents

2 Kings 1 – Ahaziah and Elijah 7
2 Kings 2 – Elijah's Ascension 14
2 Kings 3 – War Against Moab 22
2 Kings 4 – God Works Miracles Through Elisha 30
2 Kings 5 – Naaman the Leper 39
2 Kings 6 – God's Protection of Elisha 48
2 Kings 7 – God's Miraculous Provision for Samaria 55
2 Kings 8 – New Kings in Syria and Judah 62
2 Kings 9 – Jehu Takes the Throne of Israel 71
2 Kings 10 – The Reforms of Jehu 79
2 Kings 11 – The Young King Joash 87
2 Kings 12 – The Reign of King Jehoash over Judah 93
2 Kings 13 – The Death of Elisha 99
2 Kings 14 – The Reigns of Amaziah and Jeroboam II 107
2 Kings 15 – Unstable Monarchy in Israel 115
2 Kings 16 – The Compromise of Ahaz 125
2 Kings 17 – The Fall of Israel 134
2 Kings 18 – Hezekiah's Reign; Assyria's Threat 145
2 Kings 19 – God Delivers Jerusalem from Assyria 157
2 Kings 20 – God Extends Hezekiah's Life 170
2 Kings 21 – The Wicked Reigns of Manasseh and Amon 180
2 Kings 22 – King Josiah Finds the Book of the Law 188
2 Kings 23 – The Reforms of Josiah 196
2 Kings 24 – Judah Subjected Under Babylon 206
2 Kings 25 – The Fall of Jerusalem and the Captivity of Judah 213

Bibliography - Page 221
Remarks from the Author - Page 223

2 Kings 1 – Ahaziah and Elijah

A. Ahaziah's injury.

1. (1-2) Ahaziah seeks Baal-Zebub.

Moab rebelled against Israel after the death of Ahab. Now Ahaziah fell through the lattice of his upper room in Samaria, and was injured; so he sent messengers and said to them, "Go, inquire of Baal-Zebub, the god of Ekron, whether I shall recover from this injury."

a. **Moab rebelled against Israel after the death of Ahab**: The reign of Ahab was a spiritual disaster for the Northern Kingdom, but it was a time of political security and economic prosperity. After his death the kingdom of Moab found a good opportunity to remove their nation from the domination of Israel.

i. "Their land was immediately east of the Dead Sea and shared an indefinite border with Israel to the north at approximately the point where the Jordan River enters the Dead Sea." (Dilday)

ii. Moab had been under Israelite domination since the days of David (2 Samuel 8:2 and 8:11-12). This rebellion of Moab in the days of Ahaziah was a sign of the decline of Israel's power and of the judgment of God.

b. **Ahaziah fell through the lattice of his upper room in Samaria**: This was surely an unexpected crisis. Such accidents happen to kings and peasants both.

i. "The king apparently leaned against the wooden screen and fell through from the second-floor balcony to the ground below." (Dilday)

c. **Go, inquire of Baal-Zebub, the god of Ekron, whether I shall recover from this injury**: Ahaziah showed that he was a true worshipper of the pagan god Baal-Zebub because he turned to this god in his time of trouble.

i. "This could suggest that Baal-Zebub was a god who warded off plagues that were brought on by flies. There are numerous references to 'fly gods' in classical literature." (Dilday)

ii. "He was the local god of Ekron, and probably was used at first to drive away flies. Afterwards, he became a very respectable devil, and was supposed to have great power and influence. In the New Testament, Beelzebub is a common name for Satan himself, or the prince of devils." (Adam Clarke)

iii. "Men love the gods that are most like unto themselves, so it is not surprising to see Ahaziah sending to this miserable Philistine god." (Knapp)

2. (3-4) Elijah's message to Ahaziah.

But the angel of the LORD said to Elijah the Tishbite, "Arise, go up to meet the messengers of the king of Samaria, and say to them, 'Is it because *there is* no God in Israel *that* you are going to inquire of Baal-Zebub, the god of Ekron?' Now therefore, thus says the LORD: 'You shall not come down from the bed to which you have gone up, but you shall surely die.'" So Elijah departed.

a. **Is it because there is no God in Israel**: There is little doubt that King Ahaziah believed that Yahweh lived, but he *lived* as if there were **no God in Israel**. He was a practical atheist, and the way he sought Baal-Zebub *instead* of the LORD demonstrated this.

b. **You shall not come down from the bed to which you have gone up, but you shall surely die**: Ahaziah did not seek help from the *real* God; therefore he will get no *real* help. Instead this will be an occasion for the *real* God to send a message of judgment to King Ahaziah.

i. According to Wiseman, when ancients sought their gods about medical issues, "The result was usually given in medical prognostic texts as 'he will live/die' as in verses 6, 16 (*you will certainly die*)." This means that Elijah's words **but you shall surely die** were phrased as a medical diagnosis. It was as if Elijah said, "Here's your diagnosis, Ahaziah: Your condition is fatal and irreversible."

ii. In fact, this was a *mercy* to Ahaziah. God told him something that few people know. His death was imminent, and he had time to repent and prepare to meet God.

iii. This prophetic announcement might also explain why Ahaziah did not want to seek an answer from the LORD: He knew what the answer would be. In seeking Baal-Zebub for an answer, Ahaziah may have wanted to find a god to tell him what he wanted to hear.

3. (5-8) The messengers return to Ahaziah.

And when the messengers returned to him, he said to them, "Why have you come back?" So they said to him, "A man came up to meet us, and said to us, 'Go, return to the king who sent you, and say to him, "Thus says the LORD: '*Is it* because *there is* no God in Israel *that* you are sending to inquire of Baal-Zebub, the god of Ekron? Therefore you shall not come down from the bed to which you have gone up, but you shall surely die.'"'" Then he said to them, "What kind of man *was it* who came up to meet you and told you these words?" So they answered him, "A hairy man wearing a leather belt around his waist." And he said, "It *is* Elijah the Tishbite."

a. **A man came up to meet us**: Though they were sent to seek a word from the pagan priests of Baal-Zebub, the word from Elijah persuaded them so much that they didn't follow through on their original mission.

i. "This official delegation from the king would certainly not have turned back from their royal assignment just because some anonymous wayfarer asked them to. There must have been an irresistible quality to Elijah's personality, a forceful spiritual presence, that compelled them to obey this stranger even though they didn't know who he was." (Dilday)

b. **What kind of man was it who came up to meet you**: Ahaziah clearly suspected it was the Prophet Elijah who spoke this word. His suspicion was confirmed when the **man** was described as **a hairy man wearing a leather belt around his waist**.

i. The Hebrew words translated **hairy man** literally mean, "possessor of hair." "This description more than likely refers to the hairy animal skins he wore clinched around his waist with a leather belt." (Dilday)

ii. Identifying Elijah by his clothes also connected him to the ministry of John the Baptist, who dressed in hairy skins from animals (Matthew 3:4). When the priests and Levites saw him they asked, "Are you Elijah?" (John 1:19-21)

iii. "Either because Elijah had much hair on his head and face, or because, as a prophet, he wore a rough garment (Zechariah 13:4), as a pattern of repentance." (Trapp)

B. Elijah appears before Ahaziah.

1. (9-10) Judgment comes upon the arresting soldiers.

Then the king sent to him a captain of fifty with his fifty men. So he went up to him; and there he was, sitting on the top of a hill. And he

spoke to him: "Man of God, the king has said, 'Come down!'" So Elijah answered and said to the captain of fifty, "If I *am* a man of God, then let fire come down from heaven and consume you and your fifty men." And fire came down from heaven and consumed him and his fifty.

a. **The king sent to him a captain of fifty with his fifty men**: This should have been plenty of men to capture one prophet. Clearly, Ahaziah sent *more* men than were normally required.

b. **Man of God, the king has said, "Come down"**: The captain here admitted the righteousness of Elijah when he called him "**Man of God.**" Therefore they were wrong in doing this, even though they were on orders from their king.

i. The Bible clearly teaches that we owe submission to the government and governing authorities (Romans 13:1-2). Yet in the human sphere, the Biblical command to submit is never absolute, but always conditioned by the greater responsibility to submit to God (Acts 5:29). This commander should have resisted the ungodly and immoral command from King Ahaziah and obeyed God instead. His **fifty** men should have refused to obey the ungodly and immoral command of their **captain**.

c. **If I am a man of God, then let fire come down from heaven**: Elijah put the issue in stark contrast. If he really were **a man of God**, then the captain and his men were on an ungodly and immoral mission. Since Elijah could not bring down **fire** from heaven without Divine approval, he asked *God* to evaluate these men and the rightness of their actions against God's prophet.

i. "Either they did not hold him to be a prophet, or they gloried in putting the power of their master above that of Jehovah. In any case, the insult was less against Elijah than Elijah's God." (Meyer)

ii. Elijah did not say, "You bet I am a man of God." Instead, he answered **If I am a man of God**. Essentially Elijah said, "You say I am a man of God even though you are not acting like it. Maybe I am and maybe I am not. Let's let God decide by fire."

iii. "Some have blamed the prophet for destroying these men, by bringing down fire from heaven upon them. But they do not consider that it was no more possible for *Elijah* to bring down fire from heaven, than for *them* to do it. *God alone* could send the fire; and as he is *just* and *good*, he would not have destroyed these men had there not been a *sufficient cause* to justify the act." (Clarke)

d. **Fire came down from heaven and consumed him and his fifty**: God brought judgment on these men who acted as if Yahweh was not a real God and as if Elijah was not truly His servant.

i. The captain commanded Elijah to **"Come down!"** The man of God didn't come down, but the fire of God did.

ii. "It must be noted that the demands made of Elijah were wrong. A king had no right to ask such allegiance and his actions should always be subordinate to God's word. God was protecting his word and his servant." (Wiseman)

2. (11-12) Judgment also comes upon a second captain.

Then he sent to him another captain of fifty with his fifty men. And he answered and said to him: "Man of God, thus has the king said, 'Come down quickly!'" So Elijah answered and said to them, "If I *am* a man of God, let fire come down from heaven and consume you and your fifty men." And the fire of God came down from heaven and consumed him and his fifty.

a. **Man of God, thus has the king said**: The second captain repeated the same error as the first captain, but with even more guilt because *he knew what happened to the first captain*. The judgment upon the first group should have warned this second captain and his **fifty men**.

i. The specific request of the second captain (**Come down quickly!**) shows that the second captain made his request even *more* bold and demanding.

ii. The people and leaders of Israel had gone after pagan gods so long that they could not distinguish between the imaginary, impotent gods of the pagan world and Yahweh, the Lord God of Israel. They thought that Yahweh was just as powerless as their own useless gods.

b. **If I am a man of God, let fire come down from heaven and consume you and your fifty men**: Elijah left the matter in God's hands, and God again responded in dramatic judgment.

3. (13-15) The third captain comes in humility and Elijah goes with him.

Again, he sent a third captain of fifty with his fifty men. And the third captain of fifty went up, and came and fell on his knees before Elijah, and pleaded with him, and said to him: "Man of God, please let my life and the life of these fifty servants of yours be precious in your sight. Look, fire has come down from heaven and burned up the first two captains of fifties with their fifties. But let my life now be precious in your sight." And the angel of the Lord said to Elijah, "Go down with

him; do not be afraid of him." So he arose and went down with him to the king.

a. **Fell on his knees before Elijah, and pleaded with him**: The third captain approached his mission in a completely different manner. He came to Elijah humbly, recognizing that he really was a **Man of God**. Perhaps the third captain looked at the two blackened spots of scorched earth nearby before he spoke to Elijah.

b. **Go down with him; do not be afraid of him**: It wasn't that God did not want Elijah to go to King Ahaziah; it was that Ahaziah, his captains, and their soldiers all acted as if there were no God in Israel. When the request was made wisely and humbly, Elijah went.

i. There were many reasons why Ahaziah wanted to arrest Elijah, even though he already heard the prophecy through Elijah. Perhaps he wanted Elijah to reverse his word of doom and would use force to compel him to do it. Perhaps he just wanted to show his rage against this prophet who had troubled him and his father Ahab for so long. Perhaps he wanted to dramatically silence Elijah to discourage future prophets from speaking boldly against the king of Israel. God assured Elijah that he had nothing to fear from Ahaziah.

4. (16) Elijah delivers the same message to Ahaziah.

Then he said to him, "Thus says the LORD: 'Because you have sent messengers to inquire of Baal-Zebub, the god of Ekron, *is it* because *there is* no God in Israel to inquire of His word? Therefore you shall not come down from the bed to which you have gone up, but you shall surely die.'"

a. **Is it because there is no God in Israel to inquire of His word**: This was the same message Elijah gave to the men Ahaziah sent to inquire of Baal-Zebub. The message from God did not change just because Ahaziah didn't want to hear it the first time.

5. (17-18) Ahaziah dies and leaves no successor.

So *Ahaziah* died according to the word of the LORD which Elijah had spoken. Because he had no son, Jehoram became king in his place, in the second year of Jehoram the son of Jehoshaphat, king of Judah. Now the rest of the acts of Ahaziah which he did, *are* they not written in the book of the chronicles of the kings of Israel?

a. **So Ahaziah died according to the word of the LORD which Elijah had spoken**: The proof was in the result. Elijah was demonstrated to be a man of God because his prophecy was fulfilled just as spoken. Ahaziah did not recover from his fall through the lattice.

i. "Everything he did was weak, faithless, and miserable; he achieved nothing but ruin and failure. He let Moab rebel. He hurt himself in a clumsy accident. He foolishly attempted to use military force against Elijah. And worse, he sought help in the wrong place – in Philistia at the altar of a pagan god." (Dilday)

b. **Because he had no son, Jehoram became king**: This Jehoram was also the *son* of Ahab (2 Kings 3:1) and therefore the *brother* of Ahaziah. Ahaziah had no *descendant* to pass the kingdom to, so the throne went to his brother after the brief reign of Ahaziah.

i. The account becomes a little confusing here, because the king of Judah at that time was *also* named Jehoram (**the son of Jehoshaphat**).

2 Kings 2 – Elijah's Ascension

A. Elijah ascends to heaven.

1. (1-3) The awareness of Elijah's coming departure.

And it came to pass, when the LORD was about to take up Elijah into heaven by a whirlwind, that Elijah went with Elisha from Gilgal. Then Elijah said to Elisha, "Stay here, please, for the LORD has sent me on to Bethel." But Elisha said, "*As* the LORD lives, and *as* your soul lives, I will not leave you!" So they went down to Bethel. Now the sons of the prophets who *were* at Bethel came out to Elisha, and said to him, "Do you know that the LORD will take away your master from over you today?" And he said, "Yes, I know; keep silent!"

> a. **When the LORD was about to take Elijah into heaven by a whirlwind**: Apparently, this was somewhat common knowledge. Elijah, Elisha, and the **sons of the prophets** each knew that Elijah would soon be carried **into heaven by a whirlwind**; presumably there was a prophecy announcing this that at least some knew.

> b. **As the LORD lives, and as your soul lives, I will not leave you**: Elijah seemed to test the devotion of Elisha. Since it was known that Elijah would soon depart to heaven in an unusual way, Elisha wanted to stay as close as possible to his mentor.

2. (4-7) The awareness of Elijah's departure at Jericho and the Jordan.

Then Elijah said to him, "Elisha, stay here, please, for the LORD has sent me on to Jericho." But he said, "*As* the LORD lives, and *as* your soul lives, I will not leave you!" So they came to Jericho. Now the sons of the prophets who *were* at Jericho came to Elisha and said to him, "Do you know that the LORD will take away your master from over you today?" So he answered, "Yes, I know; keep silent!" Then Elijah said to him, "Stay here, please, for the LORD has sent me on to the Jordan." But he

said, *"As* the LORD lives, and *as* your soul lives, I will not leave you!" So the two of them went on. And fifty men of the sons of the prophets went and stood facing *them* at a distance, while the two of them stood by the Jordan.

   a. **Elisha, stay here, please, for the LORD has sent me on to Jericho**: Elijah continued to test the devotion of Elisha, and Elisha continued to stay with his mentor until his anticipated unusual departure.

      i. Elijah knew that God had a dramatic plan for the end of his earthly life, yet he was perfectly willing to allow it all to take place privately, without anyone else knowing. "The prophet's evident desire to die alone shames us, when we remember how eager we are to tell men, by every available medium, of what we are doing for the Lord." (Meyer)

   b. **The two of them went on**: Elisha would not leave his mentor until *God* took him away in the dramatic way promised.

3. (8-10) Elisha asks for a double portion.

Now Elijah took his mantle, rolled *it* up, and struck the water; and it was divided this way and that, so that the two of them crossed over on dry ground. And so it was, when they had crossed over, that Elijah said to Elisha, "Ask! What may I do for you, before I am taken away from you?" Elisha said, "Please let a double portion of your spirit be upon me." So he said, "You have asked a hard thing. *Nevertheless*, if you see me *when I am* taken from you, it shall be so for you; but if not, it shall not be *so*."

   a. **Elijah took his mantle, rolled it up, and struck the water; and it was divided this way and that, so that the two of them crossed over on dry ground**: This was a strange and unique miracle on a day of strange and unique miracles. Elijah walked in the steps of Moses and Joshua as ones whom God used to miraculously part waters.

   b. **Ask! What may I do for you, before I am taken away from you**: This was a big invitation, but Elisha had demonstrated his tenacity by refusing to leave his mentor.

      i. "It was with the object of testing the spirit of his friend that the departing seer had urged him again and again to leave him. And it was only when Elisha had stood the test with such unwavering resolution that Elijah was able to give him this *carte blanche*." (Meyer)

   c. **Please let a double portion of your spirit be upon me**: When invited to make a request, Elisha asked for a big thing – a **double portion** of the mighty **spirit** of Elijah. Elisha saw how greatly the Spirit of God worked through Elijah, and he wanted the same for himself.

i. He could have asked for anything, but he asked for this. "He sought neither wealth, nor position, nor worldly power; nor a share in those advantages on which he had turned his back for ever." (Meyer)

ii. The idea of a **double portion** was not to ask for *twice as much* as Elijah had, but to ask for the portion that went to the firstborn son, as in Deuteronomy 21:17. Elisha asked for the right to be regarded as the successor of Elijah, as his firstborn son in regard to ministry. Yet Elisha had *already* been designated as Elijah's successor (1 Kings 19:19). This was a request for the *spiritual power* to *fulfill* the calling he already received.

iii. It is worthwhile to consider if this was generally a *good* or a *bad* thing. Normally we don't think of one person inheriting the ministry of another. The relation between Elijah and Elisha – and God's apparent blessing on their ministries – shows that at least *sometimes* God intends one person to inherit the ministry of another.

d. **If you see me when I am taken from you, it shall be for you**: Elijah tested the devotion of his mentor by seeing if he would persistently stay with him through these last remarkable hours. If the devotion of Elisha remained strong through the testing, his request to be the successor of the first prophet would be fulfilled.

4. (11-13) Elijah ascends into heaven.

Then it happened, as they continued on and talked, that suddenly a chariot of fire *appeared* with horses of fire, and separated the two of them; and Elijah went up by a whirlwind into heaven. And Elisha saw *it*, and he cried out, "My father, my father, the chariot of Israel and its horsemen!" So he saw him no more. And he took hold of his own clothes and tore them into two pieces. He also took up the mantle of Elijah that had fallen from him, and went back and stood by the bank of the Jordan.

a. **As they continued on and talked**: "What sublime themes must have engaged them, standing as they did on the very confines of heaven, and in the vestibule of eternity! The apostasy of Israel and its approaching doom; the ministry just closing, with its solemn warnings; the outlook towards the work upon which Elisha was preparing to enter – these and cognate subjects must have occupied them." (Meyer)

b. **Suddenly a chariot of fire appeared with horses of fire, and separated the two of them; and Elijah went up by a whirlwind into heaven**: This was a strange and unique miracle. As the two prophets walked, some fiery object **separated the two of them** and then carried Elijah up to heaven.

i. "It was meet that a whirlwind-man should sweep to heaven in the very element of his life… What a contrast to the gentle upward motion of the ascending Saviour!" (Meyer)

ii. "Elijah was taken up to heaven in the *whirlwind*, not in the *chariot of fire and horses of fire* which merely 'came between the two of them' (Hebrew) and cut him off from human sight. These *chariots* and *horsemen* symbolized strong protection as well as the forces of God's spiritual presence which were the true safety of Israel." (Wiseman)

c. **My father, my father, the chariot of Israel and its horsemen**: With these words Elisha recognized the *true* strength of Israel. "Elisha saw that the strength of Israel had been that of the presence of the prophet of God. It is more than a coincidence that when presently Elisha himself passed away, Joash, the reigning king, uttered the same exclamation (13:14)." (Morgan)

i. "Who by thy example, and counsels, and prayers, and power with God, didst more for the defence and preservation of Israel, than all their chariots and horses, or other warlike provisions." (Poole)

ii. This was the end of a remarkable ministry, one that was in many ways similar to the ministry of Moses. Both Moses and Elijah:

- Stood alone for righteousness.
- Were associated with fire upon mountains.
- Were associated with the desert.
- Met God on Sinai.
- Were chased out of their countries by pagan rulers.
- Knew God's miraculous provision for food and water.
- Wandered in the desert for a period measured by 40.
- Fasted for 40 days.
- Were powerful examples of praying men.
- Parted waters.
- Had close associates who succeeded them.
- Had successors who parted waters also.
- Had mysterious or strange deaths.

d. **And Elisha saw it**: This fulfilled the requirement mentioned in 2 Kings 2:10. Elisha would indeed inherit the prophetic ministry of Elijah. Yet Elisha wasn't happy when this happened; he **took hold of his own clothes and tore them into two pieces** as an expression of deep mourning.

e. **He also took up the mantle of Elijah that had fallen from him**: Since the mantle was the special mark of a prophet, this was a demonstration of the truth that Elisha truly had inherited the ministry of Elijah.

> i. Think of what it was like for Elisha to pick up that mantle. The mantle did not fall from heaven and rest on his shoulders; he had to *decide* to pick it up and put it on. He had to decide: *Do I really want to put this on?* Elijah's ministry was one of great power, but also of great pressure and responsibility.

B. The beginning of the ministry of the prophet Elisha.

1. (14-15) Elisha continues after the pattern of Elijah.

Then he took the mantle of Elijah that had fallen from him, and struck the water, and said, "Where *is* the LORD God of Elijah?" And when he also had struck the water, it was divided this way and that; and Elisha crossed over. Now when the sons of the prophets who *were* from Jericho saw him, they said, "The spirit of Elijah rests on Elisha." And they came to meet him, and bowed to the ground before him.

> a. **Where is the LORD God of Elijah**: Elisha knew that the power in prophetic ministry did not rest in mantles or fiery chariots. It rested in the presence and work of the Living God. If the LORD **God of Elijah** were also with Elisha, then he would inherit the same power and direction of ministry.
>
> > i. This was a great question to ask. If God expected Elisha to continue on the ministry of Elijah, then He must be present for the junior prophet in the same ways He was for the senior prophet. It was as if Elisha could have asked the question more specifically:
> >
> > - Where is the God who kept Elijah faithful when the whole nation turned from God?
> > - Where is the God who mightily answered prayer from Elijah?
> > - Where is the God who provided miraculously for Elijah?
> > - Where is the God who raised the dead through Elijah?
> > - Where is the God who answers prayer by sending fire from heaven?
> > - Where is the God who encouraged the discouraged prophet?
> > - Where is the God who carried Elijah away into heaven?
>
> b. **When he also struck the water, it was divided**: This shows that Elisha immediately had the same power in ministry that Elijah had. He went back

over a divided Jordan River the same way that he and Elijah first came over the river.

> i. "And when you have got their mantle, do not waste precious time in lamentations about them any more; *get to your business.* There is a river in your way; what then? Well, go to the Jordan as the prophet Elisha did, and try to pass it. Say not, 'Where is Elijah?' but 'Where is the Lord God of Elijah?' Elijah is gone, but his God is not; Elijah has gone away, but Jehovah is present, still." (Spurgeon)

c. **The spirit of Elijah rests on Elisha**: The succession of Elisha to the power and office of Elijah was *apparent to others*. Elisha didn't need to persuade or convince them of this with words. God's blessing on his actions was enough to prove it.

2. (16-18) A futile search for Elijah.

Then they said to him, "Look now, there are fifty strong men with your servants. Please let them go and search for your master, lest perhaps the Spirit of the LORD has taken him up and cast him upon some mountain or into some valley." And he said, "You shall not send anyone." But when they urged him till he was ashamed, he said, "Send *them*!" Therefore they sent fifty men, and they searched for three days but did not find him. And when they came back to him, for he had stayed in Jericho, he said to them, "Did I not say to you, 'Do not go'?"

a. **Please let them go and search for your master**: The sons of the prophets wondered if the chariot of fire had not merely taken Elijah to another place in Israel. Elisha knew that it had carried him to heaven, so he was hesitant to give permission for what he knew would be a futile mission.

b. **Did I not say to you, "Do not go"**: Elisha knew that the mission would be futile and it was. Elijah was carried up to *heaven*, not some other place on this earth.

3. (19-22) The waters of Jericho are healed.

Then the men of the city said to Elisha, "Please notice, the situation of this city *is* pleasant, as my lord sees; but the water *is* bad, and the ground barren." And he said, "Bring me a new bowl, and put salt in it." So they brought *it* to him. Then he went out to the source of the water, and cast in the salt there, and said, "Thus says the LORD: 'I have healed this water; from it there shall be no more death or barrenness.'" So the water remains healed to this day, according to the word of Elisha which he spoke.

a. **The water is bad, and the ground barren**: At this time Jericho had a poor water supply. This made agriculture impossible and life very difficult.

b. **Thus says the Lord: "I have healed this water; from it there shall be no more death or barrenness"**: The miracle did not happen because Elisha wanted to impress others or because *he* thought it would be good to do it. This was a work of the Lord, and it was a word from the Lord that announced the healing of the water.

> i. "If God casteth into our hearts but one cruseful of the salt of his Spirit, we are whole." (Trapp)

4. (23-25) Judgment upon the youths of Bethel.

Then he went up from there to Bethel; and as he was going up the road, some youths came from the city and mocked him, and said to him, "Go up, you baldhead! Go up, you baldhead!" So he turned around and looked at them, and pronounced a curse on them in the name of the Lord. And two female bears came out of the woods and mauled forty-two of the youths. Then he went from there to Mount Carmel, and from there he returned to Samaria.

a. **Some youths came from the city and mocked him**: The ancient Hebrew word translated **youths** here means young men in a very broad sense. This term applied to Joseph when he was 39 (Genesis 41:12), to Absalom as an adult (2 Samuel 14:21, 18:5), and to Solomon when he was 20 (1 Kings 3:7).

> i. These youths were from **Bethel**, and their mocking presence shows the continuing opposition to a true prophet in Bethel, the chief center of pagan calf-worship." (Wiseman)

b. **Go up, you baldhead**: This both mocked Elisha because of his apparent baldness, and because of his connection with the prophet Elijah. The idea behind the words, "**Go up**" was that Elisha should **go up** to heaven like Elijah did. It mocked Elisha, his mentor Elijah, and the God they served.

> i. "*Go up; go up* into heaven, whither thou pretendest that Elijah is gone. Why didst not thou accompany thy friend and master into heaven? Oh that the same Spirit would take thee up also, that thou mightest not trouble us nor our Israel, as Elijah did!" (Poole)

> ii. "The lack of hair was not a result of old age; since he lived about fifty years after this incident, he was at the time a relatively young man. Elisha's baldness must have been in striking contrast to Elijah's hairy appearance." (Dilday)

c. **So he turned around and looked at them, and pronounced a curse on them in the name of the Lord**: Elisha knew these young men mocked his ministry, Elijah's ministry, and the God they both faithfully served. Yet he left any correction up to God by pronouncing **a curse on them in the name of the Lord**.

d. Two female bears came out of the woods and mauled forty-two of the youths: In response to the curse of Elisha, God sent **two female bears** and they **mauled** (literally, *cut up*) the young men.

i. "*Bears* are attested in the hill ranges until mediaeval times." (Wiseman)

ii. "Since forty-two of the boys were struck by the bears, the group may have been quite large and therefore dangerously out of control. Elisha may have needed miraculous intervention to escape." (Dilday)

iii. "Verse 24 does not say that the victims were killed. The Hebrew word translated 'mauled' might indicate less serious injuries. The ultimate outcome of the miracle was to break up the gang, frighten the offenders and the entire village." (Dilday)

2 Kings 3 – War Against Moab

The Moabite Stone (also called the Mesha Stele) was discovered in 1868 and contains a Moabite inscription that confirms many of the events of 2 Kings 3 but gives it a distinctly pro-Moabite spin.

A. Three kings gather against the Moabites.

1. (1-3) A summary of Jehoram's reign, the son of Ahab.

Now Jehoram the son of Ahab became king over Israel at Samaria in the eighteenth year of Jehoshaphat king of Judah, and reigned twelve years. And he did evil in the sight of the LORD, but not like his father and mother; for he put away the *sacred* **pillar of Baal that his father had made. Nevertheless he persisted in the sins of Jeroboam the son of Nebat, who had made Israel sin; he did not depart from them.**

> a. **Now Jehoram the son of Ahab became king over Israel**: Jehoram came from a family that was far beyond dysfunctional. His father Ahab was one of the worst kings the Northern Kingdom of Israel ever knew and his mother Jezebel was certainly the worst queen Israel ever knew.
>
> b. **But not like his father and mother**: Jehoram was better than his father and mother, but he was still a wicked man. He was the ninth consecutive bad king over the Northern Kingdom, which never had a godly king.
>
> > i. "The 'sins of Jeroboam' that Jehoram perpetuated were not related to the worship of Baal but to the false worship of Yahweh under the calf (or ox) images that Jeroboam set up in Dan and Bethel. This was primarily a political strategy rather than a religious one." (Dilday)
> >
> > ii. "He appears to have been, in spiritual matters, one of those undecided, neutral characters, who puzzle most observers, and who never seem to know themselves just where they stand, or belong. He put away the Baal statue, made by his father Ahab, but never became a real believer in Jehovah." (Knapp)

iii. Poole believed that Jehoram put away Baal worship out of bad motives – either because he was frightened when he remembered the judgment that came against his father Ahab and his brother Ahaziah, or because he wanted to impress Jehoshaphat so the Judean king would agree to an alliance. Elisha wasn't impressed with Jehoram's putting away of Baal (2 Kings 3:13).

2. (4-5) Moab's rebellion.

Now Mesha king of Moab was a sheepbreeder, and he regularly paid the king of Israel one hundred thousand lambs and the wool of one hundred thousand rams. But it happened, when Ahab died, that the king of Moab rebelled against the king of Israel.

a. **Now Mesha king of Moab was a sheepbreeder**: The Moabites lived on the eastern side of the Dead Sea, and were under tribute to Israel. When King Ahab died, the king of the Moabites saw an opportunity to escape the taxation that the king of Israel forced upon him.

3. (6-8) Israel and Judah join together to fight Moab.

So King Jehoram went out of Samaria at that time and mustered all Israel. Then he went and sent to Jehoshaphat king of Judah, saying, "The king of Moab has rebelled against me. Will you go with me to fight against Moab?" And he said, "I will go up; I *am* as you *are*, my people as your people, my horses as your horses." Then he said, "Which way shall we go up?" And he answered, "By way of the Wilderness of Edom."

a. **He went and sent to Jehoshaphat king of Judah**: Jehoshaphat was a godly king (1 Kings 22:41-43), who followed in the godly footsteps of his father Asa (1 Kings 15:9-15). Yet Asa fought against Israel (1 Kings 15:16) while Jehoshaphat made peace with the Northern Kingdom (1 Kings 22:44).

b. **Will you go with me to fight against Moab**: Though greater Israel was long since separated by a civil war, the two nations (Judah and Israel) were now willing to come together to fight this common foe.

c. **Then he said, "Which way shall we go up**: Jehoram of Israel asked Jehoshaphat of Judah for military advice because Jehoshaphat was more experienced in battle than Jehoram. The king of Judah advised Jehoram to attack Moab from the south, going through the very dry desert of the Edomites.

4. (9-10) The armies of Israel, Judah, and Edom are stranded in the desert without water.

So the king of Israel went with the king of Judah and the king of Edom, and they marched on that roundabout route seven days; and there was

no water for the army, nor for the animals that followed them. And the king of Israel said, "Alas! For the LORD has called these three kings together to deliver them into the hand of Moab."

> a. **They marched on that roundabout route seven days**: The combined armies of Judah, Israel, and Edom had to travel a considerable distance to attack Moab from the south.
>
>> i. "Verse 9 mentions the king of Edom, but we have already been told in 1 Kings 22:47 that there was no king in Edom at this time. So 'king' here must refer to a vice-regent appointed by the king of Judah." (Dilday)
>
> b. **Alas! For the LORD has called these three kings together to deliver them into the hand of Moab**: Jehoram's guilty conscience convinced him that this calamity was the judgment of God. His own sin made him think that everything that happened against him was the judgment of God.

B. Elisha speaks for the LORD.

1. (11-12) The godly Jehoshaphat seeks God's word in the matter.

But Jehoshaphat said, "*Is there* no prophet of the LORD here, that we may inquire of the LORD by him?" So one of the servants of the king of Israel answered and said, "Elisha the son of Shaphat *is* here, who poured water on the hands of Elijah." And Jehoshaphat said, "The word of the LORD is with him." So the king of Israel and Jehoshaphat and the king of Edom went down to him.

> a. **Is there no prophet of the LORD here, that we may inquire of the LORD by him**: Both Jehoram and Jehoshaphat believed there was a spiritual, divine element to their current crisis. Jehoram believed that God was to be *avoided* because of the crisis, while Jehoshaphat believed that God should be *sought* because of the crisis.
>
> b. **Who poured water on the hands of Elijah**: This is a wonderful title for any servant of God. Elisha was the humble and practical servant of Elijah. This was *spiritual* service that prepared him for further spiritual service.
>
> c. **So the king of Israel and Jehoshaphat and the king of Edom went down to him**: This was encouraging humility on the part of these three kings. Normally, kings demand that others come to see them. These three were willing to go to the prophet.

2. (13-15) Elisha agrees to speak with the three kings.

Then Elisha said to the king of Israel, "What have I to do with you? Go to the prophets of your father and the prophets of your mother." But the king of Israel said to him, "No, for the LORD has called these three kings *together* to deliver them into the hand of Moab." And Elisha said, "*As* the LORD of hosts lives, before whom I stand, surely were it not that I regard the presence of Jehoshaphat king of Judah, I would not look at you, nor see you. But now bring me a musician." Then it happened, when the musician played, that the hand of the LORD came upon him.

a. **Go to the prophets of your father and the prophets of your mother**: Elisha's call was to continue the ministry of Elijah, and here he imitated Elijah's plain speaking to powerful people. Elisha's plain speaking struck the conscience of the king of Israel.

i. **What have I to do with you**: "The Hebrew idiom… is commonly employed to express emphatic denial (cf. 2 Samuel 16:10) or differences of opinion between the persons involved (cf. John 2:4)." (Patterson and Austel)

b. **Were it not that I regard the presence of Jehoshaphat king of Judah, I would not look at you**: It wasn't that Elisha was against every king or powerful person. He was willing to speak to these three kings for the sake of Jehoshaphat, the godly king of Judah.

c. **Then it happened, when the musician played, that the hand of the LORD came upon him**: When Elisha wanted to become more sensitive to the leading and speaking of the Holy Spirit, he asked for the service of a **musician**. This demonstrates the great spiritual power in music.

i. "This he requires, that his mind, which had been disturbed and inflamed with holy anger at the sight of wicked Jehoram, might be composed, and cheered, and united within itself, and that he might be excited to the more fervent prayer to God, and joyfully praising him; whereby he was prepared to receive the prophetical announcement." (Poole)

ii. "The way to be filled with the Spirit is to edify ourselves by psalms, and hymns, and spiritual songs." (Trapp)

iii. "This nameless musician was endowed with God-given talents and he used them for the good of others. Surely it never occurred to him that by his music he would help win a military victory and have a dramatic effect on history. But when he shared his God-given ability, the power of God came upon the prophet." (Dilday)

3. (16-19) The word from God.

And he said, "Thus says the LORD: 'Make this valley full of ditches.' For thus says the LORD: 'You shall not see wind, nor shall you see rain; yet that valley shall be filled with water, so that you, your cattle, and your animals may drink.' And this is a simple matter in the sight of the LORD;

He will also deliver the Moabites into your hand. Also you shall attack every fortified city and every choice city, and shall cut down every good tree, and stop up every spring of water, and ruin every good piece of land with stones."

a. **You shall not see wind, nor shall you see rain; yet that valley shall be filled with water**: This was a strange promise from God. Water would be provided, but without any apparent rain or storm.

b. **Make this valley full of ditches**: God promised to send water to the valley, but they had to dig the **ditches** to catch what God would provide. They had to dig the ditches before the water was apparent, so they could benefit from it when it came.

i. "The dried-up river bed was to have many trenches (Hebrew 'trenches trenches') dug to retain the flash flood." (Wiseman)

ii. When the kings returned from their visit to Elisha and told their commanders to have the men dig ditches, it must have been hard to hear. Thirsty, near-dead men in the middle of the desert don't look forward to the hard work of digging ditches in dry ground. Yet this work was essential.

iii. This demonstrates the principle that God wants us to prepare for the blessing He wants to bring. Listening to Him, we are to anticipate His working and to get ready for it.

iv. Digging ditches was something the people of God could do. God didn't ask them to do more than they were able to do. When God wants us to prepare for the blessing He will bring, He gives us things that we can really do.

v. "If we expect to obtain the Holy Spirit's blessing, we must prepare for his reception. 'Make this valley full of trenches' is an order which is given me this morning for the members of this church; make ready for the Holy Ghost's power; be prepared to receive that which he is about to give; each man in his place and each woman in her sphere, make the whole of this church full of trenches for the reception of the divine water-floods." (Spurgeon)

vi. "But the most of people say, 'Well, you know, of course, if God sends a blessing, we must then enlarge.' Yes, that is the way of unbelief, and the road to the curse. But the way of faith and the road to the blessing is this: God has promised it – we will get ready for it; God is engaged to bless, now let us be prepared to receive the boon. Act not on the mere strength of what you have, but in expectation of that which you have asked." (Spurgeon)

c. **This is a simple matter in the sight of the LORD**: The kings came to Elisha inquiring about water. God wanted to give them more than their immediate need. God wanted to give them more than immediate provision; He wanted to give them complete victory over their enemies.

C. The defeat of Moab.

1. (20) God meets their need for provision when mysterious water flows through the camp.

Now it happened in the morning, when the grain offering was offered, that suddenly water came by way of Edom, and the land was filled with water.

    a. **Suddenly water came by way of Edom**: It seems that God sent an intense downpour in the nearby mountains, and this caused a flash flood though the desert of Edom.

    b. **The land was filled with water**: The water was available only because they were obedient to dig the ditches. The ditches collected the water from the flash flood.

        i. If Israel and Judah had disobeyed God's word and failed to dig the ditches, God's blessing would have passed them by. God told them to get ready and prepare to receive and catch His blessing. God often moves us to do things that may or may not make much sense for the moment, but they are things that will prepare us for what He will do in the future.

        ii. The measure of water available to these thirsty men was directly connected to how faithful they were to dig the ditches. The more ditches and the bigger the ditches, the more water was provided. Though it was hard and unpleasant work, the more they did, the more blessing they received.

        iii. The ditches were not the blessing, and they were not the victory, though they were essential parts of both the blessing and the victory. When God wants us to do something to prepare for blessing, we should not confuse the preparation with the blessing itself. Without the miraculous blessing of God, the ditches meant nothing.

2. (21-25) The Moabites attack the camp of the three kings.

And when all the Moabites heard that the kings had come up to fight against them, all who were able to bear arms and older were gathered; and they stood at the border. Then they rose up early in the morning, and the sun was shining on the water; and the Moabites saw the water on the other side *as* red as blood. And they said, "This is blood; the kings

have surely struck swords and have killed one another; now therefore, Moab, to the spoil!" So when they came to the camp of Israel, Israel rose up and attacked the Moabites, so that they fled before them; and they entered *their* land, killing the Moabites. Then they destroyed the cities, and each man threw a stone on every good piece of land and filled it; and they stopped up all the springs of water and cut down all the good trees. But they left the stones of Kir Haraseth *intact*. However the slingers surrounded and attacked it.

a. **The Moabites saw the water on the other side as red as blood**: The ditches caught the water and saved the armies of these three kings from dehydration. They were also the means of confusion and defeat to the enemies of the people of God. When they saw the sun shining on the water collected in the ditches, they thought it was blood, from the three kings fighting each other.

b. **So when they came to the camp of Israel, Israel rose up and attacked the Moabites, so that they fled before them**: God used the ditches in a completely unexpected way to supply the need *and* to defeat the enemy.

i. The whole account of God's provision in the desert gives many principles that apply to Christian leadership.

- Like digging ditches, leadership is hard work.
- Like digging ditches, leadership is done with faith in the future.
- Like digging ditches, leadership is blessed beyond reasonable expectation.
- Like digging ditches, leadership must use delegation.
- Like digging ditches, leadership matters nothing without a miracle.
- Like digging ditches, the work of leadership often feels like work without reward.
- Like digging ditches, the work of leadership comes from God's revelation.
- Like digging ditches, the work of leadership will be criticized or doubted.
- Like digging ditches, leadership means not accepting the present state of dryness.
- Like digging ditches, the work of leadership often seems unimpressive or unspectacular.

- Like digging ditches, the work of leadership is purposely used and relied on by God.

c. **And cut down all the good trees**: "But surely *fruit trees* are not intended here; for this was positively against the law of God, Deuteronomy 20:19-20." (Clarke)

3. (26-27) The king of Moab's desperate move.

And when the king of Moab saw that the battle was too fierce for him, he took with him seven hundred men who drew swords, to break through to the king of Edom, but they could not. Then he took his eldest son who would have reigned in his place, and offered him *as* a burnt offering upon the wall; and there was great indignation against Israel. So they departed from him and returned to *their own* land.

a. **He took his eldest son who would have reigned in his place, and offered him as a burnt offering upon the wall**: This shows how desperate the king of Moab was following his defeat on the field of battle. He did this to honor his pagan gods and to show his own people his determination to prevent defeat.

b. **So they departed from him and returned to their own land**: The radical determination of the king of Moab convinced the kings of Israel, Judah, and Edom that they could not completely defeat Moab. They left content with their near-complete victory.

i. "Sickened by the maddened spectacle of senseless human sacrifice, the allies lifted the siege and returned to their homes." (Patterson and Austel)

2 Kings 4 – God Works Miracles Through Elisha

A. Miracles connected with a widow and a barren woman.

1. (1-7) Provision for a widow.

A certain woman of the wives of the sons of the prophets cried out to Elisha, saying, "Your servant my husband is dead, and you know that your servant feared the LORD. And the creditor is coming to take my two sons to be his slaves." So Elisha said to her, "What shall I do for you? Tell me, what do you have in the house?" And she said, "Your maidservant has nothing in the house but a jar of oil." Then he said, "Go, borrow vessels from everywhere, from all your neighbors—empty vessels; do not gather just a few. And when you have come in, you shall shut the door behind you and your sons; then pour it into all those vessels, and set aside the full ones." So she went from him and shut the door behind her and her sons, who brought *the vessels* **to her; and she poured** *it* **out. Now it came to pass, when the vessels were full, that she said to her son, "Bring me another vessel." And he said to her,** *"There is* **not another vessel." So the oil ceased. Then she came and told the man of God. And he said, "Go, sell the oil and pay your debt; and you** *and* **your sons live on the rest."**

> a. **The creditor is coming to take my two sons to be his slaves**: This woman, the widowed wife of one of the **sons of the prophets**, had debts and no means to pay them. The legal system in Israel would not allow her to declare bankruptcy; she had to give her sons as indentured servants to her creditor as payment for the debts.
>
>> i. "However inhumane this might seem, the creditor was within his rights; for Mosaic Law allowed him to enslave the debtor and his children as far as the Year of Jubilee in order to work off a debt." (Patterson and Austel)

b. **Your maidservant has nothing in the house but a jar of oil**: There is some evidence that this jar of oil was not a larger supply held for cooking, but a smaller vessel that held only oil for anointing.

i. "A unique word here, possibly for a small anointing flask." (Wiseman)

c. **Go, borrow vessels from everywhere, from all your neighbors**: Elisha made this woman commit herself in faith to God's provision. To **borrow vessels** in this manner invited awkward questions, but she did as the word of God through His prophet commanded her.

i. "She did what she was commanded to do: she did it in faith; and the result answered the end. God takes care to deliver his servants in ways that exercise their faith. He would not have them be little in faith, for faith is the wealth of the heavenly life." (Spurgeon)

ii. "You have God in the measure in which you desire Him. Only remember that the desire that brings God must be more than a feeble, fleeting wish. Wishing is one thing; *willing* is quite another. Lazily wishing and strenuously desiring are two entirely different postures of mind; the former gets nothing and the latter gets everything, gets God, and with God all that God can bring." (Maclaren)

d. **Pour it into all those vessels, and set aside the full ones**: Elisha told the woman to take what she had – one jar of oil (*all* that she had) – and pour that out in faith into the borrowed vessels. As she did this, the oil miraculously kept pouring from the original vessel until all the borrowed vessels were filled. At the end of it, she had *a lot* of oil.

i. We notice that Elisha made *her* do this. Perhaps Elisha was tempted to gather the vessels and pour the oil himself, but he knew that *she had to trust God herself.*

ii. The original vessel of oil – the one the woman had in her house – was a smaller vessel that held only oil for anointing. This means that the distribution of the oil into the other vessels required constant pouring and allowing the oil to supernaturally fill the small vessel again.

iii. The vessels also had to be *empty* before they could be filled with oil. It did no good to bring the widow full vessels. "A full Christ is for empty sinners, and for empty sinners only, and as long as there is a really empty soul in a congregation, so long will a blessing go forth with the word, and no longer. It is not our emptiness, but our fullness which can hinder the outgoings of free grace." (Spurgeon)

e. **So the oil ceased**: The miracle was given according to the measure of her previous faith in borrowing vessels. She borrowed enough so the excess oil was sold and provided money to pay the debt to the creditor and to provide for the future. Had she borrowed more, more would have been provided; had she gathered less, less would have been provided.

    i. "If she borrowed few vessels, she would have but little oil; if she borrowed many vessels they should all be filled, and she should have much oil. She was herself to measure out what she should have; and I believe that you and I, in the matter of spiritual blessings from God, have more to do with the measurement of our mercies than we think. We make our blessings little, because our prayers are little." (Spurgeon)

    ii. The oil did not pour out on the ground or simply flow about. It was intended for a prepared vessel. Each vessel had to be prepared by being *gathered*, by being *assembled*, by being *emptied*, by being *put in the right position* and by *staying in the right position*. When there was no more prepared vessel, the oil stopped.

    iii. The principle of this miracle was the same as the principle of the ditches dug in the previous chapter. The amount of man's work with the miracle determined the amount of blessing and provision actually received. God's powerful provision *invites* our hard work and never excuses laziness.

    iv. "Men must likewise see to it, that their ministers' widows and children have a comfortable subsistence." (Trapp)

2. (8-17) A son for a barren woman.

Now it happened one day that Elisha went to Shunem, where there *was* a notable woman, and she persuaded him to eat some food. So it was, as often as he passed by, he would turn in there to eat some food. And she said to her husband, "Look now, I know that this *is* a holy man of God, who passes by us regularly. Please, let us make a small upper room on the wall; and let us put a bed for him there, and a table and a chair and a lampstand; so it will be, whenever he comes to us, he can turn in there." And it happened one day that he came there, and he turned in to the upper room and lay down there. Then he said to Gehazi his servant, "Call this Shunammite woman." When he had called her, she stood before him. And he said to him, "Say now to her, 'Look, you have been concerned for us with all this care. What *can I* do for you? Do you want me to speak on your behalf to the king or to the commander of the army?'" She answered, "I dwell among my own people." So he said, "What then *is* to be done for her?" And Gehazi answered, "Actually, she has no son, and her husband is old." So he said, "Call her." When he had called her, she stood in the doorway. Then he said, "About this time next year you shall embrace a son." And she said, "No, my lord. Man of God, do not lie to your maidservant!" But the woman conceived, and

bore a son when the appointed time had come, of which Elisha had told her.

a. **A notable woman, and she persuaded him to eat some food**: This remarkable relationship between Elisha and the Shunammite woman began when the woman *sought to do something for the prophet*. Elisha didn't seek anything from this woman; she eventually **persuaded him to eat some food** as the guest of her hospitality.

b. **Let us make a small upper room on the wall**: The Shunammite woman then sought to do *more* for the prophet. With the approval of her husband, they made a room for Elisha to stay in on his frequent travels through the area.

c. **About this time next year you shall embrace a son**: To this barren woman this promise seemed too good to be true. The stigma associated with barrenness was harsh in the ancient world, and this promised son would answer the longing of her heart and remove the stigma of barrenness.

d. **The woman conceived, and bore a son when the appointed time had come, of which Elisha had told her**: The woman who so generously provided material things for the prophet of God was now blessed by the God of the prophet, blessed *beyond* material things.

3. (18-37) The Shunammite woman's son is raised from the dead.

And the child grew. Now it happened one day that he went out to his father, to the reapers. And he said to his father, "My head, my head!" So he said to a servant, "Carry him to his mother." When he had taken him and brought him to his mother, he sat on her knees till noon, and *then* died. And she went up and laid him on the bed of the man of God, shut *the door* upon him, and went out. Then she called to her husband, and said, "Please send me one of the young men and one of the donkeys, that I may run to the man of God and come back." So he said, "Why are you going to him today? *It is* neither the New Moon nor the Sabbath." And she said, "*It is* well." Then she saddled a donkey, and said to her servant, "Drive, and go forward; do not slacken the pace for me unless I tell you." And so she departed, and went to the man of God at Mount Carmel. So it was, when the man of God saw her afar off, that he said to his servant Gehazi, "Look, the Shunammite woman! Please run now to meet her, and say to her, '*Is it* well with you? *Is it* well with your husband? *Is it* well with the child?'" And she answered, "*It is* well." Now when she came to the man of God at the hill, she caught him by the feet, but Gehazi came near to push her away. But the man of God said, "Let her alone; for her soul *is* in deep distress, and the LORD has hidden *it* from me, and has not told me." So she said, "Did I ask a son of

my lord? Did I not say, 'Do not deceive me'?" Then he said to Gehazi, "Get yourself ready, and take my staff in your hand, and be on your way. If you meet anyone, do not greet him; and if anyone greets you, do not answer him; but lay my staff on the face of the child." And the mother of the child said, "*As* the LORD lives, and *as* your soul lives, I will not leave you." So he arose and followed her. Now Gehazi went on ahead of them, and laid the staff on the face of the child; but *there was* neither voice nor hearing. Therefore he went back to meet him, and told him, saying, "The child has not awakened." When Elisha came into the house, there was the child, lying dead on his bed. He went in therefore, shut the door behind the two of them, and prayed to the LORD. And he went up and lay on the child, and put his mouth on his mouth, his eyes on his eyes, and his hands on his hands; and he stretched himself out on the child, and the flesh of the child became warm. He returned and walked back and forth in the house, and again went up and stretched himself out on him; then the child sneezed seven times, and the child opened his eyes. And he called Gehazi and said, "Call this Shunammite woman." So he called her. And when she came in to him, he said, "Pick up your son." So she went in, fell at his feet, and bowed to the ground; then she picked up her son and went out.

> a. **He sat on her knees till noon, and then died**: This was the son granted by miraculous promise, in reward to the faithful service of the Shunammite woman. The boy tragically died on the lap of his mother after a brief but severe affliction.
>
>> i. "His head was grievously pained; which possibly came from the heat of the harvest season, to which he was exposed in the field." (Poole)
>>
>> ii. "Probably affected by the *coup de soleil*, or *sun stroke*, which might, in so young a subject, soon occasion death, especially in that hot country." (Clarke)
>
> b. **She went up and laid him on the bed of the man of God, shut the door upon him, and went out**: This shows the faith of the woman. She prepared for the *resurrection* of the boy, not his burial.
>
>> i. "She had no doubt heard that Elijah had raised the widow's son of Zarephath to life; and she believed that he who had obtained this gift of God for her, could obtain his restoration to life." (Clarke)
>
> c. **And she answered, "It is well"**: The Shunammite woman didn't want Elisha to learn of her grief through his assistant Gehazi. She wanted the man of God to hear it from her own lips and sense her own grief.

i. "Nothing makes grief dumb so surely as prying and yet indifferent intrusion. A tenderer hand than Gehazi's is needed to unlock the sad secret of that burdened breast." (Maclaren)

d. **Let her alone; for her soul is in deep distress, and the LORD has hidden it from me, and has not told me**: Elisha seemed mystified that this woman (whom he presumably often prayed for) was in a crisis that was hidden from Elisha. In this circumstance Elisha was more surprised that God *didn't* speak to him than if God *had* spoken to him.

i. "How much better would it have been for the Church if its teachers had been more willing to copy his modesty, and said about a great many things, 'The Lord hath hid it from me'!" (Maclaren)

e. **Lay my staff on the face of the child**: Instead of going directly himself, Elisha sent his servant Gehazi with his staff. This seems to follow the previous pattern in Elisha's ministry: He did not do things for people directly but gave them the opportunity to work with God and to trust Him for themselves. God told the alliance of kings to have ditches dug (2 Kings 3:16). God told the widow to gather vessels and pour the oil herself (2 Kings 4:1-7).

i. It may be that the Shunammite woman failed under this test, because she thought that the power to heal was more connected with Elisha himself and she refused to leave his presence (**I will not leave you**). The child was not healed by the laying on of the staff, though (hypothetically) the child may have been healed with only the staff if the Shunammite would have embraced this promise with full faith.

f. **He went in therefore, shut the door behind the two of them, and prayed to the LORD**: God did heal the Shunammite woman's son in response to Elisha's prayer. He prayed after the pattern shown by his mentor Elijah (1 Kings 17:20-23).

i. Elisha prayed with great faith because he knew God worked this way in the life of his mentor Elijah. He also prayed with great faith because he sensed that God *wanted* to raise this boy from the dead.

ii. "Although some ceremonial uncleanness might seem to be contracted by the touch of this dead body, yet that was justly to give place to a moral duty, and to an action of so great piety and charity as this was, especially when done by a prophet, and by the instinct of God's Spirit, who can dispense with his own laws." (Poole)

iii. There is a significant contrast between the stretched-out supplication of Elijah and Elisha and the authoritative command of Jesus in raising the dead (as in John 11:43). Elijah and Elisha rightly *begged* God to raise the dead. Jesus *commanded* the dead to be raised.

iv. "This staff of his – whatever became of the other - was long enough, he knew, to reach up to heaven, to know at those gates, yea, to wrench them open." (Trapp)

g. **The flesh of the child became warm… then the child sneezed seven times, and the child opened his eyes**: "Although miracles were for the most part done in an instant, yet sometimes they were done by degrees, as here, and 1 Kings 18:44-45; Mark 8:24-25." (Poole)

i. "Of course, there is a profound and beautiful use to be made of the prophet's action in laying himself upon the dead child, mouth to mouth, and hand to hand, if we regard it as symbolic of that closeness of approach to our nature, dead in sins, which the Lord of life makes in His incarnation and in His continual drawing near." (Maclaren)

B. Miracles connected with the provision of food.

1. (38-41) The purification of the stew.

And Elisha returned to Gilgal, and *there was* a famine in the land. Now the sons of the prophets *were* sitting before him; and he said to his servant, "Put on the large pot, and boil stew for the sons of the prophets." So one went out into the field to gather herbs, and found a wild vine, and gathered from it a lapful of wild gourds, and came and sliced *them* into the pot of stew, though they did not know *what they were*. Then they served it to the men to eat. Now it happened, as they were eating the stew, that they cried out and said, "Man of God, *there is* death in the pot!" And they could not eat *it*. So he said, "Then bring some flour." And he put *it* into the pot, and said, "Serve *it* to the people, that they may eat." And there was nothing harmful in the pot.

a. **There was a famine in the land**: "The famine mentioned in verse 38 may be the seven-year famine alluded to in 2 Kings 8:1-3." (Dilday)

b. **Man of God, there is death in the pot**: Elisha felt a special responsibility to help in this situation because he told the men to gather ingredients for the stew, and they gathered the **wild vine** that poisoned the pot.

i. "The gourds were probably colocynth. Popularly called 'wild cucumber,' the vine still grows near the Dead Sea. When the gourds are cut open the pulp dries rapidly and forms a powder, which in that part of the world is still used as a cathartic medicine. It has a very bitter taste. If eaten in enough quantity, it induces colic and can be fatal." (Dilday)

ii. "You have been trying to find pleasure in the world, and you have found wild vines… you have gathered wild gourds, a lap full, almost a heart full. You have been shredding death into the pot, and now you cannot feel as you used to feel, the poison is stupefying your soul. While we were singing just now, you said, 'I want to sing as saints do, but there is no praise in me'… If you are a worldling, and not God's child, you can live on that which would poison a Christian, but if you are a child of God, you will cry out, 'O thou man of God, there is death in the pot!'" (Spurgeon)

c. **And there was nothing harmful in the pot**: There was nothing inherently purifying in the flour Elisha put in the pot. The real purification was a miraculous work of God.

i. "There is death in the pot; how is the Church to meet it? I believe it is to imitate Elisha. We need not attempt to get the wild gourds out of the pot; they are cut too small, and are too cunningly mixed up; they have entered too closely into the whole mass of teaching to be removed. Who shall extract the leaven from the leavened loaf? What then? We must look to God for help, and use the means indicated here. '*Bring meal*.' Good wholesome food was cast into the poisonous stuff, and by God's gracious working it killed the poison; and the Church must cast the blessed gospel of the grace of God into the poisoned pottage, and false doctrine will not be able to destroy men's souls as it now does." (Spurgeon)

2. (42-44) The multiplication of loaves.

Then a man came from Baal Shalisha, and brought the man of God bread of the firstfruits, twenty loaves of barley bread, and newly ripened grain in his knapsack. And he said, "Give *it* to the people, that they may eat." But his servant said, "What? Shall I set this before one hundred men?" He said again, "Give it to the people, that they may eat; for thus says the LORD: 'They shall eat and have *some* left over.'" So he set *it* before them; and they ate and had *some* left over, according to the word of the LORD.

a. **Bread of the firstfruits, twenty loaves of barley bread**: "These had been brought to Elisha as firstfruits (verse 42). Normally these portions were reserved for God (Leviticus 23:20) and the Levitical priests (Numbers 18:13; Deuteronomy 18:4-5). Because the religion in the Northern Kingdom was apostate, the loaves had been brought by their owner to the one whom he considered to be the true repository of godly religion in Israel." (Patterson and Austel)

b. **Give it to the people, that they may eat**: In a miracle that anticipated Jesus' miracle of feeding the 5,000, Elisha commanded that a small amount of bread be served to 100 men.

> i. "This is something like our Lord's feeding the multitude miraculously. Indeed, there are many things in this chapter similar to facts in our Lord's history; and this prophet might be more aptly considered a type of our Lord, than most of the other persons in the Scripture who have been thus honored." (Clarke)

c. **For thus says the Lord: "They shall eat and have some left over"**: God promised not only to provide, but to provide *beyond* the immediate need. Elisha trusted the promise of God, acted upon it, and saw the promise miraculously fulfilled.

> i. "What can these few cakes do towards feeding a hundred men? They forget that God can multiply them. Ye limit the Holy One of Israel. Do you think he needs our numbers? Do you think he is dependent upon human strength? I tell you, our weakness is a better weapon for God than our strength." (Spurgeon)

2 Kings 5 – Naaman the Leper

A. Naaman comes to Elisha.

1. (1) Naaman's problem.

Now Naaman, commander of the army of the king of Syria, was a great and honorable man in the eyes of his master, because by him the LORD had given victory to Syria. He was also a mighty man of valor, *but* a leper.

   a. **Naaman, commander of the army of the king of Syria, was a great and honorable man**: Naaman was the chief military commander of a persistent enemy to both Israel and Judah. As recently as the days of Ahab and Jehoshaphat, Syria had fought and won against Israel (1 Kings 22:35-36). His position and success made him a **great and honorable man**, and personally he was a **mighty man of valor**.

      i. This same title was applied to Gideon (Judges 6:12), Jephthah (Judges 11:1), David (1 Samuel 16:18), Jeroboam (1 Kings 11:28), and Eliada (2 Chronicles 17:17). It seems that this is the only *specific* Gentile mentioned as a **mighty man of valor**.

      ii. According to Jewish legends, "The Rabbins tell us that it was he [Naaman] who shot the arrow wherewith Ahab was slain." (Trapp)

   b. **But a leper**: Naaman had a lot going for him, but what he had against him was devastating. He was **a leper**, which meant that he had a horrible, incurable disease that would slowly result in his death. No matter how good and successful everything else was in Naaman's life, he was **a leper**.

      i. "Here was a heavy tax upon his grandeur; he was afflicted with a disorder the most loathsome and the most humiliating that could possibly disgrace a human being." (Clarke)

      ii. Ancient leprosy began as small, red spots on the skin. Before too long the spots got bigger, and started to turn white, with sort of a shiny, or scaly appearance. Pretty soon the spots spread over the whole body and hair began to fall out – first from the head, then even from the eyebrows. As things got worse, fingernails and toenails become loose; they start to rot and eventually fell off. Then the joints of fingers and toes began to rot and fall off piece by piece. Gums began to shrink and they couldn't hold the teeth anymore, so each of them was lost. Leprosy kept eating away at the face until literally the nose, the palate, and even the eyes rotted – and the victim wasted away until death.

2. (2-3) The testimony from the servant girl.

And the Syrians had gone out on raids, and had brought back captive a young girl from the land of Israel. She waited on Naaman's wife. Then she said to her mistress, "If only my master *were* with the prophet who *is* in Samaria! For he would heal him of his leprosy."

> a. **Had brought back captive a young girl from the land of Israel**: This girl was an unwilling missionary, taken **captive** from Israel and now in Syria. Yet God allowed the tragedy of her captivity to accomplish a greater good.
>
>> i. The **young girl** illustrates the mysterious ways God works. She was probably raised in a godly home, yet taken from her family at a young age. It was an irreplaceable loss for her parents, and one they no doubt grieved over every day. Yet, she was greatly used in a simple way.
>
> b. **If only my master were with the prophet who is in Samaria**: This **young girl** was an outstanding example of a faithful witness in her current circumstance. She *cared* enough to speak up, and she had *faith* enough to believe that Elisha **would heal him of his leprosy.**
>
>> i. "And see the benefits of a religious education! Had not this little maid been brought up in the knowledge of the true God, she had not been the instrument of so great a salvation." (Clarke)

3. (4-7) Naaman comes to the king of Israel looking for healing.

And *Naaman* went in and told his master, saying, "Thus and thus said the girl who *is* from the land of Israel." Then the king of Syria said, "Go now, and I will send a letter to the king of Israel." So he departed and took with him ten talents of silver, six thousand *shekels* of gold, and ten changes of clothing. Then he brought the letter to the king of Israel, which said, "Now be advised, when this letter comes to you, that I have sent Naaman my servant to you, that you may heal him of his leprosy." And it happened, when the king of Israel read the letter, that he tore his clothes and said, "*Am* I God, to kill and make alive, that this man sends

a man to me to heal him of his leprosy? Therefore please consider, and see how he seeks a quarrel with me."

a. **Go now, and I will send a letter to the king of Israel**: Considering the record of wars between Israel and Syria described in the previous chapters, it seems strange that the king of Syria would send a letter of recommendation with his General Naaman. It seems that 2 Kings is not necessarily arranged chronologically, so this probably occurred during a time of lowered tension between Israel and Syria.

i. **And took with him ten talents of silver**: Dilday estimated that by the values of his own day, Naaman took more than $1.2 million with him to Israel. All this together shows how *desperate* Naaman's condition was, and how badly the king of Syria wanted to help him.

b. **I have sent Naaman my servant to you, that you may heal him of his leprosy**: When the king of Israel (Jehoram) read the letter, he was understandably upset. First, it was obviously out of his power to heal Naaman's leprosy. Second, he had no relationship with the prophet of the God who *did* have the power to heal. He thought the king of Syria sought a **quarrel**.

i. The king of Syria assumed that the king of Israel was on a much better relationship with Elisha than he really was. It is easy for others to assume that we have a better relationship with God than we really do.

4. (8-9) Naaman comes to Elisha's house.

So it was, when Elisha the man of God heard that the king of Israel had torn his clothes, that he sent to the king, saying, "Why have you torn your clothes? Please let him come to me, and he shall know that there is a prophet in Israel." Then Naaman went with his horses and chariot, and he stood at the door of Elisha's house.

a. **Why have you torn your clothes**: Elisha gave a gentle rebuke to the king of Israel. "This is a crisis to you, because you have no relationship with the God who can heal lepers. But it is a needless crisis, because you *could* have a relationship with this God."

b. **Please let him come to me, and he shall know that there is a prophet in Israel**: Naaman would never know there was a prophet in Israel by hanging around the royal palace. The true **prophet** in Israel wasn't welcome at the palace.

B. **Naaman is healed.**

1. (10-12) Naaman's anger at Elisha's instructions.

And Elisha sent a messenger to him, saying, "Go and wash in the Jordan seven times, and your flesh shall be restored to you, and *you shall* be clean." But Naaman became furious, and went away and said, "Indeed, I said to myself, 'He will surely come out *to me,* and stand and call on the name of the LORD his God, and wave his hand over the place, and heal the leprosy.' *Are* not the Abanah and the Pharpar, the rivers of Damascus, better than all the waters of Israel? Could I not wash in them and be clean?" So he turned and went away in a rage.

> a. **Elisha sent a messenger to him**: Naaman took the trouble to come to the home of Elisha, but Elisha refused to give him a personal audience. He simply **sent a messenger**. This was humbling to Naaman, who was accustomed to being honored.
>
> b. **Go and wash in the Jordan seven times, and your flesh shall be restored to you, and you shall be clean**: These were simple, uncomplicated instructions. Yet as Naaman's reaction demonstrates, these were humbling instructions.
>
> c. **He will surely come out to me and stand and call on the name of the LORD his God, and wave his hand over the place, and heal the leprosy**: Naaman had it all figured out. In his great need, he anticipated a way God would work, and he was offended when God didn't work the way he expected.
>
> d. **He turned and went away in a rage**: Because his expectation of how God *should* work was crushed, Naaman wanted nothing to do with Elisha. If the answer was in washing in a river, Naaman knew there were better rivers in his own land.

2. (13) The good advice of Naaman's servants.

And his servants came near and spoke to him, and said, "My father, *if* the prophet had told you *to do* something great, would you not have done *it?* How much more then, when he says to you, 'Wash, and be clean'?"

> a. **His servants came near and spoke to him**: Thank God for faithful subordinates who will speak to their superiors in such a way. Naaman was obviously angry, yet they were bold enough to give him the good advice he needed to hear.
>
> b. **If the prophet had told you to do something great, would you not have done it**: The servants of Naaman used a brilliantly logical approach. If Elisha had asked Naaman to sacrifice 100 or 1,000 animals to the God of Israel, Naaman would have done it immediately. Yet because his request was easy to do and humbling, Naaman first refused.

3. (14) Naaman is healed.

So he went down and dipped seven times in the Jordan, according to the saying of the man of God; and his flesh was restored like the flesh of a little child, and he was clean.

> a. **According to the saying of the man of God**: Naaman did exactly what Elisha told him to do. Therefore we can say that each dunk in the Jordan was a step of faith, trusting in the word of God through His prophet.
>
>> i. Wiseman on the ancient Hebrew word translated **dipped**: "Naaman 'plunged' in the River Jordan. This signified total obedience to the divine word."
>>
>> ii. Spurgeon saw Naaman attacked by two enemies: *Proud Self*, who internally demanded that Elisha come out and see him, and *Evil Questioning*, who questioned why he should wash in the Jordan when he had better rivers back in his homeland. Naaman overcame these two enemies and did what God told him to do.
>
> b. **And his flesh was restored like the flesh of a little child, and he was clean**: Naaman's response of faith was generously rewarded. God answered his faith with complete and miraculous healing.
>
>> i. "The simple method of this miracle, performed without the prophet there, did give God the credit. It was obvious that the healing came from Yahweh rather than from the sort of magical incantation that Naaman had anticipated." (Dilday)

4. (15-16) Naaman offers to reward Elisha but the prophet refuses.

And he returned to the man of God, he and all his aides, and came and stood before him; and he said, "Indeed, now I know that *there is* no God in all the earth, except in Israel; now therefore, please take a gift from your servant." But he said, *"As* the LORD lives, before whom I stand, I will receive nothing." And he urged him to take *it,* but he refused.

> a. **And he returned to the man of God**: This was a fine display of gratitude. Naaman was like the one leper out of the ten Jesus healed who came back to thank Jesus (Luke 17:12-19). He was also a foreigner, like the one thankful leper of Luke 17.
>
>> i. Before, Naaman expected the prophet to come to him. Now he **returned to the man of God** and **stood before him.**
>>
>> ii. "It is often the case that those who have least to value themselves on are proud and haughty; whereas the most excellent of the earth are the most humble, knowing that they have nothing but what they have

received. Naaman, the *leper*, was more proud and dictatorial than he was when *cleansed* of his leprosy." (Clarke)

b. **Now I know that there is no God in all the earth, except in Israel**: It wasn't just the healing that persuaded Naaman of this. It was the healing connected with the word of the prophet. Together, this was convincing evidence to Naaman that the God Elisha represented was the true **God in all the earth**.

c. **Please take a gift from your servant**: We can say that Naaman only meant well by this gesture. He felt it was appropriate to support the ministry of this man of God whom the LORD had used so greatly to bring healing. However, Elisha steadfastly insisted that he would receive nothing from Naaman.

5. (17-19) Naaman's new faith.

So Naaman said, "Then, if not, please let your servant be given two mule-loads of earth; for your servant will no longer offer either burnt offering or sacrifice to other gods, but to the LORD. Yet in this thing may the LORD pardon your servant: when my master goes into the temple of Rimmon to worship there, and he leans on my hand, and I bow down in the temple of Rimmon—when I bow down in the temple of Rimmon, may the LORD please pardon your servant in this thing." Then he said to him, "Go in peace." So he departed from him a short distance.

a. **Let your servant be given two mule-loads of earth**: Like many new believers, Naaman was superstitious in his faith. He held the common opinion of the ancient world that particular deities had power over particular places. He thought that if he took a piece of Israel back with him to Syria, he could better worship the God of Israel.

i. "The transporting of holy soil was a widespread custom. Naaman's faith was yet untaught; and with his personal need to follow publicly the state cults, Elisha may have felt that available Israelite soil may have afforded Naaman with some tangible reminder of his cleansing and new relationship to God." (Patterson and Austel)

b. **When I bow down in the temple of Rimmon, may the LORD please pardon your servant in this thing**: As an official in the government of Syria, Naaman was expected to participate in the worship of the Syrian gods. He asked Elisha for allowance to direct his heart to Yahweh even when he was in the temple of **Rimmon**.

i. "The Hebrew 'lean on the hand' does not imply physical support but that he was the king's 'right hand man' (cf. 2 Kings 7:2, 17)." (Wiseman)

c. **Go in peace**: By generally approving but not saying specifically "yes" or "no," it seems that Elisha left the matter up to Naaman and God. Perhaps he trusted that the LORD would personally convict Naaman of this and give him the integrity and strength to avoid idolatry.

i. Some commentators (Clarke and Trapp among them) believe that Naaman asked forgiveness for his *previous* idolatry in the **temple of Rimmon**, instead of asking permission for future occasions. Apparently, the Hebrew will allow for this translation, although it is not the most natural way to understand the text.

ii. Nevertheless, we can certainly agree with Trapp's application: "Let none by Naaman's example plead an upright soul in a prostrate body."

C. The greed of Gehazi.

1. (20-24) Gehazi follows after Naaman.

But Gehazi, the servant of Elisha the man of God, said, "Look, my master has spared Naaman this Syrian, while not receiving from his hands what he brought; but *as* the LORD lives, I will run after him and take something from him." So Gehazi pursued Naaman. When Naaman saw *him* running after him, he got down from the chariot to meet him, and said, *"Is* all well?" And he said, "All *is* well. My master has sent me, saying, 'Indeed, just now two young men of the sons of the prophets have come to me from the mountains of Ephraim. Please give them a talent of silver and two changes of garments.'" So Naaman said, "Please, take two talents." And he urged him, and bound two talents of silver in two bags, with two changes of garments, and handed *them* to two of his servants; and they carried *them* on ahead of him. When he came to the citadel, he took *them* from their hand, and stored *them* away in the house; then he let the men go, and they departed.

a. **I will run after him and take something from him**: As Gehazi heard Naaman and Elisha speak, he was shocked that his master refused to take anything from such a wealthy, influential, and grateful man. He figured that *someone* should benefit from such an opportunity, and he took the initiative to **run after** Naaman and **take something from him**.

i. Gehazi thought that Elisha *deserved* a reward (**my master has spared Naaman**). He also became exactly what Elisha avoided: becoming a *taker* (**take something from him**).

b. **Please, take two talents**: Gehazi probably thought that God was blessing his venture. After all, he asked for **a talent of silver** and Naaman was happy to give him **two talents**.

i. The fact that he **handed them to two of his servants** shows that this was a lot of silver. "It required two servants to carry these two talents, for, according to the computation above, each talent was about 120 lbs. weight." (Clarke)

c. **Stored them away in the house**: He deliberately hid them from Elisha. Gehazi knew that he did wrong.

2. (25-27) Gehazi's reward.

Now he went in and stood before his master. Elisha said to him, "Where *did you go*, Gehazi?" And he said, "Your servant did not go anywhere." Then he said to him, "Did not my heart go *with you* when the man turned back from his chariot to meet you? *Is it* time to receive money and to receive clothing, olive groves and vineyards, sheep and oxen, male and female servants? Therefore the leprosy of Naaman shall cling to you and your descendants forever." And he went out from his presence leprous, *as white* as snow.

a. **Did not my heart go with you**: Elisha *knew*. We don't know if this was supernatural knowledge or simply gained from observation and knowing Gehazi's character. One way or another, Elisha knew. All Gehazi's attempts to cover his sin failed.

b. **Is it time to receive money**: It seems that Elisha had no absolute law against receiving support from those who were touched by his ministry. Yet it was spiritually clear to Elisha, and should have been clear to Gehazi, that it was not appropriate at this **time** and circumstance.

i. **Money… clothing… olive groves and vineyards, sheep and oxen, male and female servants**: Obviously, Gehazi did not bring all of these things home with him from Naaman. Yet he *wanted* all of these things, and Elisha exposed his greedy heart.

ii. "The deepest wrong in the action of Gehazi was that it involved the Divine witness which had been borne to the Syrian, Naaman, by the action of the little serving maid in his house, and the prophet Elisha. Their actions had been wholly disinterested, and for the glory of God." (Morgan)

c. **Therefore the leprosy of Naaman shall cling to you and your descendants forever**: This was a severe judgment, but as a man in ministry Gehazi was under a stricter judgment. When he allowed himself to covet what Naaman had, he thought only in terms of the *money* Naaman possessed. God allowed him to keep the riches, but also gave him the *other* thing Naaman had – severe leprosy.

i. "Gehazi is not the last who has got money in an unlawful way, and has got God's curse with it." (Clarke)

ii. "We see here a pagan who by an act of faith is cured of leprosy and an Israelite who by an act of dishonor is cursed with it." (Dilday)

2 Kings 6 – God's Protection of Elisha

A. The recovery of the ax head.

1. (1-3) The sons of the prophets need to expand.

And the sons of the prophets said to Elisha, "See now, the place where we dwell with you is too small for us. Please, let us go to the Jordan, and let every man take a beam from there, and let us make there a place where we may dwell." So he answered, "Go." Then one said, "Please consent to go with your servants." And he answered, "I will go."

a. **The place where we dwell with you is too small for us**: This indicates that at this time Elisha had a significant impact on the nation. The old facility for housing the **sons of the prophets** was not large enough to meet the needs of all those who wanted to be trained in ministry.

b. **Please consent to go with your servants**: Elisha did not initiate or lead this work of building a new center for training the prophets, but it could not happen without his approval and blessing.

2. (4-7) The recovery of the ax head – another miracle of provision.

So he went with them. And when they came to the Jordan, they cut down trees. But as one was cutting down a tree, the iron *ax head* fell into the water; and he cried out and said, "Alas, master! For it was borrowed." So the man of God said, "Where did it fall?" And he showed him the place. So he cut off a stick, and threw *it* in there; and he made the iron float. Therefore he said, "Pick *it* up for yourself." So he reached out his hand and took it.

a. **The iron ax head fell into the water**: This was a significant loss. Iron was certainly present at this time in Israel, but it was not common enough to be cheap.

b. **Alas, master! For it was borrowed**: The man who lost the ax head was rightly sensitive to the fact that he lost something that belonged to someone else, making the loss more acute.

   i. "The *iron axe-head* (Hebrew 'iron') had been asked for, that is, begged or prayed for, and not necessarily 'borrowed.'" (Wiseman)

c. **So he cut off a stick, and threw it in there; and he made the iron float**: This was an obvious and unique miracle. There was no trickery in the way that Elisha put the stick in the water; it was simply an expression of his faith that God honored.

   i. "God can do all things, he can make iron swim – we cannot – and yet you see the prophet did it, and he did it by the use of a stick. He cut down a stick. Was there any connection between the stick and the iron? I can't see any, and yet God does use means, and he would have us use means." (Spurgeon)

   ii. "The chief value of the story lies in its revelation of the influence Elisha was exerting in the nation. The growth of the school of the prophets was most remarkable." (Morgan)

d. **Pick it up for yourself**: Conceivably, God could have arranged a way for the ax head to appear right in the man's hand without any effort on his part. But this miracle worked in a familiar way – God did the part only He could do, but He left to man the part that he could do.

   i. "Elisha then caused the submerged ax head to surface and instructed the pupil to retrieve the ax; thus he would personally participate in the miracle." (Patterson and Austel)

B. God protects Elisha from the Syrians.

1. (8-13) The king of Syria plots the capture of Elisha.

Now the king of Syria was making war against Israel; and he consulted with his servants, saying, "My camp *will be* in such and such a place." And the man of God sent to the king of Israel, saying, "Beware that you do not pass this place, for the Syrians are coming down there." Then the king of Israel sent *someone* to the place of which the man of God had told him. Thus he warned him, and he was watchful there, not just once or twice. Therefore the heart of the king of Syria was greatly troubled by this thing; and he called his servants and said to them, "Will you not show me which of us *is* for the king of Israel?" And one of his servants said, "None, my lord, O king; but Elisha, the prophet who *is* in Israel, tells the king of Israel the words that you speak in your bedroom." So he said, "Go and see where he *is*, that I may send and get him." And it was told him, saying, "Surely *he is* in Dothan."

a. **And the man of God sent to the king of Israel**: Elisha did not support the corrupt monarchs of Israel, but he knew that it was even worse for Israel to be conquered and subjugated under Syria. Therefore, he gave the **king of Israel** information from divinely inspired espionage.

i. "A more sensible king, Jehoram, now sits on the throne of Ahab, and the prophet of the Lord is no longer a dreaded antagonist, but the king's trusted counselor. Elijah was a fugitive constantly on the run from a wrathful king, but now Elisha is a welcome visitor in Jehoram's court." (Dilday)

b. **Will you not show me which of us is for the king of Israel**: The king of Syria was naturally mystified by the way the king of Israel knew all of Syria's plans beforehand. He was convinced there was a traitor among them until one servant revealed that **Elisha, the prophet who is in Israel**, knew and revealed these things.

2. (14-17) Elisha sees his invisible, spiritual protection.

Therefore he sent horses and chariots and a great army there, and they came by night and surrounded the city. And when the servant of the man of God arose early and went out, there was an army, surrounding the city with horses and chariots. And his servant said to him, "Alas, my master! What shall we do?" So he answered, "Do not fear, for those who *are* with us *are* more than those who *are* with them." And Elisha prayed, and said, "Lord, I pray, open his eyes that he may see." Then the Lord opened the eyes of the young man, and he saw. And behold, the mountain *was* full of horses and chariots of fire all around Elisha.

a. **Alas, my master! What shall we do**: When Elisha's servant saw the **horses and chariots and a great army** surrounding their city, he was naturally afraid. He knew that there was little chance of escaping or surviving an attack from so many.

b. **Do not fear, for those who are with us are more than those who are with them**: This seemed unbelievable to Elisha's servant. He saw the **horses**, the **chariots**, and the **great army** surrounding them. He could not see *anyone* who was **with** Elisha and him.

i. We also notice that Elisha gave his servant a *reason* to **not fear**. This was not empty hope or wishful thinking; it was a real *reason* for confidence, even if the servant could not see it.

c. **Lord, I pray, open his eyes that he may see**: Elisha did not pray that God would change anything in the situation. His only request was that his servant could actually *see* the reality of the situation. Yet, Elisha also did not try to persuade the servant of the reality of **those who are with us**. The servant could not have this explained to him nor could he be persuaded into it. He had to **see** it.

d. Then the LORD opened the eyes of the young man, and he saw: God answered Elisha's prayer. When a person is blind to spiritual reality, only God can open his eyes. God may do it through the words someone speaks, but the work of spiritually opening eyes is spiritual work and belongs to God alone.

e. And behold, the mountain was full of horses and chariots of fire all around Elisha: When his eyes were opened, the servant saw the reality that he could not see before. He saw that there really were more with him and Elisha than those assembled against them.

i. The previous lack of perception on the part of Elisha's servant did not make the reality of the spiritual army any less real. If there are 50 people who do not see something, it doesn't invalidate the perception of one who *does* see.

ii. "Faith is never the imagining of unreal things. It is the grip of things which cannot be demonstrated to the senses, but which are real. The chariots of horses and fire were actually there." (Morgan)

iii. "That you have not perceived spiritual things is true; but it is no proof that there are none to perceive. The whole case is like that of the Irishman who tried to upset evidence by non-evidence. Four witnesses saw him commit a murder. He pleaded that he was not guilty, and wished to establish his innocence by producing forty persons who did not see him do it. Of what use would that have been? So, if forty people declare that there is no power of the Holy Ghost going with the word, this only proves that the forty people do not know what others do know." (Charles Spurgeon, *Three Sights Worth Seeing*)

iv. **Horses and chariots** were the most sophisticated and mighty military instruments of the day. But the invisible army of God had literally more firepower than the horses and chariots of the Syrians. The spiritual army had **chariots of fire all around Elisha**.

v. "If our eyes were opened, we should see the angel-hosts as an encircling fence of fire; but whether we see them or not, they are certainly there." (Meyer)

3. (18-23) The blinded Syrians are led to Samaria.

So when *the Syrians* came down to him, Elisha prayed to the LORD, and said, "Strike this people, I pray, with blindness." And He struck them with blindness according to the word of Elisha. Now Elisha said to them, "This *is* not the way, nor *is* this the city. Follow me, and I will

bring you to the man whom you seek." But he led them to Samaria. So it was, when they had come to Samaria, that Elisha said, "LORD, open the eyes of these *men,* that they may see." And the LORD opened their eyes, and they saw; and there *they were,* inside Samaria! Now when the king of Israel saw them, he said to Elisha, "My father, shall I kill *them?* Shall I kill *them?"* But he answered, "You shall not kill *them.* Would you kill those whom you have taken captive with your sword and your bow? Set food and water before them, that they may eat and drink and go to their master." Then he prepared a great feast for them; and after they ate and drank, he sent them away and they went to their master. So the bands of Syrian *raiders* came no more into the land of Israel.

> a. **Strike this people, I pray, with blindness**: The Syrian soldiers could not see the spiritual army, so they did not hesitate to approach Elisha. But just as he previously prayed that God would give sight to his servant, he then asked God to **strike this people... with blindness**. God answered this prayer, just as He previously answered the prayer to give perception to the servant.
>
>> i. This shows us that God may grant sight or send blindness, according to His wisdom and in response to the prayers of His people.
>>
>> ii. "Not with a total blindness, that they could see nothing, for then they would not have followed him; but with a partial blindness, that they could not distinctly discern the man they sought; which might be by some alteration made by God in their brain, or in the air." (Poole)
>
> b. **Follow me, and I will bring you to the man whom you seek**: Here Elisha told a technical truth but certainly intended to deceive. He did in fact bring them to the man they sought (when their eyes were opened, Elisha was there with them). However, he led them back to Samaria – the capital city of the kingdom of Israel and an unfriendly place for a group of Syrian soldiers.
>
>> i. Yet, Elisha's gentle deception demonstrates a principle: *the blind are easily deceived.* Those who are spiritually blind should appreciate that they can be easily deceived regarding spiritual things.
>
> c. **You shall not kill them**: Instead of killing these enemy soldiers, Elisha instead commanded the king of Israel to treat them with kindness and generosity. This practice of answering evil with good successfully changed the policy of free-lance raiders from Syria (**So the bands of Syrian raiders came no more into the land of Israel**).

C. The siege of Samaria.

1. (24-29) Terrible famine in the besieged city of Samaria.

And it happened after this that Ben-Hadad king of Syria gathered all his army, and went up and besieged Samaria. And there was a great famine in Samaria; and indeed they besieged it until a donkey's head was *sold* for eighty *shekels* of silver, and one-fourth of a kab of dove droppings for five *shekels* of silver. Then, as the king of Israel was passing by on the wall, a woman cried out to him, saying, "Help, my lord, O king!" And he said, "If the Lord does not help you, where can I find help for you? From the threshing floor or from the winepress?" Then the king said to her, "What is troubling you?" And she answered, "This woman said to me, 'Give your son, that we may eat him today, and we will eat my son tomorrow.' So we boiled my son, and ate him. And I said to her on the next day, 'Give your son, that we may eat him'; but she has hidden her son."

> a. **Ben-Hadad king of Syria gathered all his army, and went up and besieged Samaria**: Though the kindness of Elisha and the king of Israel changed the heart of the Syrian raiders, it did not change the heart of the **king of Syria**. He launched a large, full-scale attack against his neighbor to the south.
>
>> i. He used the common method of attack in those days against securely walled cities: He **besieged Samaria**. A siege was intended to surround a city, prevent all business and trade from entering or leaving the city, and to eventually starve the population into surrender.
>
> b. **There was a great famine in Samaria**: The siege strategy successfully starved Samaria. The famine was so bad that a **donkey's head** or **dove droppings** became so expensive that only the rich could afford them.
>
>> i. Wiseman says that **dove droppings** is better translated as *carob beans*, and that **five shekels of silver** were more than a month's wages for a laborer.
>>
>> ii. Yet, Poole writes: "That dove's dung, though it be hotter than ordinary, might in other respects be fitter for nourishment than other, as being made of the best and purest grains, and having some moisture in it."
>>
>> iii. "When Hannibal besieged Casiline, one mouse was sold for two hundred pence. Puddings made of dogs' guts were dear bought at the siege of Scodra." (Trapp)
>
> c. **Give your son, that we may eat him**: This shows how terrible the famine was. Mothers were so hungry that they ate their own children.
>
>> i. Deuteronomy 28 contains an extended section where God warned Israel about the curses that would come upon them if they rejected the

covenant He made with them. Part of that chapter describes the horrors fulfilled in this chapter: *They shall besiege you at all your gates until your high and fortified walls, in which you trust, come down throughout all your land; and they shall besiege you at all your gates throughout all your land which the LORD your God has given you. You shall eat the fruit of your own body, the flesh of your sons and your daughters whom the LORD your God has given you, in the siege and desperate straits in which your enemy shall distress you.* (Deuteronomy 28:52-53)

ii. These terrors came upon Israel because they disobeyed Gpd, rejected Him, and abandoned the covenant He made with them.

2. (30-33) The anger of the king of Israel against Elisha.

Now it happened, when the king heard the words of the woman, that he tore his clothes; and as he passed by on the wall, the people looked, and there underneath *he had* sackcloth on his body. Then he said, "God do so to me and more also, if the head of Elisha the son of Shaphat remains on him today." But Elisha was sitting in his house, and the elders were sitting with him. And *the king* sent a man ahead of him, but before the messenger came to him, he said to the elders, "Do you see how this son of a murderer has sent someone to take away my head? Look, when the messenger comes, shut the door, and hold him fast at the door. *Is* not the sound of his master's feet behind him?" And while he was still talking with them, there was the messenger, coming down to him; and then *the king* said, "Surely this calamity *is* from the LORD; why should I wait for the LORD any longer?"

a. **God do so to me and more also**: The king was deeply grieved and angry – but not with himself, with Israel, or with their sin. The king was angry against the prophet of God.

b. **Surely this calamity is from the LORD; why should I wait for the LORD any longer**: The king of Israel was honest enough to admit that his real anger was against the LORD.

2 Kings 7 – God's Miraculous Provision for Samaria

A. God's promise and what the lepers discovered.

1. (1-2) God's promise and the doubt of the king's officer.

Then Elisha said, "Hear the word of the Lord. Thus says the Lord: 'Tomorrow about this time a seah of fine flour *shall be sold* for a shekel, and two seahs of barley for a shekel, at the gate of Samaria.'" So an officer on whose hand the king leaned answered the man of God and said, "Look, *if* the Lord would make windows in heaven, could this thing be?" And he said, "In fact, you shall see *it* with your eyes, but you shall not eat of it."

a. **Hear the word of the Lord**: Though the king of Israel blamed the Lord for the calamity that came upon Israel and Samaria, God still had a word for the king and the nation – and it was a good word.

b. **Tomorrow about this time**: God's promise through Elisha was that in 24 hours the economic situation in Samaria would be completely reversed. Instead of scarcity, there would be such abundance that food prices would radically drop in the city.

i. "The *gate* was the market-place as well as the local court of justice." (Wiseman)

ii. By the standards of that time, the prices listed were not cheap; but they were nothing compared to the famine conditions associated with the siege. "By the next day conditions would so improve that good products would be available again, even though at a substantial price." (Patterson and Austel)

c. **Look, if the Lord would make windows in heaven, could this thing be**: The king's officer doubted the prophecy, and his doubt was based on several faulty premises.

i. First, he doubted the *power* of God. If God willed it, He certainly could **make windows in heaven** and drop down food from the sky for the hungry, besieged city of Samaria.

ii. Second, he doubted the *creativity* of God. In the mind of the king's officer, the way food could come to the city was from above, because the city was surrounded by a hostile, besieging army. He had no idea that God could bring provision in a completely unexpected way. "How often faith breaks down in this way! It knows that God is, and that He can act. But it only sees one way, and refuses to believe that such a way will be taken. The supply came without the opening of heaven's windows." (Morgan)

iii. Third, he doubted the *messenger* of God. Though the promise was admittedly hard to believe, the king's officer could have and should have believed it because it came from a man with an established track record of reliability.

iv. All in all, the officer well illustrates the conduct of unbelief:

- Unbelief dares to question the truthfulness of God's promise itself.
- Unbelief says, "This is a *new* thing and cannot be true."
- Unbelief says, "This is a *sudden* thing and cannot be true."
- Unbelief says, "There is no way to accomplish this thing."
- Unbelief says, "There is only one way God can work."
- Unbelief says, "Even if God does something, it won't be enough."

d. **In fact, you shall see it with your eyes, but you shall not eat of it**: Through Elisha, God pronounced a harsh judgment upon the king's doubting officer. He would see the word fulfilled, but not benefit from its fulfillment.

i. "Unbelievers do not really enjoy the things of this life. The mass of them find that wealth does not yield them satisfaction, their outward riches cannot conceal their inner poverty. To many men it is given to have all that heart can wish, and yet not to have what their heart does wish. They have everything except contentment." (Spurgeon)

2. (3-5) Four lepers come upon the deserted Syrian camp.

Now there were four leprous men at the entrance of the gate; and they said to one another, "Why are we sitting here until we die? If we say, 'We will enter the city,' the famine *is* in the city, and we shall die there. And if we sit here, we die also. Now therefore, come, let us surrender to

the army of the Syrians. If they keep us alive, we shall live; and if they kill us, we shall only die." And they rose at twilight to go to the camp of the Syrians; and when they had come to the outskirts of the Syrian camp, to their surprise no one *was* there.

a. **Now there were four leprous men**: These men stayed at the **entrance of the gate** because they were not welcome in the city. Their leprous condition made them outcasts and untouchables.

i. "If you were to take out of the Scriptures all the stories that have to do with poor, afflicted men and women, what a very small book the Bible would become, especially if together with the stories you removed all the psalms of the sorrowful, all the promises for the distressed, and all the passages which belong to the children of grief! This Book, indeed, for the most part is made up of the annals of the poor and despised." (Spurgeon)

ii. Unfounded Jewish traditions say these four were actually Gehazi and his three sons. Gehazi was afflicted with leprosy because of his greed toward Naaman (2 Kings 5:27).

b. **Why are we sitting here until we die**: Their logic was perfect. They would soon die from the famine if they stayed by the city. If any food became available, they would certainly be the last to receive it. So they decided that their chances were better if they surrendered to the Syrians.

i. "Now you perceive that there are just two courses open to you; you can sit still, but then you know that you must perish; or you can go to Christ, and your fear is that you will perish then. Yet you can but die if you go to him, and he rejects you; whereas, if you do not go to him, you must surely perish." (Spurgeon)

c. **When they had come to the outskirts of the Syrian camp, to their surprise no one was there**: This huge army surrounded the city of Samaria for many months, and the camp was the home and supply center for thousands of men. When the lepers came upon it that morning, they discovered an empty army camp – fully supplied, but empty of men.

i. The words **to the outskirts of the Syrian camp** imply that they came not only to the edge of the camp, but that they walked around to the *furthermost part* of the **Syrian camp**, the part *away* from the city. They came to the camp as someone from afar would approach, not as someone from Syria. They figured that this was their best chance, coming as if they were not from the besieged city and to the least fortified positions of the camp.

ii. This approach of the lepers to the camp "… may provide the occasion for the miracle itself; perhaps the Lord had in some way magnified the stumbling footsteps of the men as they made their way around the camp's opposite end." (Patterson and Austel)

3. (6-7) How God caused the Syrians to abandon their camp.

For the LORD had caused the army of the Syrians to hear the noise of chariots and the noise of horses—the noise of a great army; so they said to one another, "Look, the king of Israel has hired against us the kings of the Hittites and the kings of the Egyptians to attack us!" Therefore they arose and fled at twilight, and left the camp intact—their tents, their horses, and their donkeys—and they fled for their lives.

a. **For the LORD had caused the army of the Syrians to hear the noise of chariots… the noise of a great army**: Israel was powerless against this besieging army, but God wasn't powerless. He attacked the Syrian army simply by causing them to **hear** the **noise** of an army.

i. Perhaps God did this by putting the noise into the air; perhaps He simply created the perception of the noise in the minds of the Syrian soldiers. However God did it, it happened.

ii. The same God who struck one Syrian army so they could not see what *was* there now struck another Syrian army so that they heard things that *were not* there.

b. **And left the camp intact**: Everything was left behind, leaving the unlikely lepers to spoil the camp. As a result, *the siege for Samaria was over* – even though no one in the city *knew* it or *enjoyed* it.

i. "Everybody who went to bed that night felt that he was still in that horrible den where grim death seemed actually present in the skeleton forms of the hunger-bitten. They were as free as the harts of the wilderness had they known it: but their ignorance held them in vile durance [imprisonment]." (Spurgeon)

4. (8-9) After enjoying it all, the lepers realize their responsibility.

And when these lepers came to the outskirts of the camp, they went into one tent and ate and drank, and carried from it silver and gold and clothing, and went and hid *them*; then they came back and entered another tent, and carried *some* from there *also*, and went and hid *it*. Then they said to one another, "We are not doing right. This day *is* a day of good news, and we remain silent. If we wait until morning light, some punishment will come upon us. Now therefore, come, let us go and tell the king's household."

a. **They went into one tent and ate and drank**: Of course they did. After the long period of famine, this was the answer to every hope and prayer they had.

b. **And went and hid it**: They knew that their discovery of the camp could not remain secret forever. They hid some of the valuables so they could profit by them even when the camp was discovered by others.

c. **We are not doing right… come, let us go and tell**: The lepers rightly enjoyed the miracle God provided. But they also realized that the gift gave them a responsibility to share it with others. They understood that to **remain silent** and to selfishly enjoy their blessings would be sin. They had a responsibility to share the **good news**.

i. "If the only result of our religion is the comfort of our poor little souls, if the beginning and the end of piety is contained within one's self, why, it is a strange thing to be in connection with the unselfish Jesus, and to be the fruit of his gracious Spirit. Surely, Jesus did not come to save us that we might live unto ourselves. He came to save us from selfishness." (Spurgeon)

ii. Yet, *they enjoyed the feast first* before they told others about it. We cannot properly share the good news of Jesus Christ unless we ourselves are enjoying it.

B. The plundering of the camp of the Syrians.

1. (10-15) The king discovers the empty camp of the Syrian army.

So they went and called to the gatekeepers of the city, and told them, saying, "We went to the Syrian camp, and surprisingly no one *was* there, not a human sound—only horses and donkeys tied, and the tents intact." And the gatekeepers called out, and they told *it* to the king's household inside. So the king arose in the night and said to his servants, "Let me now tell you what the Syrians have done to us. They know that we *are* hungry; therefore they have gone out of the camp to hide themselves in the field, saying, 'When they come out of the city, we shall catch them alive, and get into the city.'" And one of his servants answered and said, "Please, let several *men* take five of the remaining horses which are left in the city. Look, they *may either become* like all the multitude of Israel that are left in it; or indeed, *I say,* they *may become* like all the multitude of Israel left from those who are consumed; so let us send them and see." Therefore they took two chariots with horses; and the king sent them in the direction of the Syrian army, saying, "Go and see." And they went after them to the Jordan; and indeed all the road *was* full

of garments and weapons which the Syrians had thrown away in their haste. So the messengers returned and told the king.

a. **They went and called to the gatekeepers of the city**: Since the lepers were not welcome in the city, they could only communicate with the **gatekeepers**. There were many people they could *not* speak to, but they were faithful to speak to the ones they *could* speak to.

b. **And the gatekeepers called out, and they told it**: The good news from the lepers was communicated in the simplest way possible. It went from one person to another, until the news reached the king himself.

c. **So let us send them and see**: This was the sensible reaction to the good news that started with the report of the lepers. The report might be true or it might not be; it only made sense to test it and see.

2. (16) The fulfillment of Elisha's prophecy.

Then the people went out and plundered the tents of the Syrians. So a seah of fine flour was *sold* for a shekel, and two seahs of barley for a shekel, according to the word of the LORD.

a. **Then the people went out and plundered the tents of the Syrians**: When the good news that started with the report of the lepers was found to be true, there was no stopping the people. Because they knew their need, they were happy to receive God's provision to meet that need.

i. The king's officer "derided the possibility of the prophet's prediction; and no doubt had plenty of adherents. But the leper's report swept away all his words to the winds. They had known, tasted, and handled." (Meyer)

b. **According to the word of the LORD**: Through Elisha, God announced the exact prices in the Samaritan markets, and the prophecy was proven to be precisely true.

3. (17-20) The death of the king's doubting officer.

Now the king had appointed the officer on whose hand he leaned to have charge of the gate. But the people trampled him in the gate, and he died, just as the man of God had said, who spoke when the king came down to him. So it happened just as the man of God had spoken to the king, saying, "Two seahs of barley for a shekel, and a seah of fine flour for a shekel, shall be *sold* tomorrow about this time in the gate of Samaria." Then that officer had answered the man of God, and said, "Now look, *if* the LORD would make windows in heaven, could such a thing be?" And he had said, "In fact, you shall see *it* with your eyes, but you shall not

eat of it." And so it happened to him, for the people trampled him in the gate, and he died.

a. **The king had appointed the officer on whose hand he leaned to have charge of the gate**: Perhaps the king did this to rebuke his **officer**. The man would have to personally supervise the people responding to the provision he said could never come, because he could not understand how God could bring the supply despite the siege.

b. **For the people trampled him in the gate, and he died**: The prediction regarding the officer proved just as true as the prediction regarding the prices of food in the markets of Samaria. Because of his unbelief, he saw others enjoy God's blessings but he did not.

2 Kings 8 – New Kings in Syria and Judah

A. The restoration of the Shunammite woman's land.

1. (1-3) The Shunammite woman returns to Israel after seven years.

Then Elisha spoke to the woman whose son he had restored to life, saying, "Arise and go, you and your household, and stay wherever you can; for the LORD has called for a famine, and furthermore, it will come upon the land for seven years." So the woman arose and did according to the saying of the man of God, and she went with her household and dwelt in the land of the Philistines seven years. It came to pass, at the end of seven years, that the woman returned from the land of the Philistines; and she went to make an appeal to the king for her house and for her land.

> a. **Elisha spoke to the woman whose son he had restored to life**: 2 Kings 4 describes Elisha's previous dealings with this woman. She and her husband were godly, generous people who helped the prophet. Through Elisha's prayer they were blessed with a son, who was also brought miraculously back to life.
>
> b. **She went with her household and dwelt in the land of the Philistines seven years**: On the advice of the prophet, the woman and her family left Israel because of a coming famine. In **the land of the Philistines**, they were spared the worst of the famine.
>
> c. **She went to make an appeal to the king for her house and for her land**: Upon leaving Israel and going to the land of the Philistines, the woman forfeited her claim to her ancestral lands. She made this **appeal** so she would not be a loser for listening to God's prophet and for saving her family from famine.

2. (4-6) Her land is restored.

Then the king talked with Gehazi, the servant of the man of God, saying, "Tell me, please, all the great things Elisha has done." Now it happened, as he was telling the king how he had restored the dead to life, that there was the woman whose son he had restored to life, appealing to the king for her house and for her land. And Gehazi said, "My lord, O king, this *is* the woman, and this *is* her son whom Elisha restored to life." And when the king asked the woman, she told him. So the king appointed a certain officer for her, saying, "Restore all that *was* hers, and all the proceeds of the field from the day that she left the land until now."

a. **Then the king talked with Gehazi**: This was the same servant of Elisha who was cursed with leprosy in 2 Kings 5:20-27. It seems strange that a severely afflicted leper would be a counselor to a king, so it seems that either Gehazi was granted healing from his leprosy or that this actually took place *before* the events of 2 Kings 5.

i. Of course, it is still possible that the king had this conversation with Gehazi when the former prophet's assistant was a leper and the king simply kept his distance. "Some think that this conversation might have taken place after Gehazi became leprous; the king having an insatiable curiosity to know the private history of a man who had done such astonishing things: and from whom could he get this information, except from the prophet's own confidential servant?" (Clarke)

b. **Tell me, please, all the great things Elisha has done**: Perhaps his motive was nothing more than curiosity, yet it was still a significant testimony to the king of Israel. He knew that God was with the actions of Elisha, giving evidence that He was also with the word of Elisha.

c. **As he was telling the king**: The woman came to make her request at the *exact time* Gehazi told the king about the miracles associated with her life. This was perfect, God-ordained timing.

d. **Restore all that was hers, and all the proceeds of the field from the day that she left**: The king understood that if *God* was obviously supportive of this woman, then it also made sense for him to support her and to answer her request. In the end, her obedience to God's word was not penalized.

i. "This act was in striking contrast to the notorious land-grabbing of Jehoram's father, Ahab." (Dilday)

B. A new king in Syria.

1. (7-9) Elisha is questioned by Ben-Hadad.

Then Elisha went to Damascus, and Ben-Hadad king of Syria was sick; and it was told him, saying, "The man of God has come here." And the king said to Hazael, "Take a present in your hand, and go to meet the

man of God, and inquire of the LORD by him, saying, 'Shall I recover from this disease?' " So Hazael went to meet him and took a present with him, of every good thing of Damascus, forty camel-loads; and he came and stood before him, and said, "Your son Ben-Hadad king of Syria has sent me to you, saying, 'Shall I recover from this disease?' "

> a. **The man of God has come here**: The leaders of Syria once tried to capture or kill Elisha. Since God miraculously delivered the prophet so many times, he was now respected and welcomed in the courts of the Syrian king. He was especially welcome on account of the king's illness.
>
> b. **Take a present in your hand**: Wanting to know the outcome of his present illness, the king of Syria asked the prophet – and with his extravagant gift did whatever he could to prompt a favorable message.
>
>> i. "Whether the prophet received it or not, is not here mentioned; but it is most probable that he did not, from his former practice, chapter 5, and because the reasons which then swayed him were still of the same force." (Poole)

2. (10-13) Elisha's enigmatic revelation.

And Elisha said to him, "Go, say to him, 'You shall certainly recover.' However the LORD has shown me that he will really die." Then he set his countenance in a stare until he was ashamed; and the man of God wept. And Hazael said, "Why is my lord weeping?" He answered, "Because I know the evil that you will do to the children of Israel: Their strongholds you will set on fire, and their young men you will kill with the sword; and you will dash their children, and rip open their women with child." So Hazael said, "But what *is* your servant—a dog, that he should do this gross thing?" And Elisha answered, "The LORD has shown me that you *will become* king over Syria."

> a. **Go, say to him, "You shall certainly recover." However the LORD has shown me that he will really die**: God gave Elisha insight into more than the health of the king of Syria. He also saw the inevitable and ultimately God-ordained political machinations that would unfold.
>
>> i. Elisha rightly said that the king would **certainly recover** from his illness, and he did. However, he also saw that the same servant he spoke with at that moment would engineer an assassination and take the throne.
>>
>> ii. This is how Elisha's statement was true. The king **certainly** did **recover** from his illness, and he really did die soon – but not from the illness.

b. **He set his countenance in a stare… I know the evil that you will do**: This was a dramatic, personal confrontation between this prophet and the high official of the king of Syria. Elisha stared at him so because he had prophetic knowledge of future events, and how this man would trouble Israel in the future.

> i. "The prophet gazed long and fixedly into the eyes of Hazael. It would seem that he saw far more in the soul of the man than any other had seen, perhaps more than the man himself was conscious of." (Morgan)

c. **And the man of God wept**: God told Elisha more about the coming situation than he wanted to know. He showed the prophet that the messenger of the king (**Hazael**), after he took the throne from the present king of Syria, would do **evil** to the **children of Israel**.

> i. Elisha's prophetic calling and gift was at times more of a burden than a blessing. He could clearly see what would befall Israel through Hazael, but he was powerless to prevent it.

> ii. "The nearer we live to God, the more we deserve to be known as men and women of God, the more will our tears flow for the slain of the daughters of our people." (Meyer)

> iii. "His tears were in themselves signs of his understanding of the necessity for those severe judgments which must fall upon the guilty nation; but they were the outcome of his deep love for his people." (Morgan)

d. **But what is your servant – a dog, that he should do this gross thing**: Perhaps Hazael had planned this assassination and simply acted ignorant at Elisha's announcement. Perhaps he had not yet planned it, but did not know the evil capabilities in his own heart.

> i. Either way, his offense was inappropriate. He should have taken this warning as an opportunity to confront himself and to *do right*, instead of turning an accusation back upon Elisha.

> ii. "Our ignorance of the depravity of our own hearts is a startling fact. Hazael did not believe that he was bad enough to do any of the things here anticipated… I appeal to you, Christian men and women, if anyone had told you that you would have loved your Savior so little as you have done; if any prophet had told you, in the hour of your conversion, that you would have served him so feebly as you have done, would you have believed it!" (Spurgeon)

e. **The LORD has shown me that you will become king over Syria**: It may be asked if Elisha should have told Hazael this; perhaps he set in motion a self-fulfilling prophecy and actually *inspired* the assassination of the king of Syria.

    i. However, there are many reasons for thinking that Elisha did exactly the right thing when he said this to Hazael.

- Elisha did not tell Hazael how the king would die; he did not reveal that it would be through assassination.
- Elisha did not tell Hazael *how* he would become the next king of Syria; he did not *tell* Hazael to assassinate the king.
- Elisha went against his own compassionate and patriotic interests in telling Hazael this, making it more likely that he did it at God's prompting.
- Elisha perhaps hoped that this amazing prophecy would touch Hazael's heart and turn him away from the evil he would later commit against Israel.

    ii. As it turned out, God knew the actions of Hazael, but He did not *make* Hazael do it. "It was absolutely foretold that Hazael would be king of Syria. The prophet knew the fact right well, and he clearly descried the means; else, why should he look into Hazael's face, and weep? God foreknew the mischief that he would do when he came to the throne; yet that foreknowledge did not in the least degree interfere with his free agency." (Spurgeon)

3. (14-15) The assassination of the king of Syria.

Then he departed from Elisha, and came to his master, who said to him, "What did Elisha say to you?" And he answered, "He told me you would surely recover." But it happened on the next day that he took a thick cloth and dipped *it* in water, and spread *it* over his face so that he died; and Hazael reigned in his place.

    a. **He told me you would surely recover**: The king certainly did recover, or would have, had not the wicked Hazael committed murder.

        i. "He represents the prophet's answer by halves, that by his master's security he might have the fitter opportunity to execute his treasonable design." (Poole)

    b. **So that he died**: Hazael took an evil inference from Elisha's prophecy and seized the throne. He should have taken the prophet's announcement as a warning to check his own heart; instead he acted on that evil – and was fully responsible for his own actions.

        i. "The predestination of God does not destroy the free agency of man, or lighten the responsibility of the sinner. It is true, in the matter of salvation, when God comes to save, his free grace prevails over our free agency, and leads the will in glorious captivity to the obedience of faith. But in sinning, man is free, – free in the widest sense of the term, never being compelled to do any evil deed, but being left to follow the turbulent passions of his own corrupt heart, and carry out the prevailing tendencies of his own depraved nature." (Spurgeon)

ii. "An ancient Assyrian inscription, called the Berlin inscription, says, 'Hazael the son of nobody, seized the throne.' This designation indicates that he was an usurper with no dynastic line." (Dilday)

C. Two new kings in Judah.

1. (16-24) The reign of Jehoram over Judah.

Now in the fifth year of Joram the son of Ahab, king of Israel, Jehoshaphat *having been* king of Judah, Jehoram the son of Jehoshaphat began to reign as king of Judah. He was thirty-two years old when he became king, and he reigned eight years in Jerusalem. And he walked in the way of the kings of Israel, just as the house of Ahab had done, for the daughter of Ahab was his wife; and he did evil in the sight of the Lord. Yet the Lord would not destroy Judah, for the sake of his servant David, as He promised him to give a lamp to him *and* his sons forever. In his days Edom revolted against Judah's authority, and made a king over themselves. So Joram went to Zair, and all his chariots with him. Then he rose by night and attacked the Edomites who had surrounded him and the captains of the chariots; and the troops fled to their tents. Thus Edom has been in revolt against Judah's authority to this day. And Libnah revolted at that time. Now the rest of the acts of Joram, and all that he did, *are* they not written in the book of the chronicles of the kings of Judah? So Joram rested with his fathers, and was buried with his fathers in the City of David. Then Ahaziah his son reigned in his place.

a. **Jehoram, the son of Jehoshaphat began to reign as king of Judah**: The story of the kings of Judah really paused at 1 Kings 22:50, where Jehoshaphat the son of Asa ended his 25-year reign and his son Jehoram came to the throne. Now we pick up the story of Jehoram again.

i. This King **Jehoram** of Judah should not be confused with the King Jehoram of Israel mentioned in 2 Kings 3. That Jehoram is called **Joram** in this passage and following.

b. **He walked in the way of the kings of Israel**: This was not a compliment. While the Southern Kingdom of Judah had a mixture of godly and wicked kings, the Northern Kingdom of Israel had nothing but evil, God-rejecting kings.

> i. The Chronicler adds that Jehoram made all Judah to sin according to the religion of the Canaanites (2 Chronicles 21:11).

c. **For the daughter of Ahab was his wife**: The wickedness of Jehoram was not a surprise, considering how much he allowed himself to be influenced by the house of Ahab. Perhaps this marriage made sense politically or socially, but it was a spiritual calamity for Judah.

> i. Arranged by his father, Jehoram married the daughter of Ahab and Jezebel – her name was Athaliah. In order to consolidate his throne, he murdered his many brothers and many other leaders (1 Chronicles 21:1-6). "Josephus expands on this, indicating that he committed the murders at the prompting of Athaliah." (Dilday)
>
> ii. Perhaps some people thought that the marriage between the royal families of the kingdom of Judah and the kingdom of Israel would lift up the kingdom of Israel spiritually. It didn't work that way. Instead, it brought the kingdom of Judah *down* spiritually.
>
> iii. "It was all the result of his ill-advised alliance with the ungodly house of Ahab, and what he sowed he, by dread anticipation at least, reaped. And his posterity were made to reap it actually, in a most terrible way." (Knapp)

d. **Yet the LORD would not destroy Judah, for the sake of his servant David**: The implication is that Jehoram's evil was great enough to justify such judgment, but God withheld it out of faithfulness to his ancestor David.

> i. "The *lamp* was more than a symbol of life and of testimony; it reminded the hearer of the covenant (Psalm 132:17, *c.f.* 2 Chronicles 21:7)." (Wiseman)

e. **In his days Edom revolted against Judah's authority**: This is evidence of the weakness of Jehoram. He thought that the marriage alliance with Ahab and the kingdom of Israel would make Judah stronger, but this act of disobedience only made them weaker.

f. **So Joram rested with his fathers**: It is easy to get confused with the variation between **Jehoram** and **Joram**, but they are two variant names for the same king of Judah. He died and was buried in Jerusalem, but not in the honored tombs of his ancestors (2 Chronicles 21:20).

> i. According to 2 Chronicles 21:12-15, Elijah wrote Jehoram a letter, condemning him for his sins and predicting that judgment would come

upon him and disaster upon the nation. At the age of 40, Jehoram was struck with a fatal intestinal disease and he died in terrible pain (2 Chronicles 21:19).

ii. "He is one of the most unlovely of all the kings of Judah. 'Exalted by Jehovah,' he was for his wickedness thrust down to a dishonoured grave." (Knapp)

2. (25-29) The reign of Ahaziah over Judah.

In the twelfth year of Joram the son of Ahab, king of Israel, Ahaziah the son of Jehoram, king of Judah, began to reign. Ahaziah *was* twenty-two years old when he became king, and he reigned one year in Jerusalem. His mother's name *was* Athaliah the granddaughter of Omri, king of Israel. And he walked in the way of the house of Ahab, and did evil in the sight of the LORD, like the house of Ahab, for he *was* the son-in-law of the house of Ahab. Now he went with Joram the son of Ahab to war against Hazael king of Syria at Ramoth Gilead; and the Syrians wounded Joram. Then King Joram went back to Jezreel to recover from the wounds which the Syrians had inflicted on him at Ramah, when he fought against Hazael king of Syria. And Ahaziah the son of Jehoram, king of Judah, went down to see Joram the son of Ahab in Jezreel, because he was sick.

a. **Ahaziah the son of Jehoram, king of Judah, began to reign**: The short life and reign of Jehoram (he reigned only eight years and died at 40 years of age) should have warned Ahaziah. His brief reign (**one year**) shows he was even *less* blessed than his father Jehoram.

i. "Ahaziah succeeded his father, Jehoram, in the critical year 841 B.C. He was not to survive the momentous waves of the political events that were to inundate the ancient Near East in that year. Indeed, in 841 B.C. Shalmaneser III of Assyria (859-824 B.C.) at last was able to break the coalition of western allies with whom he had previously fought a long series of battles (853, 848, 845)." (Patterson and Austel)

ii. **Twenty-two years old**: This is at odds with 2 Chronicles 22:2, which says that Ahaziah took the throne when 42 years old. "I am satisfied the reading in 2 Chronicles 22:2, is a *mistake*; and that we should read there, as here, *twenty-two* instead of *forty-two* years… "Is there a single ancient author of any kind, but particularly those who have written on matters of *history* and *chronology*, whose works have been transmitted to us free of similar errors, owing to the negligence of transcribers?" (Clarke)

b. **Now he went with Joram the son of Ahab to war against Hazael king of Syria**: His close association with the wicked house of Ahab developed into a war alliance with Israel against Syria. His connection with his mother's family (she was a daughter of Ahab and Jezebel, 2 Kings 8:18) was so strong and sympathetic that he paid a visit to the injured and sick king of Israel (**Joram**).

2 Kings 9 – Jehu Takes the Throne of Israel

It is indeed a terrible chapter in which the truth of the divine government is written no longer in the gentle words of patient mercy, but in flames of fire. (Morgan)

A. Jehu is anointed and declared king.

1. (1-3) Elisha's instructions to the young prophet.

And Elisha the prophet called one of the sons of the prophets, and said to him, "Get yourself ready, take this flask of oil in your hand, and go to Ramoth Gilead. Now when you arrive at that place, look there for Jehu the son of Jehoshaphat, the son of Nimshi, and go in and make him rise up from among his associates, and take him to an inner room. Then take the flask of oil, and pour *it* on his head, and say, 'Thus says the LORD: "I have anointed you king over Israel."' Then open the door and flee, and do not delay."

> a. **Called one of the sons of the prophets**: This was a young man from the association for training prophets in Israel. We might imagine that Elisha gave him this duty as a class assignment.
>
>> i. "This unnamed young prophet is identified in Jewish tradition (*Seder Olam*) with Jonah (2 Kings 14:25)." (Wiseman)
>
> b. **I have anointed you king over Israel**: At this time, Joram the son of Ahab was the king of Israel (also called *Jehoram* in 2 Kings 3). This was the dynasty of Omri, but this dynasty was about to come to an end. The next king would be Jehu, who would begin a new – albeit a brief – dynasty.
>
>> i. Though Israel had abandoned God, God had not abandoned Israel. He still had the right to interfere among them. He would appoint and allow kings as He chose, either to bless an obedient Israel or to curse a disobedient nation, according to the terms of His covenant with them at Mount Sinai.

ii. "Jehu is mentioned twice in the cuneiform inscriptions on the Black Obelisk of Shalmaneser III…. The Shalmaneser inscriptions also give us an objective date for this period in Hebrew chronology, 841 b.c." (Dilday)

2. (4-10) Jehu is anointed and commissioned.

So the young man, the servant of the prophet, went to Ramoth Gilead. And when he arrived, there *were* the captains of the army sitting; and he said, "I have a message for you, Commander." Jehu said, "For which *one* of us?" And he said, "For you, Commander." Then he arose and went into the house. And he poured the oil on his head, and said to him, "Thus says the Lord God of Israel: 'I have anointed you king over the people of the Lord, over Israel. You shall strike down the house of Ahab your master, that I may avenge the blood of My servants the prophets, and the blood of all the servants of the Lord, at the hand of Jezebel. For the whole house of Ahab shall perish; and I will cut off from Ahab all the males in Israel, both bond and free. So I will make the house of Ahab like the house of Jeroboam the son of Nebat, and like the house of Baasha the son of Ahijah. The dogs shall eat Jezebel on the plot *of ground* at Jezreel, and *there shall be* none to bury *her*.'" And he opened the door and fled.

a. **There were the captains of the army sitting**: Jehu was a commander in the army of Israel, under King Ahab and his son, King Joram. Jehu was previously anointed as a future king of Israel, who would overthrow the dynasty of Omri and Ahab (1 Kings 19:16-18). Yet that was a long time previous to this, and now he was anointed again to show that the time of fulfillment of the previous prophecy was now at hand.

b. **And he poured the oil on his head**: He was anointed, but was not to take the throne immediately. Both Saul and David were anointed as king over Israel before they actually possessed the throne.

i. "Elisha's insistence that the anointing ceremony be secret would allow the new king to choose the right time to raise the standard of his revolt without alerting Jehoram. The surprise would prevent the king from making preparation to oppose it." (Dilday)

ii. "Jehu is the only king of the Northern Kingdom (Israel) to have been anointed, perhaps to indicate that he should follow in the Davidic tradition, as Saul had been anointed by Samuel; David by Samuel, to mark the Spirit of God endowing him for the task." (Wiseman)

iii. "The anointing of the king over Israel was not an established custom, or rule. It was done when the circumstances were out of the ordinary, or when there might be some question as to his title to the crown." (Knapp)

c. **That you may strike down the house of Ahab your master**: This was more than we were told Elisha told this man from the school of prophets to say (2 Kings 9:1-3). Either Elisha told him to say this and it was not recorded previously, or he came under the inspiration of the Spirit when he did what Elisha told him to do, and spoke this in spontaneous prophecy to Jehu.

d. **The whole house of Ahab shall perish; and I will cut off from Ahab all the males in Israel... dogs shall eat Jezebel**: Clearly, God intended to use Jehu as a tool of judgment against the royal **house of Ahab**.

i. The King James Version translates this line from 2 Kings 9:8: *And I will cut off from Ahab him that pisseth against the wall*. Dilday says of this translation, "The graphic and explicit language used by the King James Version in verse 8 is the literal translation of the Hebrew word for 'male.'"

3. (11-13) Jehu is declared as the king over Israel.

Then Jehu came out to the servants of his master, and *one* said to him, "*Is* all well? Why did this madman come to you?" And he said to them, "You know the man and his babble." And they said, "A lie! Tell us now." So he said, "Thus and thus he spoke to me, saying, 'Thus says the LORD: "I have anointed you king over Israel."'" Then each man hastened to take his garment and put *it* under him on the top of the steps; and they blew trumpets, saying, "Jehu is king!"

a. **Why did this madman come to you... You know the man and his babble**: It was easy to dismiss this prophet as a crazed, babbling madman. It was easy for both Jehu and his associates to think of any God-honoring man as demented. Yet Jehu knew – and the others soon did also – that the man was a true prophet of God.

i. Yet when Jehu emerged from the tent with his head drenched with oil, it was easier to think that the man who did it was a **madman**. "So God's prophets were ever counted and called by the mad world." (Trapp)

b. **Jehu is king**: A moment before, these men regarded the prophet as a **madman**; now they took his word seriously and proclaimed the reluctant Jehu as the king of Israel. This shows the sense of dissatisfaction they had with Joram.

i. "The act of spreading out the garment was one of recognition, loyalty and promise of support." (Wiseman)

B. Jehu brings God's judgment to the house of Omri.

1. (14-20) Jehu's approach to Jezreel, the city where Joram was recovering.

So Jehu the son of Jehoshaphat, the son of Nimshi, conspired against Joram. (Now Joram had been defending Ramoth Gilead, he and all Israel, against Hazael king of Syria. But King Joram had returned to Jezreel to recover from the wounds which the Syrians had inflicted on him when he fought with Hazael king of Syria.) And Jehu said, "If you are so minded, let no one leave *or* escape from the city to go and tell *it* in Jezreel." So Jehu rode in a chariot and went to Jezreel, for Joram was laid up there; and Ahaziah king of Judah had come down to see Joram. Now a watchman stood on the tower in Jezreel, and he saw the company of Jehu as he came, and said, "I see a company of men." And Joram said, "Get a horseman and send him to meet them, and let him say, '*Is it* peace?' " So the horseman went to meet him, and said, "Thus says the king: '*Is it* peace?' " And Jehu said, "What have you to do with peace? Turn around and follow me." So the watchman reported, saying, "The messenger went to them, but is not coming back." Then he sent out a second horseman who came to them, and said, "Thus says the king: '*Is it* peace?' " And Jehu answered, "What have you to do with peace? Turn around and follow me." So the watchman reported, saying, "He went up to them and is not coming back; and the driving *is* like the driving of Jehu the son of Nimshi, for he drives furiously!"

> a. **Is it peace**: Upon seeing the **company of Jehu** approach, King Joram wanted to know if this mysterious group came in **peace**. As he waited to recover full strength in Jezreel, Joram was fundamentally insecure in his hold on the throne and easily suspected threats.
>
> b. **What have you to do with peace**: Jehu meant that the soldier should not regard this as a time of peace, but a time of conflict – a time to violently overthrow the throne of Joram and the dynasty he came from.
>
>> i. When two messengers did not return but instead *joined* the **company of Jehu**, it showed that he enjoyed popular support among the troops of Israel, and King Joram did not.
>
> c. **The driving is like the driving of Jehu the son of Nimshi, for he drives furiously**: Jehu was such an intense man that his personality could be easily seen in the way he drove a chariot.

2. (21-24) Jehu kills King Joram.

Then Joram said, "Make ready." And his chariot was made ready. Then Joram king of Israel and Ahaziah king of Judah went out, each in his chariot; and they went out to meet Jehu, and met him on the property

of Naboth the Jezreelite. Now it happened, when Joram saw Jehu, that he said, "*Is it* peace, Jehu?" So he answered, "What peace, as long as the harlotries of your mother Jezebel and her witchcraft *are so* many?" Then Joram turned around and fled, and said to Ahaziah, "Treachery, Ahaziah!" Now Jehu drew his bow with full strength and shot Jehoram between his arms; and the arrow came out at his heart, and he sank down in his chariot.

a. **Met him on the property of Naboth the Jezreelite**: This was the land that Ahab and Jezebel had so wickedly obtained by murdering the innocent owner of the land – **Naboth**. On this very land – which, as far as God was concerned, still belonged to **Naboth** – the dynasty of Omri would meet its judgment.

b. **Is it peace, Jehu**: The wicked, compromising Joram wanted **peace** with Jehu. None of the dynasty of Omri wanted peace with God; nor did Ahab and Jezebel want peace with Naboth.

i. Joram's demeanor towards Jehu shows that he did not suspect his treachery. "These never dreamt of an enemy, though the messengers were detained, but thought, likely, that Jehu came with good news from the army, whereof himself would be the first messenger." (Trapp)

c. **What peace, as long as the harlotries of your mother Jezebel and her witchcraft are so many**: This shows that Jehu took his previous anointing by Elijah (1 Kings 19:16-17) and his more recent anointing by one from the school of the prophets seriously. At this point, Jehu's mind was not filled with thoughts of political gain and royal glory. He did this for the honor of God, as a conscious executor of divine judgment against the house of Ahab.

d. **Shot Jehoram between his arms**: Despite the confusing variation of the names Jehoram and Joram, it is clear that Jehu killed the king of Israel with a powerful shot through his back while he fled in his chariot.

i. Wiseman on **drew his bow with full strength**: "A technical archery term is used: 'filled his hand with the bow,' that is, stretched the bow 'with his full strength.'"

ii. "Jehu was an excellent marksman; but it was God that guided his hand, strengthened his arm (Ezekiel 30:24), and ordered his arrow (Jeremiah 1:9)." (Trapp)

3. (25-26) Joram's body is dumped in Naboth's vineyard.

Then *Jehu* said to Bidkar his captain, "Pick *him* up, *and* throw him into the tract of the field of Naboth the Jezreelite; for remember, when you and I were riding together behind Ahab his father, that the Lord laid

this burden upon him: 'Surely I saw yesterday the blood of Naboth and the blood of his sons,' says the LORD, 'and I will repay you in this plot,' says the LORD. Now therefore, take *and* throw him on the plot *of ground,* according to the word of the LORD."

    a. **Throw him on the plot of ground, according to the word of the LORD**: This confirms that Jehu saw himself as a fulfiller of God's will in bringing judgment on the house of Ahab.

4. (27-29) Jehu also kills Ahaziah, king of Judah.

But when Ahaziah king of Judah saw *this,* he fled by the road to Beth Haggan. So Jehu pursued him, and said, "Shoot him also in the chariot." *And they shot him* **at the Ascent of Gur, which is by Ibleam. Then he fled to Megiddo, and died there. And his servants carried him in the chariot to Jerusalem, and buried him in his tomb with his fathers in the City of David. In the eleventh year of Joram the son of Ahab, Ahaziah had become king over Judah.**

    a. **So Jehu pursued him**: Jehu had no direct command or commission from God to bring judgment upon the king of Judah, but he did anyway. Consciously or unconsciously, he was guided by God and he killed Ahaziah.

    b. **He fled to Megiddo, and died there**: Ahaziah was happy to associate himself with the Northern Kingdom of Israel and their wicked kings. Therefore he died in the same judgment that came upon the king of Israel.

        i. Ahaziah was also a blood relative of Ahab (Ahab was his grandfather), therefore making him liable under the judgment that came upon Ahab and his descendants.

        ii. 2 Chronicles 22:1-9 also records the reign of Ahaziah and his inglorious end at the hands of Jehu. The reconciliation of the details of the death of Ahaziah between 2 Chronicles 22 and 2 Kings 9 is complicated, but definitely possible. Adam Clarke – among other commentators – carefully works out the details.

        iii. When Ahaziah was killed in battle, they gave him a dignified burial – not for his own sake, but only because his ancestor Jehoshaphat was a godly man (2 Chronicles 22:9).

5. (30-37) Jezebel is killed in exact fulfillment of God's promise.

Now when Jehu had come to Jezreel, Jezebel heard *of it;* **and she put paint on her eyes and adorned her head, and looked through a window. Then, as Jehu entered at the gate, she said, "Is *it* peace, Zimri, murderer of your master?" And he looked up at the window, and said, "Who *is* on my side? Who?" So two** *or* **three eunuchs looked out at him. Then**

he said, "Throw her down." So they threw her down, and *some* of her blood spattered on the wall and on the horses; and he trampled her underfoot. And when he had gone in, he ate and drank. Then he said, "Go now, see to this accursed *woman*, and bury her, for she was a king's daughter." So they went to bury her, but they found no more of her than the skull and the feet and the palms of *her* hands. Therefore they came back and told him. And he said, "This *is* the word of the LORD, which He spoke by His servant Elijah the Tishbite, saying, 'On the plot *of ground* at Jezreel dogs shall eat the flesh of Jezebel; and the corpse of Jezebel shall be as refuse on the surface of the field, in the plot at Jezreel, so that they shall not say, "Here *lies* Jezebel."'"

a. **Is it peace, Zimri**: Jezebel called Jehu **Zimri** after the man who assassinated King Baasha of Israel (1 Kings 16:9-12), when Zimri was also the servant of Baasha, a commander in his army. It was her way of calling Jehu a despicable rebel.

i. It was also an implied threat, because the brief reign of Zimri was ended by Omri, who was the father of Ahab and the father-in-law of this same **Jezebel**. By implication Jezebel said, "The dynasty of Omri will defeat you just like it defeated Zimri."

ii. "Doubtless Jezebel's adornment was intended to create a queenly appearance in the face of impending death and served as a royal burial preparation." (Patterson and Austel)

iii. "Her innate vanity manifested itself up till the last." (Knapp)

b. **So they threw her down**: The eunuchs at the window probably worked for Jezebel, but they quickly responded to Jehu's request for support. They probably had long despised this wicked, pagan queen.

i. Jehu emphatically answered her question about **peace**. "There cannot be true peace so long as we permit the infidelities and charms of some Jezebel of the soul-life to attract and affect us… Whatever its charms, it must be flung out the window before we can be at peace." (Meyer)

c. **He trampled her underfoot**: In ancient near eastern cultures, this desecration of the dead body was a fate *worse* than death. Yet Jehu was completely untroubled at the ugly end of Jezebel; **he ate and drank** after trampling over her dead body and passing over the pavement splattered with her blood.

i. "Her brains, that devised mischief against the servants of God, are strewed upon the walls." (Trapp)

d. **This is the word of the LORD:** God's promise against Jezebel and the house of Ahab was exactly and righteously fulfilled (1 Kings 21:19, 21:23-25).

i. "Jehoram's blood manureth that plat that was wrung from Naboth, and Jezebel shall add to this compost. Oh, garden of herbs dearly bought, royally dunged!" (Trapp)

ii. Yet as the house of Jehu became corrupt, it also would face judgment. Hosea 1:4 speaks of judgment to come upon the house of Jehu: *I will avenge the bloodshed of Jezreel on the house of Jehu, and bring an end to the kingdom of the house of Israel.*

2 Kings 10 – The Reforms of Jehu

A. Jehu executes the house of Ahab.

1. (1-11) Ahab's descendants are executed at Jezreel.

Now Ahab had seventy sons in Samaria. And Jehu wrote and sent letters to Samaria, to the rulers of Jezreel, to the elders, and to those who reared Ahab's *sons,* saying: "Now as soon as this letter comes to you, since your master's sons *are* with you, and you have chariots and horses, a fortified city also, and weapons, choose the best qualified of your master's sons, set *him* on his father's throne, and fight for your master's house." But they were exceedingly afraid, and said, "Look, two kings could not stand up to him; how then can we stand?" And he who *was* in charge of the house, and he who *was* in charge of the city, the elders also, and those who reared *the sons,* sent to Jehu, saying, "We *are* your servants, we will do all you tell us; but we will not make anyone king. Do *what is* good in your sight." Then he wrote a second letter to them, saying: "If you *are* for me and will obey my voice, take the heads of the men, your master's sons, and come to me at Jezreel by this time tomorrow." Now the king's sons, seventy persons, *were* with the great men of the city, *who* were rearing them. So it was, when the letter came to them, that they took the king's sons and slaughtered seventy persons, put their heads in baskets and sent *them* to him at Jezreel. Then a messenger came and told him, saying, "They have brought the heads of the king's sons." And he said, "Lay them in two heaps at the entrance of the gate until morning." So it was, in the morning, that he went out and stood, and said to all the people, "You *are* righteous. Indeed I conspired against my master and killed him; but who killed all these? Know now that nothing shall fall to the earth of the word of the LORD which the LORD spoke concerning the house of Ahab; for the LORD has done what He spoke by His servant Elijah." So Jehu killed all who remained of the house of Ahab in Jezreel, and all his great men and his close acquaintances and his priests, until he left him none remaining.

a. **Ahab had seventy sons in Samaria**: These were a significant danger to the anointed King Jehu. First, they were the descendants of Ahab and had a great interest in battling back to keep the throne of Israel among the dynasty of Omri. Second, they were in **Samaria**, the capital city of Israel – meaning they were away from Jehu, who killed King Joram in Jezreel.

b. **Fight for your master's house**: Jehu challenged any partisans of the house of Omri to declare themselves and prepare to **fight for** their **master's house**.

c. **When the letter came to them, that they took the king's sons and slaughtered seventy persons**: Jehu's letter – and his previous bold action against Joram and Ahaziah – powerfully persuaded the leaders of Israel to execute the **sons** of Ahab on behalf of Jehu.

d. **Put their heads in baskets and sent them to him**: The nobles were so afraid of Jehu that they sent this grim evidence of their obedience.

   i. "It was a contemporary custom throughout the ancient east to 'pile-up' the heads of the captured rebels by the main city gate as a public warning against rebellion." (Wiseman)

   ii. "This was suitable to Ahab's sin. He had sent for baskets of grapes out of Naboth's vineyard at Jezreel; and now the heads of his sons are brought thither in baskets." (Trapp)

e. **You are righteous**: When the people saw the severed heads of 70 descendants of Ahab, they feared that judgment had gone too far and they would be punished for it. Jehu assured them that they had done right – and that none had the right to accuse him, because he acted at the command of God.

   i. "*You are righteous* in your own eyes, and you look upon me as a traitor, and rebel, and murderer, because I have risen against and slain my master, which I acknowledge I have done. But if I am guilty, you are not innocent, and therefore cannot accuse me; for I have killed one, but you a great number." (Poole)

2. (12-14) Jehu meets 42 members of Ahaziah's family and executes them.

And he arose and departed and went to Samaria. On the way, at Beth Eked of the Shepherds, Jehu met with the brothers of Ahaziah king of Judah, and said, "Who *are* you?" So they answered, "We *are* the brothers of Ahaziah; we have come down to greet the sons of the king and the sons of the queen mother." And he said, "Take them alive!" So

they took them alive, and killed them at the well of Beth Eked, forty-two men; and he left none of them.

a. **Jehu met with the brothers of Ahaziah king of Judah**: This was to the great misfortune of these men. Since Jehu was committed to execute all those connected with the house of Ahab, these men were also targets of judgment. Ahaziah was a descendant of King Ahab through his mother (who was the daughter of Ahab and Jezebel). Therefore, their mention of **the queen mother** did not help them.

b. **He left none of them**: This was characteristic of Jehu: whole-hearted and energetic obedience.

i. Some believe that the execution of Ahaziah's family was an example of Jehu going too far. "The sword of judgment, so far as the expressed purpose of Jehovah was concerned, should have been confined to the house of Ahab. But a reckless and ambitious hand was wielding it, and it devoured beyond the allotted limits." (Knapp)

3. (15-17) Jehu executes the remainder of Ahab's family at Samaria.

Now when he departed from there, he met Jehonadab the son of Rechab, *coming* **to meet him; and he greeted him and said to him, "Is your heart right, as my heart** *is* **toward your heart?" And Jehonadab answered, "It is."** *Jehu said,* **"If it is, give** *me* **your hand." So he gave** *him* **his hand, and he took him up to him into the chariot. Then he said, "Come with me, and see my zeal for the LORD." So they had him ride in his chariot. And when he came to Samaria, he killed all who remained to Ahab in Samaria, till he had destroyed them, according to the word of the LORD which He spoke to Elijah.**

a. **He met Jehonadab the son of Rechab**: This was the mysterious founder of the Rechabites, who were a reform movement among the people of God, protesting the immoral and impure lives of many in Israel and Judah.

i. In Jeremiah 35, God used the Rechabites, and the memory of Jehonadab as an example of faithfulness and obedience, to rebuke His unfaithful and disobedient people.

ii. "Jeremiah records that Jehonadab was the leader of an aesthetic group that lived an austere, nomadic life in the desert, drinking no wine and depending solely on the Lord for their sustenance. Separatists to the core and strong patriots, they lived in protest to the materialism and religious compromise in Israel." (Patterson and Austel)

iii. "According to Josephus, Jehu and Jehonadab were friends of long standing, and both detested the luxurious surrounding of the royal family." (Dilday)

b. **Is your heart right, as my heart is toward your heart**: Jehu wanted to know if Jehonadab was on his side. Jehonadab was optimistic at the emergence of this energetic reformer; Jehu was hungry for the approval of this popular religious leader and reformer. It isn't too cynical to think that Jehu wanted to use Jehonadab to add legitimacy to his reign as king.

> i. "Jehonadab was doubtless a very honourable man in Israel; and by carrying him about with him in his chariot, Jehu endeavoured to acquire the public esteem. 'Jehu must be acting right, for Jehonadab is with him, and approves his conduct.'" (Clarke)

c. **Come with me, and see my zeal for the** LORD: The zeal of Jehu was noted in his complete and energetic obedience to the LORD, to the disregard of his own safety and comfort. Yet this statement reveals the dangerous root of pride in Jehu – he is proud of his own zeal.

> i. "When proceeding against Baal worship, his words to Jehonadab, 'Come with me, and see my zeal for Jehovah,' are in themselves a revelation of a proud spirit." (Morgan)

> ii. "His ostentatious display of his reforming zeal revealed how little he had God's glory in mind in the midst of all his feverish activity and abolition." (Knapp)

B. Jehu strikes against Baal worship.

1. (18-23) Jehu arranges a big sacrifice for Baal.

Then Jehu gathered all the people together, and said to them, "Ahab served Baal a little, Jehu will serve him much. Now therefore, call to me all the prophets of Baal, all his servants, and all his priests. Let no one be missing, for I have a great sacrifice for Baal. Whoever is missing shall not live." But Jehu acted deceptively, with the intent of destroying the worshipers of Baal. And Jehu said, "Proclaim a solemn assembly for Baal." So they proclaimed *it*. **Then Jehu sent throughout all Israel; and all the worshipers of Baal came, so that there was not a man left who did not come. So they came into the temple of Baal, and the temple of Baal was full from one end to the other. And he said to the one in charge of the wardrobe, "Bring out vestments for all the worshipers of Baal." So he brought out vestments for them. Then Jehu and Jehonadab the son of Rechab went into the temple of Baal, and said to the worshipers of Baal, "Search and see that no servants of the** LORD **are here with you, but only the worshipers of Baal."**

> a. **Ahab served Baal a little, Jehu will serve him much**: Jehu feigned devotion to Baal to lure the priests and worshippers of Baal into a trap.

Jehu acted deceptively, with the intent of destroying the worshippers of Baal.

> i. **I have a great sacrifice**: "The person who made the sacrifice is not stated, it may be indefinite… The text does not say that Jehu acted as sacrificing priest." (Wiseman)
>
> ii. The priests of Baal believed the deception. "They were excited that their new king, Jehu, and the famous sheik of the Rechabites, Jehonadab, were now distinguished converts and were joining them in a ceremonial sacrifice to Baal." (Dilday)

b. **Search and see that no servants of the LORD are here with you, but only worshippers of Baal**: Jehu wanted to be certain that all the worshippers of the true God were put out of the place.

2. (24-28) Jehu wipes out Baal worship in Israel.

So they went in to offer sacrifices and burnt offerings. Now Jehu had appointed for himself eighty men on the outside, and had said, "*If* any of the men whom I have brought into your hands escapes, *whoever lets him escape, it shall be* his life for the life of the other." Now it happened, as soon as he had made an end of offering the burnt offering, that Jehu said to the guard and to the captains, "Go in *and* kill them; let no one come out!" And they killed them with the edge of the sword; then the guards and the officers threw *them* out, and went into the inner room of the temple of Baal. And they brought the *sacred* pillars out of the temple of Baal and burned them. Then they broke down the *sacred* pillar of Baal, and tore down the temple of Baal and made it a refuse dump to this day. Thus Jehu destroyed Baal from Israel.

> a. **As soon as he had made an end of offering the burnt offering**: Jehu chose to offer the sacrifice to Baal first, and then to call for the execution of the worshippers of Baal.
>
> b. **And tore down the temple of Baal and made it a refuse dump**: Ahab built this temple for his wife Jezebel (1 Kings 16:32); Jehu tore it down. He worked to completely eliminate the worship of Baal from Israel, making him a unique king among the other rulers of the Northern Kingdom.
>
> > i. Beginning with the first king of Israel – Jeroboam – Israel was steeped in idolatry. Jeroboam began with false representations of the true God (the golden calves described in 1 Kings 12:25-33). The successive kings of Israel continued his idolatry (Nadab, Baasha, Elah, Zimri, and Omri), until the reign of Ahab. Under King Ahab, Israel moved from the *false worship* of the *true God* to the *state-supported worship of Baal* (1 Kings 16:29-34). The son of Ahab (Jehoram/Joram) continued

this practice until he was assassinated by Jehu, who destroyed the infrastructure of state-sponsored Baal worship in Israel.

ii. He destroyed this temple of Baal and utterly desecrated it. To say he made it **a refuse dump** is literally that he made it a public toilet. "A place for human excrement; so all the *versions* understand it. Nothing could be more degrading than this." (Clarke)

3. (29-31) The half-way obedience of Jehu.

However Jehu did not turn away from the sins of Jeroboam the son of Nebat, who had made Israel sin, *that is,* **from the golden calves that** *were* **at Bethel and Dan. And the LORD said to Jehu, "Because you have done well in doing** *what is* **right in My sight,** *and* **have done to the house of Ahab all that** *was* **in My heart, your sons shall sit on the throne of Israel to the fourth** *generation.***" But Jehu took no heed to walk in the law of the LORD God of Israel with all his heart; for he did not depart from the sins of Jeroboam, who had made Israel sin.**

a. **However Jehu did not turn away from the sins of Jeroboam**: Jehu aggressively worked against the worship of Baal in Israel. However, he promoted the *false* worship of the *true* God, after the pattern of Jeroboam who set up **the golden calves that were at Bethel and Dan**.

i. "Do not be content to be strong against evil; be eagerly ambitious of good. It is easier to be vehement against the abominations of others than to judge and put away your own secret sins." (Meyer)

ii. "Jehu did obey God up to a certain point. It happened to be a profitable thing to him to exterminate the old royal house of Ahab, because it would confirm himself upon his own throne; but anything beyond that did not pay, and therefore Jehu did not touch it." (Spurgeon)

b. **Because you have done well in doing what is right in My sight**: Clearly, there was much good in the reign of Jehu. He was absolutely committed to fulfilling God's judgment against the house of Ahab and driving the worship of Baal out of Israel. For this, he would be rewarded with a dynasty that would last four generations.

i. This was clear praise of Jehu's actions; yet Hosea 1:4 condemns them. *For in a little while I will avenge the bloodshed of Jezreel on the house of Jehu, and bring an end to the kingdom of the house of Israel.* We can see that both 2 Kings 10:30 and Hosea 1:4 are true, in that Jehu was both good and bad.

- Jehu carried out God's will, but he went too far and executed more people than God intended.

- Jehu carried out God's will, but he did it for personal glory and out of pride.
- Jehu carried out God's will, but he only did it partially. He stopped the idolatry of Baal, but he continued the sinful idolatry of Jeroboam.

c. **But Jehu took no heed to walk in the law of the LORD God of Israel with all his heart**: Yet, Jehu was also clearly disobedient and did not obey or serve God **with all his heart.**

i. "Herein he discovers his hypocrisy, that he follows God as far as his interest would permit… but no further." (Poole)

ii. We might see Jehu as a great Israeli *patriot*. He protested against Joram and the house of Ahab for the harm they did to Israel, and knew that to be strong, Israel must be cleansed of Baal worship. He knew that Israel had to come back to the true God, but he was *unconcerned about how they did it*. For Jehu, it was just as good to worship Yahweh at the temple of the golden calves at Dan or Bethel, and it was *better* for Israel if they did it at those places rather than at Jerusalem.

iii. When we compare Jehu to the other kings of Israel, we see that he was the best of a bad group. No other king in Israel fought against idolatry as much as Jehu did; sadly, even he did not fight against it **with all his heart**.

iv. By not taking **heed to walk in the law of the LORD God**, Jehu showed that he did not live a life of fellowship with God. He was a success in one regard, but a successful failure. "How terrible a warning is the story of this man – that it is possible to be an instrument in the hand of God and yet never be in fellowship with Him." (Morgan)

v. "Jehu's zeal, on the contrary, consumed and destroyed everybody and everything that stood in the way of his own advantage or aggrandizement, but never touched himself. He appears to have been a total stranger to real exercise of soul." (Knapp)

vi. "Hating one sin he loved another, and thus proved that the fear of the Most High did not reign in his breast. He was merely a hired servant, and received the throne as his wages, but a child of God he never was." (Spurgeon)

C. A summary of Jehu's reign.

1. (32-33) Syria captures large portions of Israel's territory.

In those days the LORD began to cut off *parts* of Israel; and Hazael conquered them in all the territory of Israel from the Jordan eastward:

all the land of Gilead—Gad, Reuben, and Manasseh—from Aroer, which *is* by the River Arnon, including Gilead and Bashan.

    a. **In those days the LORD began to cut off parts of Israel**: This was the work of the LORD. These neighboring rulers and their kingdoms were prompted and made successful by God.

    b. **All the territory of Israel from the Jordan eastward**: For hundreds of years before this – since the time of the entry into the Promised Land more than 600 years before – Israel held substantial portions of land on the *eastern* side of the Jordan River. This land was held by the tribes of **Gad, Reuben, and Manasseh**. Now this land was taken by the enemies of Israel, because of their sin and unfaithfulness to the covenant.

        i. This included the rich and fruitful lands of **Gilead and Bashan**.

2. (34-36) The summary of the reign of Jehu.

Now the rest of the acts of Jehu, all that he did, and all his might, *are* they not written in the book of the chronicles of the kings of Israel? So Jehu rested with his fathers, and they buried him in Samaria. Then Jehoahaz his son reigned in his place. And the period that Jehu reigned over Israel in Samaria *was* twenty-eight years.

    a. **And they buried him in Samaria**: Though incomplete in his own goodness, this man was the best of a bad group. Jehu's goodness was rewarded with a long reign (**twenty-eight years**).

    b. **Twenty-eight years**: This was a long reign, but notable only at its beginning. Jehu had the energy and influence to truly turn the nation back to God, but his half-commitment to God left that potential unfulfilled and points to a lack of any real relationship with God.

        i. "We have no chronicles in which there is any thing further spoken of this bad man. His reign was long, *twenty-eight* years; and yet we know nothing of it but the commencement." (Clarke)

        ii. "The great lesson to be drawn from this remarkable man's life is that of being constantly on guard, as servants of God, lest we be found doing His work – whether it be in the exercise of discipline, or the accomplishment of reformation – in a spirit of unbrokenness and without due exercise of heart and conscience between Him who is 'a God of judgment,' and by whom 'actions are *weighed*.'" (Knapp)

2 Kings 11 – The Young King Joash

A. The preservation of Joash.

1. (1-3) The queen mother reigns over Judah.

When Athaliah the mother of Ahaziah saw that her son was dead, she arose and destroyed all the royal heirs. But Jehosheba, the daughter of King Joram, sister of Ahaziah, took Joash the son of Ahaziah, and stole him away from among the king's sons *who were* **being murdered; and they hid him and his nurse in the bedroom, from Athaliah, so that he was not killed. So he was hidden with her in the house of the LORD for six years, while Athaliah reigned over the land.**

a. **When Athaliah the mother of Ahaziah saw that her son was dead**: Ahaziah was executed by Jehu, as recorded in 2 Kings 9:27-29. She used the occasion of her son's death to take power for *herself*, and she **reigned over the land** for six years.

i. We remember that Athaliah was the daughter of Ahab and Jezebel, and was given to King Jehoram of Judah as a bride. She was a bad influence on both her husband (Jehoram of Judah) and her son (King Ahaziah of Judah).

b. **And destroyed all the royal heirs**: Athaliah was from the family of Ahab, and Jehu had completely destroyed all of Ahab's descendants in Israel. Now, after Jehu's coup, Athaliah tried to save something for Ahab's family by trying to eliminate the house of David in Judah.

i. "How dreadful is the lust of reigning! It destroys all the charities of life; and turns fathers, mothers, brothers, and children, into the most ferocious savages!" (Clarke)

ii. Years before, the king of Judah – Jehoshaphat – married his son to this daughter of Ahab and Jezebel, hoping to make an alliance with those wicked and apostate leaders. "And this was the fruit of

Jehoshaphat's marrying his son to a daughter of that idolatrous and wicked house of Ahab, even the extirpation of all his posterity but one." (Poole)

iii. "No character in history, sacred or secular, stands out blacker or more hideous than this daughter-in-law of the godly Jehoshaphat." (Knapp)

c. **But Jehosheba**: This little-known woman had an important place in God's plan of the ages. Through her courage and ingenuity, she preserved the royal line of David through which the Messiah would come. Evil people like Athaliah will begin their work, **but** God can always raise up a **Jehosheba**.

i. "Thus evil always breaks down. It is extremely clever, it calculates on all the changes, and seems to leave no unguarded place; but with unvarying regularity it fails somewhere to cover up its tracks, or to insure its victory." (Morgan)

ii. 2 Chronicles 22:11 tells us that Jehosheba was the wife of Jehoiada, the high priest. Yet, "It is not likely that Jehosheba was the daughter of *Athaliah*; she was a sister, we find, to Ahaziah the son of Athaliah, but probably by a different mother." (Clarke)

d. **He was hidden with her in the house of the LORD for six years**: Though Ahaziah was a bad king who made evil alliances, he was still a descendant of David and the successor of his royal line. For the sake of David, God remembered His promise and spared this one young survivor to the massacre of Athaliah. The line of David was almost extinguished and continued only in the presence of a small boy, but God preserved that flickering flame.

i. "Josephus (*Antiquities* 9.7.1) says that the *bedroom* where the child and his nurse hid was a room where spare furniture and mattresses were stored." (Wiseman)

ii. Like the boy Samuel, Joash grew up in the temple. Like Samuel, he probably found little ways to help the priests, whatever could be done without attracting too much attention.

2. (4-11) Jehoiada plans to reveal the hidden heir to the throne.

In the seventh year Jehoiada sent and brought the captains of hundreds—of the bodyguards and the escorts—and brought them into the house of the LORD to him. And he made a covenant with them and took an oath from them in the house of the LORD, and showed them the king's son. Then he commanded them, saying, "This *is* what you shall do: One-third of you who come on duty on the Sabbath shall be

keeping watch over the king's house, one-third *shall be* at the gate of Sur, and one-third at the gate behind the escorts. You shall keep the watch of the house, lest it be broken down. The two contingents of you who go off duty on the Sabbath shall keep the watch of the house of the Lord for the king. But you shall surround the king on all sides, every man with his weapons in his hand; and whoever comes within range, let him be put to death. You are to be with the king as he goes out and as he comes in." So the captains of the hundreds did according to all that Jehoiada the priest commanded. Each of them took his men who were to be on duty on the Sabbath, with those who were going off duty on the Sabbath, and came to Jehoiada the priest. And the priest gave the captains of hundreds the spears and shields which *had belonged* to King David, that were in the temple of the Lord. Then the escorts stood, every man with his weapons in his hand, all around the king, from the right side of the temple to the left side of the temple, by the altar and the house.

a. **Jehoiada sent and brought captains**: Jehoiada was a godly man who was concerned with restoring the throne of David to the line of David, and taking it away from this daughter of Ahab and Jezebel.

b. **On the Sabbath**: Jehoiada chose the Sabbath for the day of the coup because that was the day when the guards changed their shifts, and they could assemble two groups of guards at the temple at the same time without attracting attention.

c. **He made a covenant with them and took an oath from them in the house of the Lord**: From the *place* where the oath was made and the *context* of the oath, we learn that the worship of the true God was not dead in Judah. These **captains** and **bodyguards** and **escorts** could respond to their responsibility before the Lord.

d. **And showed them the king's son**: This was a dramatic moment. For six years everyone believed there were no more surviving heirs of David's royal line, and there was no legitimate ruler to displace the wicked Athaliah. The secret had to be secure, because **the king's son** would be immediately killed if his existence were revealed. The **captains** and **bodyguards** and **escorts** must have been shocked by the sight of this six-year-old heir to the throne.

  i. One reason Athaliah was able to reign for six years was that *no one knew any alternative*. Many people live under the reign of Satan because they don't really know there is a legitimate king ready to take reign in their lives.

e. **The priest gave the captains of hundreds the spears and shields which had belonged to King David, that were in the temple of the Lord**: It was fitting for these soldiers who would set the heir of David's royal line back on the throne of Judah to use these weapons **which had belonged to King David**.

3. (12) Joash is crowned and received as king.

And he brought out the king's son, put the crown on him, and *gave him* **the Testimony; they made him king and anointed him, and they clapped their hands and said, "Long live the king!"**

    a. **He brought out the king's son**: First the **king's son** had to be *revealed*. No one could support him and he could not take his rightful throne until he was **brought out** before the people.

    b. **Put the crown on him**: Next the **king's son** had to be *crowned*. This was the public and official recognition of him as king.

    c. **And gave him the Testimony**: The **king's son** had to come *with the Word of God*. Joash appeared before the people holding the scrolls of God's Word.

        i. Deuteronomy 17:18 says that the king should have his own copy of the Scriptures. "This is the basis for the British custom of presenting the monarch with a copy of the Bible during the coronation service." (Wiseman)

    d. **They made him king**: The **king's son** had to be received. He had the royal right to impose his reign, but he instead allowed his rule to be received.

    e. **And anointed him**: The **king's son** could never fulfill his office without a divine anointing.

    f. **They clapped their hands and said, "Long live the king"**: The **king's son** received praise once he was recognized as their king.

        i. We can and should follow the same pattern in our reception of Jesus Christ, the *true* **king's son**.

        ii. "Is not the spiritual condition of too many children of God represented by the condition of the Temple, during the early years of the life of Joash? The king was within its precincts, the rightful heir of the crown and defender of the worship of Jehovah; but as a matter of fact, the crown was on the head of the usurper Athaliah, who was exercising a cruel and sanguinary tyranny. The king was limited to a chamber, and the majority of the priests, with all the people, had not even heard of his existence. There needs to be an anointing, an enthroning, a determination that He shall exercise his power over the entire Temple of our Being." (Meyer)

B. The death of the Queen Mother Athaliah.

1. (13-14) Joash, the rightful heir, is revealed to Athaliah.

Now when Athaliah heard the noise of the escorts *and* the people, she came to the people *in* the temple of the LORD. When she looked, there was the king standing by a pillar according to custom; and the leaders and the trumpeters were by the king. All the people of the land were rejoicing and blowing trumpets. So Athaliah tore her clothes and cried out, "Treason! Treason!"

> a. **When she looked, there was the king**: For the usurper queen mother this was a horrifying sight. For six years she ruled because she believed there were no legitimate claimants to the throne of David. Now she sees that one son of Ahaziah – Joash, *her own grandson* – escaped her murderous intent.
>
> b. **All the people of the land were rejoicing**: They were obviously weary of the wicked reign of Athaliah.
>
> c. **Treason! Treason**: The charge was not unfounded. This was treason against her government, but it was a well-founded and godly treason against a tyrannical, wicked ruler.

2. (15-16) Jehoiada commands the execution of Athaliah and her supporters.

And Jehoiada the priest commanded the captains of the hundreds, the officers of the army, and said to them, "Take her outside under guard, and slay with the sword whoever follows her." For the priest had said, "Do not let her be killed in the house of the LORD." So they seized her; and she went by way of the horses' entrance *into* the king's house, and there she was killed.

> a. **Take her outside under guard, and slay with the sword whoever follows her**: This was both righteous and prudent. It was a just sentence against this woman who had murdered so many, and prudent precautions were taken so she could not mount a resistance.
>
> b. **Do not let her be killed in the house of the LORD**: As a priest, Jehoiada had a great concern for the sanctity and reputation of the temple. Yet in the place where horses entered **the king's house, and there she was killed**.
>
>> i. "Thus Athaliah, the most infamous queen of Judah, died at the hands of her executioners, much as did her mother, Jezebel, queen of Israel." (Patterson and Austel)

3. (17) Jehoiada establishes a new covenant.

Then Jehoiada made a covenant between the LORD, the king, and the people, that they should be the Lord's people, and *also* between the king and the people.

a. **That they should be the Lord's people**: The covenant was between the LORD and the king and the people. They re-committed themselves to honor, obey, and serve God.

b. **And also between the king and the people**: This shows that God intends that both kings and citizens have mutual obligations towards the other. Neither have absolute rights over or against the other.

4. (18-21) The reforms of Joash.

And all the people of the land went to the temple of Baal, and tore it down. They thoroughly broke in pieces its altars and images, and killed Mattan the priest of Baal before the altars. And the priest appointed officers over the house of the LORD. Then he took the captains of hundreds, the bodyguards, the escorts, and all the people of the land; and they brought the king down from the house of the LORD, and went by way of the gate of the escorts to the king's house. Then he sat on the throne of the kings. So all the people of the land rejoiced; and the city was quiet, for they had slain Athaliah with the sword *in* the king's house. Jehoash *was* seven years old when he became king.

a. **And all the people of the land went to the temple of Baal, and tore it down**: In 2 Kings 10 Jehu supervised the destruction of the temple of Baal in Samaria. Here the temple of Baal in Jerusalem was destroyed, and appropriately destroyed by **the people of the land**.

i. They didn't stop at destroying the building itself; they went on to destroy both the sacred objects dedicated to Baal and to kill **Mattan the priest of Baal**.

ii. One reason the people resented this worship of Baal in Jerusalem so much was because Athaliah had directed that sacred objects from the temple of the LORD be put into the temple of Baal: *For the sons of Athaliah, that wicked woman, had broken into the house of God, and had also presented all the dedicated things of the house of the LORD to the Baals* (2 Chronicles 24:7).

b. **Then he sat on the throne of the kings**: After more than six dark years, the rightful king of Judah once again ruled over his grateful people.

2 Kings 12 – The Reign of King Jehoash over Judah

Joash and Jehoash are simply variant spellings of the same name.

A. Jehoash repairs the temple.

1. (1-3) A summary of the reign of Jehoash.

In the seventh year of Jehu, Jehoash became king, and he reigned forty years in Jerusalem. His mother's name *was* Zibiah of Beersheba. Jehoash did *what was* right in the sight of the LORD all the days in which Jehoiada the priest instructed him. But the high places were not taken away; the people still sacrificed and burned incense on the high places.

> a. **He reigned forty years in Jerusalem**: This was a long and mostly blessed reign. Jehoash fell short of full commitment and complete godliness, but he did advance the cause of God in the kingdom of Judah.
>
> b. **Jehoash did what was right in the sight of the LORD all the days in which Jehoiada the priest instructed him**: This implies that when Jehoiada died, Jehoash no longer did what was right in the sight of the LORD. 2 Chronicles 24:15-23 tells us that he turned to idolatry when Jehoiada died, and judgment followed.
>
>> i. "After the death of the godly high priest, Jehoash fell into the hands of godless advisors who turned his heart to Canaanite practices." (Patterson and Austel)
>
> c. **The high places were not taken away**: This indicates that Jehoash implemented a half-way reformation and not a total reforming of Israel's worship. He did not take on the more difficult job of removing **the high places**.
>
>> i. "The people were so fondly and strangely addicted to *the high places*, that the foregoing kings, though men of riper years, and great power and courage, and finally settled in their thrones, could not take them

away; and therefore it is not strange if Jehoiada could not now remove them." (Poole)

2. (4-5) Jehoash makes a decree regarding the repair of the temple.

And Jehoash said to the priests, "All the money of the dedicated gifts that are brought into the house of the L‍ord—each man's census money, each man's assessment money—*and* all the money that a man purposes in his heart to bring into the house of the L‍ord, let the priests take *it* themselves, each from his constituency; and let them repair the damages of the temple, wherever any dilapidation is found."

a. **All the money of the dedicated gifts**: There was a regular income coming into the temple from several different sources. King Jehoash wanted to put that money towards a particular purpose.

i. This money was received in three ways:

- **Each man's census money**: This was the half shekel each Israelite older than the age of twenty had to pay every year (Exodus 20:13).

- **Each man's assessment money**: "That is, literally, 'each man the money of his souls of his estimating.' This was a kind of property tax based on the personal assessment of each individual (Leviticus 27:2)." (Dilday)

- **All the money that a man purposes in his heart to bring into the house of the L‍ord**: These were freely given offerings over and above the required donations.

ii. "All these sources had ever been in some measure open, but instead of repairing the dilapidations in the Lord's house, the priests and the Levites had converted the income to their own use." (Clarke) King Joash, working through the priests, corrected this problem.

b. **Let them repair the damages of the temple**: It was natural for Joash to have a high regard for the condition of the temple, because it was his home as a young boy.

i. The temple needed restoration because it was vandalized by Athaliah and her sons (2 Chronicles 24:7).

3. (6-13) Money is gathered for the rebuilding work.

Now it was so, by the twenty-third year of King Jehoash, *that* the priests had not repaired the damages of the temple. So King Jehoash called Jehoiada the priest and the *other* priests, and said to them, "Why have you not repaired the damages of the temple? Now therefore, do not take *more* money from your constituency, but deliver it for repairing

the damages of the temple." And the priests agreed that they would neither receive *more* money from the people, nor repair the damages of the temple. Then Jehoiada the priest took a chest, bored a hole in its lid, and set it beside the altar, on the right side as one comes into the house of the LORD; and the priests who kept the door put there all the money brought into the house of the LORD. So it was, whenever they saw that *there was* much money in the chest, that the king's scribe and the high priest came up and put it in bags, and counted the money that was found in the house of the LORD. Then they gave the money, which had been apportioned, into the hands of those who did the work, who had the oversight of the house of the LORD; and they paid it out to the carpenters and builders who worked on the house of the LORD, and to masons and stonecutters, and for buying timber and hewn stone, to repair the damage of the house of the LORD, and for all that was paid out to repair the temple. However there were not made for the house of the LORD basins of silver, trimmers, sprinkling-bowls, trumpets, any articles of gold or articles of silver, from the money brought into the house of the LORD.

a. **By the twenty-third year of King Jehoash, that the priests had not repaired the damages of the temple**: Building projects take a long time, and renovating an old building is almost always more difficult and expensive than building a new one. Nevertheless, it appears that King Jehoash had to wait a very long time until the damages of the temple were repaired. The work was going far too slowly.

i. "In what year Jehoash gave the orders for these repairs, we cannot tell; but the account here plainly intimates that they had been long given, and that nothing was done, merely through the inactivity and *negligence of the priests*." (Clarke)

b. **The priest took a chest, bored a hole in its lid, and set it beside the altar**: Under the direction of King Jehoash, the priests gave the people the opportunity to give. Even willing givers should be given an opportunity.

i. "Then he placed a collection chest in a strategic location on the right side of the altar, giving the repair project a high priority and a corresponding high visibility." (Dilday)

c. **Now therefore, do not take more money from your constituency, but deliver it for repairing the damages of the temple**: King Joash got to the heart of the problem – the building project was plagued by poor administration and financial mismanagement. Through Jehoiada the priest, he implemented a system where the money would be set aside, saved, and then wisely spent for the repair and refurbishing of the temple.

i. "When the people were assured that the money would really be used for the purpose for which it was given, they responded generously and so similar arrangements were continued by Josiah (2 Kings 22:3-7)." (Wiseman)

ii. "So successful had been the king's program and so well did all concerned carry out their duties that there was even money left over for the provision of sacred vessels for the sanctuary service (2 Chronicles 24:14)." (Patterson and Austel)

4. (14-16) The temple is repaired.

But they gave that to the workmen, and they repaired the house of the LORD with it. Moreover they did not require an account from the men into whose hand they delivered the money to be paid to workmen, for they dealt faithfully. The money from the trespass offerings and the money from the sin offerings was not brought into the house of the LORD. It belonged to the priests.

a. **Moreover they did not require an account from the men into whose hand they delivered the money**: Through good administration of the project, they were able to find men who could be trusted to use the money wisely and honestly. The project was previously stalled, not because of a *lack* of money, but because of *poor money management*.

b. **It belonged to the priests**: The point is made that the project succeeded without taking anything away from the priests. The temple was not repaired and refurbished at their expense; they still received money from the **trespass offerings** and from the **sin offerings**.

B. **The decline of King Jehoash.**

1. (17-18) King Jehoash pays King Hazael of Syria tribute money to avoid an attack against Jerusalem.

Hazael king of Syria went up and fought against Gath, and took it; then Hazael set his face to go up to Jerusalem. And Jehoash king of Judah took all the sacred things that his fathers, Jehoshaphat and Jehoram and Ahaziah, kings of Judah, had dedicated, and his own sacred things, and all the gold found in the treasuries of the house of the LORD and in the king's house, and sent *them* to Hazael king of Syria. Then he went away from Jerusalem.

a. **Then Hazael set his face to go up to Jerusalem**: At this time, the kingdom of Syria attacked Judah with an inferior army, but God used them as an instrument of judgment against the disobedient Joash. King Joash was wounded in a battle outside of Jerusalem.

i. 2 Chronicles 24:23-24 tells the story: *So it happened in the spring of the year that the army of Syria came up against him; and they came to Judah and Jerusalem, and destroyed all the leaders of the people from among the people, and sent all their spoil to the king of Damascus. For the army of the Syrians came with a small company of men; but the LORD delivered a very great army into their hand, because they had forsaken the LORD God of their fathers. So they executed judgment against Joash.*

b. **And Jehoash king of Judah took all the sacred things… and sent them to Hazael king of Syria**: Instead of trusting God, Jehoash traded prior blessing – the sacred treasures of the temple – to protect his capital and kingdom against the attacking Syrians.

i. He was in a difficult place: wounded, with an attacking and successful army bearing down on Jerusalem. He found it hard to trust God in this difficult place because he had stopped trusting God in easier circumstances long before.

2. (19-21) The assassination of Joash.

Now the rest of the acts of Joash, and all that he did, *are* they not written in the book of the chronicles of the kings of Judah? And his servants arose and formed a conspiracy, and killed Joash in the house of the Millo, which goes down to Silla. For Jozachar the son of Shimeath and Jehozabad the son of Shomer, his servants, struck him. So he died, and they buried him with his fathers in the City of David. Then Amaziah his son reigned in his place.

a. **Now the rest of the acts of Joash**: There is no record of repentance on Joash's part. He never came back to or fulfilled his bright early promise.

i. "O how *few* of the *few* who begin to live to God *continue unto the end!*" (Clarke)

b. **His servants arose and formed a conspiracy, and killed Joash**: This is startling, and shows that the blessing of God long before vanished from the compromised king who began so well, but failed to finish well.

i. "The murder of Joash by his *officials* or servants implies that it may have been the result of disaffection following the defeat by Hazael." (Wiseman)

ii. "So disobedience brings its own bitter reward, and what God's people sow they always, in some way or another, reap. Joash abundantly deserved his inglorious and terrible end." (Knapp)

iii. "Thus ended a reign full of promise and hope in the beginning, but profligate, cruel, and ruinous in the end. Never was the hand of

God's justice more signally stretched out against an apostate king and faithless people, than at this time." (Clarke)

2 Kings 13 – The Death of Elisha

A. The reigns of Jehoahaz and Jehoash, kings of Israel.

1. (1-4) A summary of the reign of Jehoahaz and an answer to prayer.

In the twenty-third year of Joash the son of Ahaziah, king of Judah, Jehoahaz the son of Jehu became king over Israel in Samaria, *and reigned* seventeen years. And he did evil in the sight of the Lord, and followed the sins of Jeroboam the son of Nebat, who had made Israel sin. He did not depart from them. Then the anger of the Lord was aroused against Israel, and He delivered them into the hand of Hazael king of Syria, and into the hand of Ben-Hadad the son of Hazael, all *their* days. So Jehoahaz pleaded with the Lord, and the Lord listened to him; for He saw the oppression of Israel, because the king of Syria oppressed them.

> a. **Jehoahaz, the son of Jehu became king over Israel**: This was the beginning of the fulfillment of a promise made to Jehu, recorded in 2 Kings 10:30. God promised him that his descendants would sit on the throne of Israel to the fourth generation. This dynasty – though founded on a violent overthrow of the previous royal house – continued because Jehu came to the throne doing the will of God.

> b. **He did evil in the sight of the Lord, and followed in the sins of Jeroboam**: His father Jehu also continued in the idolatry of Jeroboam (2 Kings 10:31). Jehoahaz followed in the footsteps of *both* Jeroboam and his father Jehu.

> c. **He delivered them into the hand of Hazael king of Syria**: The Northern Kingdom of Israel still had its own name and king, but they were a tributary and subservient nation to **Syria**.

>> i. In the general history of this time, the Assyrian Empire kept the Syrians weak and unable to expand their domain into Israel. But there

was a period when internal problems made the Assyrians bring back their troops from the frontiers of their empire, and the Syrians took advantage of this time of Assyrian distraction.

d. So Jehoahaz pleaded with the Lord, and the Lord listened to him: Jehoahaz was an ungodly man, and this prayer did not mark a lasting or real revival in his life. Yet God listened to his prayer because of His great mercy and because of His care for Israel.

i. "The term '*pleaded with the Lord*' comes from a word meaning 'to be sick,' implying weakness and dependency. Jehoahaz was at the end of his rope." (Dilday)

ii. "This restoration to prosperity began under Joash son of Jehoahaz, and culminated during the reign of his grandson Jeroboam II. So prayer is frequently answered after the petitioner has passed away." (Knapp)

2. (5-9) The rest of Jehoahaz's reign.

Then the Lord gave Israel a deliverer, so that they escaped from under the hand of the Syrians; and the children of Israel dwelt in their tents as before. Nevertheless they did not depart from the sins of the house of Jeroboam, who had made Israel sin, *but* walked in them; and the wooden image also remained in Samaria. For He left of the army of Jehoahaz only fifty horsemen, ten chariots, and ten thousand foot soldiers; for the king of Syria had destroyed them and made them like the dust at threshing. Now the rest of the acts of Jehoahaz, all that he did, and his might, *are* they not written in the book of the chronicles of the kings of Israel? So Jehoahaz rested with his fathers, and they buried him in Samaria. Then Joash his son reigned in his place.

a. **Then the Lord gave Israel a deliverer**: This reminds us of the pattern often seen in the Book of Judges. Israel slipped into apostasy, God allowed them to be humbled under the enemies, they cried out to the Lord, and then He sent a deliverer, so that Israel **escaped from under the hand of the Syrians**.

i. We don't know the name of this **deliverer**, but he is well known in heaven. One does not need a great name to do a great work for the Lord.

b. **Nevertheless they did not depart from the sins of the house of Jeroboam**: Though God answered their prayer and sent a **deliverer**, Israel continued in their *false* worship of the *true* God. Men often consider this to be a small and inconsequential sin, and excuse the idolatry under the claim of good intentions.

i. "Israel's repentance was only half-hearted; they repented because they suffered. They repented because of the suffering rather than because of the sin. They went back to the sin after they escaped from the sorrow." (Spurgeon)

c. **He left of the army of Jehoahaz only fifty horsemen**: Israel was *delivered*; they were *apostate*; and they were *weak*. Their lack of fellowship with the true God made them weak; or actually, *God* made them weak because of their lack of true relationship.

3. (10-13) Summary of Jehoash's reign over Israel.

In the thirty-seventh year of Joash king of Judah, Jehoash the son of Jehoahaz became king over Israel in Samaria, *and reigned* sixteen years. And he did evil in the sight of the LORD. He did not depart from all the sins of Jeroboam the son of Nebat, who made Israel sin, but walked in them. Now the rest of the acts of Joash, all that he did, and his might with which he fought against Amaziah king of Judah, *are* they not written in the book of the chronicles of the kings of Israel? So Joash rested with his fathers. Then Jeroboam sat on his throne. And Joash was buried in Samaria with the kings of Israel.

a. **Jehoash the son of Jehoahaz became king over Israel in Samaria**: He was the grandson of King Jehu, founder of this dynasty. He continued in the same sins as his father and grandfather.

b. **His might with which he fought against Amaziah king of Judah**: The reign of Jehoash saw a civil war among the people of God, with the Southern Kingdom of Judah and the Northern Kingdom of Israel at war.

i. "This war with Amaziah may be seen in ample detail in 2 Chronicles 25; it ended in the total defeat of Amaziah who was taken prisoner by Joash, and afterwards slain in a conspiracy at Lachish." (Clarke)

B. The death of Elisha.

1. (14a) Elisha's sickness unto death.

Elisha had become sick with the illness of which he would die.

a. **Elisha had become sick**: Even men of faith and miracles are not immune to sickness and disease. This great man became **sick** like others whom he had healed as a channel of the power and blessing of God.

b. **With the illness of which he would die**: Though God used Elisha on many occasions to heal others, God appointed this illness to be the means of taking Elisha from this world. God has no one single way that He does this; it is a mistake to believe that all the godly die in their sleep without a hint of prior illness.

2. (14b-17) King Joash and his final audience with Elisha the prophet.

Then Joash the king of Israel came down to him, and wept over his face, and said, "O my father, my father, the chariots of Israel and their horsemen!" And Elisha said to him, "Take a bow and some arrows." So he took himself a bow and some arrows. Then he said to the king of Israel, "Put your hand on the bow." So he put his hand *on it*, and Elisha put his hands on the king's hands. And he said, "Open the east window"; and he opened *it*. Then Elisha said, "Shoot"; and he shot. And he said, "The arrow of the Lord's deliverance and the arrow of deliverance from Syria; for you must strike the Syrians at Aphek till you have destroyed *them*."

a. **Joash the king of Israel came down to him, and wept over his face**: This reaction of the king of Israel might seem strange, having just read the description of the sin and evil that marked his reign. However, it is important to remember that Joash was not a worshipper of the false gods; he was a *false* worshipper of the true God. He had some respect for the true God, and therefore some regard and honor for Elisha.

i. "Dear friends, let us seek so to live that even ungodly men may miss us when we are gone." (Spurgeon)

b. **The chariots of Israel and their horsemen**: Elisha said these words to Elijah at the end of the elder prophet's days on this earth. When he said this to Elijah in 2 Kings 2:12, he recognized the *true* strength of Israel. He knew that the strength of Israel was really in the presence of the prophet of God. Now Joash sees the same strength slipping from this earth and mourns it.

c. **Take a bow and some arrows**: Joash was concerned that the true strength of Israel was about to depart from this earth. Therefore, Elisha used this illustration of the arrow shot through the window to show him that the **arrow of the Lord's deliverance** was still present, and all Joash had to do was to **shoot** the arrow in faith.

d. **For you must strike the Syrians at Aphek**: Elisha made it clear that there was a connection between the shooting of the arrows towards the east and a **strike** against the Syrians that would bring **deliverance** to Israel.

i. "The window was opened eastward toward Syria and specifically toward Aphek, the most strategic site between Damascus and Samaria. Aphek was the city where Ahab had defeated the Syrians years earlier (1 Kings 20:26)." (Dilday)

ii. "It was an ancient custom to *shoot an arrow* or *cast a spear* into the country which an army intended to invade… The *dart, spear,* or *arrow* thrown, was an emblem of the commencement of hostilities." (Clarke)

3. (18-19) King Joash fails to fully take the opportunity.

Then he said, "Take the arrows"; so he took *them*. And he said to the king of Israel, "Strike the ground"; so he struck three times, and stopped. And the man of God was angry with him, and said, "You should have struck five or six times; then you would have struck Syria till you had destroyed *it*! But now you will strike Syria *only* three times."

a. **Take the arrows**: Joash *just heard* Elisha make the connection between the arrows shot through the window and coming victory over the Syrian army. He knew that these arrows represented the Lord's deliverance of Israel against Syria.

b. **Strike the ground**: Joash timidly received this invitation of the prophet to shoot the arrows at no particular target so that they hit the ground. He shot three arrows and stopped, not sensing what he should have – that the arrows represented victories in battle over the Syrians, and he should have received the prophet's invitation more boldly.

i. The phrase "**Strike the ground**" can be for shot arrows hitting the ground. Elisha asked Joash to shoot the arrows through the window at no particular target, not to pound them on the floor.

ii. Elisha clearly asked Joash to do something that modeled *prayer*.

- Shooting the arrows required *effort* and *aim*.
- Shooting the arrows required *instruction* and *help* from the prophet of God.
- Shooting the arrows had to be done *through an open window*.
- Shooting the arrows had to be done without knowing the *exact outcome* ahead of time. The *target* was only fully known by faith.
- Shooting the arrows was *ineffective* because it was not *repeated enough*, reflecting a lack of confidence in the process.
- Shooting the arrows had its *strategic moment*, and when that moment passed it was gone.
- Failing to shoot the arrows *hurt others*, not only himself.

c. **The man of God was angry with him**: Because King Joash did not seize the strategic moment, Israel would enjoy only three victories over the Syrian army, instead of the many more they *could have* enjoyed.

i. "The prophet himself did not yet know how many victories Jehoash should obtain against the Syrians, but God had signified to him that he should learn that by the number of the king's strokes." (Poole)

ii. There are many situations in which we should keep "shooting the arrows," but we content ourselves with a small effort. "He should have continued smiting till the prophet had said, Enough." (Trapp)

- Keep shooting in the battle against sin.
- Keep shooting in the attainment of Christian knowledge.
- Keep shooting in the attainment of faith.
- Keep shooting to do more for the kingdom of God.
- Keep shooting because the world, the flesh, and the devil will not stop their shooting.

iii. When God invites us to take something by faith, we must receive it boldly – and ask Him knowing that He is a great king and giver who is honored by bold, reverent requests.

iv. "Only Joash's lack of faith, manifested in his half-hearted smiting the ground with arrows but thrice, prevented his destroying the Syrians utterly. And it was unto him according to his faith." (Knapp)

d. **But now you will strike Syria only three times**: As it happened, life and death depended on how many arrows Joash shot to the ground. When King Joash had the opportunity to shoot the arrows, it probably seemed to be a small thing to him. He did not know that God's plan for a nation and his seemingly small actions were vitally connected.

i. "It is a fact that God has purposed all things both great and little; neither will anything happen but according to his eternal purpose and decree. It is also a sure and certain fact that, oftentimes, events hang upon the choice of men. Their will has a singular potency." (Spurgeon)

ii. We think of all the excuses that Joash could have made; yet none of them are valid.

- "I stopped shooting because I didn't want to be presumptuous and ask for too much."
- "I stopped shooting because I'm not a very good archer."
- "I stopped shooting because Elisha didn't help me more."
- "I stopped shooting because I thought three was plenty."
- "I stopped shooting because I didn't think it would do any good."

- "I stopped shooting because I wasn't in a shooting mood. I didn't feel like it."
- "I stopped shooting because I didn't want to get over-excited."

iii. "So there be some who think that hearing the gospel is a little thing. Life, death, and hell, and worlds unknown, may hang upon the preaching and hearing of a sermon. To hear attentively, and not be disturbed in the sermon, may seem a very insignificant thing; and yet upon the catching of the word may result either the attainment of faith or the absence of faith, and so the salvation that comes by faith." (Spurgeon)

4. (20-21) The continuing power of God at work in Elisha, even after his death.

Then Elisha died, and they buried him. And the *raiding* bands from Moab invaded the land in the spring of the year. So it was, as they were burying a man, that suddenly they spied a band *of raiders;* and they put the man in the tomb of Elisha; and when the man was let down and touched the bones of Elisha, he revived and stood on his feet.

a. **Then Elisha died**: Perhaps he expected or hoped that he would be carried up into heaven after the dramatic pattern of his mentor, Elijah. Yet that was not God's plan or will for Elisha. Like many others, he simply became old, sick, and then died.

b. **When the man was let down and touched the bones of Elisha, he revived and stood on his feet**: This is one of the more strange and unusual miracles in the Bible. There is little explanation and the silence of the record suggests that there was not inherent power in the bones of Elisha to resuscitate others. This seems to be a unique, one-time miracle to bring honor to the memory of this great prophet.

i. "This is the *first*, and I believe the *last*, account of a *true miracle* performed by the bones of a dead man; and yet on it and such like the whole system of miraculous working *relics* has been founded by the popish Church." (Clarke)

ii. We can also be brought to life by our contact with these dead prophets.

C. God's mercy unto Israel.

1. (22-23) God's kindness to Israel.

And Hazael king of Syria oppressed Israel all the days of Jehoahaz. But the LORD was gracious to them, had compassion on them, and regarded them, because of His covenant with Abraham, Isaac, and Jacob, and would not yet destroy them or cast them from His presence.

a. **Hazael king of Syria oppressed Israel**: This was allowed – even planned – by God as a way to discipline this wayward nation. In 2 Kings 8:12, it records Elisha's prior knowledge of the calamity Hazael would bring upon Israel.

b. **But the LORD was gracious to them**: Israel deserved this discipline, yet God refused to forsake them. He gave them many blessings and saved them from many problems and **would not yet destroy them or cast them from His presence**.

2. (24-25) The victories of King Joash against the Syrians.

Now Hazael king of Syria died. Then Ben-Hadad his son reigned in his place. And Jehoash the son of Jehoahaz recaptured from the hand of Ben-Hadad, the son of Hazael, the cities which he had taken out of the hand of Jehoahaz his father by war. Three times Joash defeated him and recaptured the cities of Israel.

a. **Three times Joash defeated him**: Elisha had promised Joash these three victories over the Syrians. We can suppose that, especially after the third victory, King Joash wished he had shot more arrows through the window at the invitation of Elisha.

2 Kings 14 – The Reigns of Amaziah and Jeroboam II

A. The reign of Amaziah over Judah.

1. (1-4) A summary of his reign.

In the second year of Joash the son of Jehoahaz, king of Israel, Amaziah the son of Joash, king of Judah, became king. He was twenty-five years old when he became king, and he reigned twenty-nine years in Jerusalem. His mother's name was Jehoaddan of Jerusalem. And he did *what was* **right in the sight of the LORD, yet not like his father David; he did everything as his father Joash had done. However the high places were not taken away, and the people still sacrificed and burned incense on the high places.**

a. **He did what was right in the sight of the LORD**: Amaziah, son of the great reformer Joash, continued the generally godly reign began by his father.

i. "He made a good beginning in thus adhering closely to the law. Happy would it have been for him and for his kingdom had he continued as he began." (Knapp)

b. **Yet not like his father David; he did everything as his father Joash had done**: Compared to Joash, Amaziah faithfully continued his policies. Yet some of those policies allowed compromises, such as the allowing of continued sacrifices and incense offerings **on the high places**. Compared to **David** – the greatest merely human king to reign over the people of God – Amaziah did not match up favorably.

i. "The constantly repeated story of limitation in loyalty is told again." (Morgan)

2. (5-6) An example of Amaziah's obedience.

Now it happened, as soon as the kingdom was established in his hand, that he executed his servants who had murdered his father the king. But the children of the murderers he did not execute, according to what is written in the Book of the Law of Moses, in which the LORD commanded, saying, "Fathers shall not be put to death for their children, nor shall children be put to death for their fathers; but a person shall be put to death for his own sin."

> a. **He executed his servants who had murdered his father the king**: This was both just and in the best interest of Amaziah. It was good for him to eliminate those who found the assassination of the king a reasonable way to change the kingdom.
>
>> i. It also fulfilled God's command to punish murderers with execution, first given in Genesis 9:5-7.
>
> b. **But the children of the murderers he did not execute, according to what is written in the Book of the Law of Moses**: It was the standard practice of the ancient world to execute not only the guilty party in such a murder, but also his family. Amaziah went against the conventional practice of his day and obeyed the word of God instead (Deuteronomy 24:16).
>
>> i. "Wherein he showed some faith and courage, that he would obey this command of God, though it was very hazardous to himself, such persons being likely to seek revenge for their father's death." (Poole)

3. (7) His victory over the Edomites.

He killed ten thousand Edomites in the Valley of Salt, and took Sela by war, and called its name Joktheel to this day.

> a. **He killed ten thousand Edomites**: This shows the military might of Amaziah, and that he successfully subdued the weaker nations surrounding Judah.
>
> b. **And took Sela by war**: Some believe this was the ancient rock city in the desert also known as *Petra*; others believe it was a different place. One way or another, this was a significant victory for Amaziah.
>
>> i. 2 Chronicles 25:5-16 gives more background to this event. Amaziah gathered a huge army in Judah to go against Edom – *three hundred thousand choice men, able to go to war, who could handle spear and shield.* He also hired 100,000 mercenary soldiers from Israel. But a prophet came and warned him *not* to use the soldiers from Israel, because God was not with that rebellious and idolatrous kingdom. Amaziah was convinced to trust God, send the mercenaries from Israel away, and accept the loss of the money used to hire them. God blessed this step of faith, and gave them a convincing victory over the Edomites.

ii. Amaziah trusted God for the victory over Edom; but immediately after the victory his heart turned from God: *Now it was so, after Amaziah came from the slaughter of the Edomites, that he brought the gods of the people of Seir, set them up to be his gods, and bowed down before them and burned incense to them.* (2 Chronicles 25:14)

4. (8-12) His defeat at the hands of Jehoash of Israel.

Then Amaziah sent messengers to Jehoash the son of Jehoahaz, the son of Jehu, king of Israel, saying, "Come, let us face one another *in battle*." And Jehoash king of Israel sent to Amaziah king of Judah, saying, "The thistle that *was* in Lebanon sent to the cedar that *was* in Lebanon, saying, 'Give your daughter to my son as wife'; and a wild beast that *was* in Lebanon passed by and trampled the thistle. You have indeed defeated Edom, and your heart has lifted you up. Glory *in that*, and stay at home; for why should you meddle with trouble so that you fall—you and Judah with you?" But Amaziah would not heed. Therefore Jehoash king of Israel went out; so he and Amaziah king of Judah faced one another at Beth Shemesh, which *belongs* to Judah. And Judah was defeated by Israel, and every man fled to his tent.

a. **Come, let us face one another in battle**: Proud from his success against Edom, Amaziah decided to make war against the Northern Kingdom of Israel.

i. Again, 2 Chronicles 25:5-16 gives more background to this event. When Amaziah sent away the Israelite mercenaries, they were not happy – even though he paid them for *not* fighting against Edom (they probably counted on receiving much more from the spoil of battle). As they returned to Israel, *they raided the cities of Judah from Samaria to Beth Horon, killed three thousand in them, and took much spoil* (2 Chronicles 25:13). This was the *political* motivation for Amaziah's attack against Israel.

ii. He had reason to believe he would be successful. He had recently assembled a 300,000 man army that killed 20,000 Edomites in a victory over Edom (2 Chronicles 25:5, 11-12). Jehoahaz seemed very weak, having only 50 horsemen, 10 chariots, and 10,000 foot soldiers after being defeated by the Syrians (2 Kings 13:7).

b. **The thistle that was in Lebanon**: The reply of Jehoash king of Israel was both wise and diplomatic. With this little story and its application, he counseled Amaziah to glory in his previous victory over Edom but then to **stay at home**.

i. "The thistle, imagining himself to be equal with the cedar, presumptuously suggested a marriage alliance between them. The difference between the two was made obvious when a wild beast passed through and crushed the thistle underfoot. Of course the beast was powerless to injure the cedar." (Dilday)

c. **Why should you meddle with trouble so that you fall – you and Judah with you**: Amaziah should have listened to this word from Jehoash, but he didn't. He provoked a fight he should have avoided, and did not consider both the likelihood of success and the effect his defeat would have on the whole kingdom of Judah.

5. (13-14) The result of Amaziah's foolish war against Israel.

Then Jehoash king of Israel captured Amaziah king of Judah, the son of Jehoash, the son of Ahaziah, at Beth Shemesh; and he went to Jerusalem, and broke down the wall of Jerusalem from the Gate of Ephraim to the Corner Gate—four hundred cubits. And he took all the gold and silver, all the articles that were found in the house of the LORD and in the treasuries of the king's house, and hostages, and returned to Samaria.

a. **Israel captured Amaziah king of Judah**: Because of his foolish attack against Israel, Amaziah *lost his freedom* and for a time became a prisoner of the king of Israel.

i. Amaziah had a mighty army and Jehoash had a weak army. Yet God gave Israel the victory over Judah to rebuke the idolatry of Amaziah. *It came from God, that He might give them into the hand of their enemies, because they sought the gods of Edom.* (2 Chronicles 25:20)

ii. "His name means 'strength of Jah'; but we read, 'he strengthened *himself*' (2 Chronicles 25:11); his character of self-sufficiency thus belying his name – a thing not uncommon in our day." (Knapp)

b. **He went to Jerusalem, and broke down the wall of Jerusalem**: Because of his foolish attack against Israel, Amaziah *saw the defenses of Jerusalem broken down*. Not only did they lose the battle at Beth Shemesh, but they were also in a weaker position to face future attacks.

c. **And he took all the gold and silver**: Because of his foolish attack against Israel, Amaziah *lost the treasure of the people of God*. It wasn't just a loss of his *personal* wealth (**the treasuries of the king's house**), but also of the **gold and silver** of God's people. Amaziah didn't have the wisdom to see how losing this battle would hurt others as well as himself.

i. This even extended to **hostages** who were taken from Jerusalem to Samaria. The decision to attack Israel was his alone, but the price paid for the foolish attack was paid by the whole kingdom of Judah. It is a sober warning to all leaders, to consider how their foolish decisions affect many other people.

ii. "The quarrel of Amaziah was certainly *just*, yet he was put to the rout; he did *meddle to his hurt; he fell*, and *Judah fell with him*, as Jehoash had said." (Clarke)

6. (15-22) Amaziah is rejected as king over Judah for his son.

Now the rest of the acts of Jehoash which he did—his might, and how he fought with Amaziah king of Judah—*are* they not written in the book of the chronicles of the kings of Israel? So Jehoash rested with his fathers, and was buried in Samaria with the kings of Israel. Then Jeroboam his son reigned in his place. Amaziah the son of Joash, king of Judah, lived fifteen years after the death of Jehoash the son of Jehoahaz, king of Israel. Now the rest of the acts of Amaziah, *are* they not written in the book of the chronicles of the kings of Judah? And they formed a conspiracy against him in Jerusalem, and he fled to Lachish; but they sent after him to Lachish and killed him there. Then they brought him on horses, and he was buried at Jerusalem with his fathers in the City of David. And all the people of Judah took Azariah, who *was* sixteen years old, and made him king instead of his father Amaziah. He built Elath and restored it to Judah, after the king rested with his fathers.

a. **They formed a conspiracy against him in Jerusalem**: The embarrassing loss against Israel undermined Amaziah's support among the leaders of Judah.

i. He lived **fifteen years** after the death of Jehoash (which probably prompted his release from imprisonment in Israel). "But it was a kind of a lifeless life... He lay all the while under the hatred and contempt of his subjects." (Trapp)

b. **He fled to Lachish; but they sent after him to Lachish and killed him there**: Amaziah tried but was unable to escape the conspirators. He was assassinated, just like his father was (2 Kings 12:20-21).

i. "Lachish was the first of the cities of Judah to adopt the idolatries of the kingdom of Israel ('the beginning of the sin to the daughter of Zion: for the transgressions of Israel were found in thee,' Micah 1:13), and it was natural for the idolatrous Amaziah to seek an asylum there." (Knapp)

ii. "Some commentators believe the assassins who put Amaziah to death in verse 19 may have been the very children whom Amaziah had spared. They, in turn, were exacting vengeance for Amaziah's executions." (Dilday)

c. **And all the people of Judah took Azariah, who was sixteen years old, and made him king instead of his father**: This was the start of the illustrious reign of **Azariah** (also known as *Uzziah*). He was the greatest king of Judah after David.

i. "The election of Amaziah's son Azariah may refer to an earlier time when 'all the people had taken Azariah, when he was sixteen years old, and made him king while Amaziah had been a prisoner." (Wiseman)

B. The reign of Jeroboam II in Israel.

1. (23-27) A summary of his reign and God's assistance to Jeroboam.

In the fifteenth year of Amaziah the son of Joash, king of Judah, Jeroboam the son of Joash, king of Israel, became king in Samaria, *and reigned* forty-one years. And he did evil in the sight of the Lord; he did not depart from all the sins of Jeroboam the son of Nebat, who had made Israel sin. He restored the territory of Israel from the entrance of Hamath to the Sea of the Arabah, according to the word of the Lord God of Israel, which He had spoken through His servant Jonah the son of Amittai, the prophet who *was* from Gath Hepher. For the Lord saw *that* the affliction of Israel *was* very bitter; and whether bond or free, there was no helper for Israel. And the Lord did not say that He would blot out the name of Israel from under heaven; but He saved them by the hand of Jeroboam the son of Joash.

a. **He did evil in the sight of the Lord**: Jeroboam II was a wicked king, who continued the politically-motivated idolatry of his namesake **Jeroboam the son of Nebat**. During his reign the prophets Jonah and Amos spoke for God.

b. **He restored the territory of Israel… for the Lord saw that the affliction of Israel was very bitter**: Out of great mercy, God showed kindness to a disobedient Israel ruled by an evil king.

i. "It seems to suggest amazement in his mind as he contemplated the patience of Jehovah with the sinning nation." (Morgan)

c. **According to the word of the Lord God of Israel, which He had spoken through His servant Jonah the son of Amittai, the prophet**: This is almost certainly the same Jonah who is famous for his missionary trip to Nineveh. Apparently he also had a ministry among his own people, not only among the people of Nineveh.

i. "God sent them *Jonah* to encourage them, and to assure them of better days." (Clarke)

2. (28-29) Summary of the reign of Jeroboam II.

Now the rest of the acts of Jeroboam, and all that he did—his might, how he made war, and how he recaptured for Israel, from Damascus and Hamath, *what had belonged* **to Judah—***are* **they not written in the book of the chronicles of the kings of Israel? So Jeroboam rested with his fathers, the kings of Israel. Then Zechariah his son reigned in his place.**

a. **His might, how he made war, and how he recaptured for Israel, from Damascus and Hamath, what had belonged to Judah**: The reign of Jeroboam II was a time of economic, political, and material prosperity for Israel. Yet it was not because of their own merit or goodness, but because of God's great mercy to Israel.

i. Archaeology confirms the economic **might** of Jeroboam II. In the age prior to Jeroboam II, the houses in Israel's cities were roughly the same size. But archaeologists find a change starting in the eighth century B.C. – ancient cities like Tirzah have a neighborhood of large, expensive houses and another neighborhood of small, crowded structures, smaller than the houses from previous years. The larger houses are filled with the marks of prosperity, and the oppressive rich of Israel thought they could find safety there – but God's judgment came against those houses as well (Amos 3:13-15).

ii. "The resultant prosperity, however, which ended in the wrong use of power in luxury and the oppression of the poor, was denounced by the contemporary prophets, especially Amos (2:6-7; 8:4-6); Isaiah (3:18-26; 5:8-13) and Micah (2:2)." (Wiseman)

iii. In the days of King Jehoahaz of Israel, God promised to send a deliverer to Israel, one who helped them to escape from under the hand of the Syrians (2 Kings 13:4-5). It is likely that Jeroboam II was this promised deliverer.

b. **From Damascus**: Though the hand of the LORD was behind these events, God used the strength of the Assyrian Empire to bless Israel. For most of its history, the Northern Kingdom of Israel struggled against Syria, her neighbor to the north. But around the year 800, the mighty Assyrian Empire defeated Syria, and neutralized this power that hindered Israel's expansion and prosperity. With Syria in check, Israel enjoyed great prosperity during the reign of Jeroboam II.

i. The Book of Amos shows that Israel *did not* handle this prosperity well, and the wickedness under the prosperity of Jeroboam II heaped judgment up for themselves.

ii. "Israel was blessed with the ministries of both Hosea and Amos during Jeroboam's reign. From their writings it will readily be seen that though there was political revival under his rule, there was no real moral or spiritual awakening among the people." (Knapp)

iii. "When Jeroboam II died in 752 B.C., he left behind a strong kingdom but, unfortunately, one whose core foundation was so spiritually rotten that the edifice of state would not long withstand the rising tides of international intrigue and pressure." (Patterson and Austel)

c. **Then Zechariah his son reigned in his place**: Zechariah was the fourth generation of the Jehu dynasty, and it was prophesied that the dynasty of Jehu would continue for four generations (2 Kings 10:30).

i. "From the time of Jeroboam's death, declension set in, ending less than seventy years later in its final overthrow and dissolution. Prophetic ministry was from this time greatly increased. 'Such is the way of our gracious God,' an unknown writer says, 'that when judgment is near to approach, then testimony is multiplied.'" (Knapp)

2 Kings 15 – Unstable Monarchy in Israel

A. The reign of Azariah (Uzziah) over Judah.

1. (1-4) A summary of his reign.

In the twenty-seventh year of Jeroboam king of Israel, Azariah the son of Amaziah, king of Judah, became king. He was sixteen years old when he became king, and he reigned fifty-two years in Jerusalem. His mother's name *was* Jecholiah of Jerusalem. And he did *what was* right in the sight of the LORD, according to all that his father Amaziah had done, except that the high places were not removed; the people still sacrificed and burned incense on the high places.

a. **He did what was right in the sight of the LORD**: The reign of Azariah (also called *Uzziah* in 2 Kings 15:13 and many other places in 2 Kings, 2 Chronicles, and Isaiah) was largely characterized by the good he did **in the sight of the LORD**. His godliness was rewarded with a long reign of 52 years.

i. Azariah came to the throne in a difficult era: "Following the tragic events that brought King Amaziah's reign to an end, Jerusalem was in disarray, a major section of its protective wall destroyed, its temple and palace emptied of their treasures, and some of its inhabitants taken away to Israel as hostages." (Dilday)

ii. 2 Chronicles 26 tells us much more about the successful reign of Uzziah (**Azariah**):

- He began his reign when he was only 16 years old (26:3).
- He reigned during the ministry of Zechariah the prophet (26:5).
- He defeated the Philistines and took many of their cities, and also kept the Ammonites in tribute (26:6-8).
- He was internationally famous as a strong king (26:8).

- He was an ambitious builder and skilled in agriculture (26:9-10). "He probably gave special attention to the tillage of the soil because of the prophecies of Hosea and Amos concerning the scarcity about to come. (See Hosea 2:9; 4:3; 9:2; Amos 1:2; 4:6-9; 5:16-19)." (Knapp)
- He built up and organized the army, introducing several new items of military technology (26:11-15).

iii. Knapp suggests that Azariah became king in an unusual manner: "He seems to have come by the throne, not in the way of ordinary succession, but by the direct choice of the people. The princes had been destroyed by the Syrians toward the close of his grandfather Joash's reign (2 Chronicles 24:23), leaving the people a free hand."

b. **Except that the high places were not removed**: As with Jehoash (2 Kings 12:3) and Amaziah (2 Kings 14:4), the reforms of Azariah did not reach so far as to remove these traditional places of sacrifice to the LORD.

i. "The apparent compromise is indicative of a basic spiritual shallowness that was to surface in the prophecies of the great writing prophets of the eighth century B.C." (Patterson and Austel)

ii. "This, if it did not loose, yet it lessened his crown of glory." (Trapp)

2. (5-7) The sad end of his reign.

Then the LORD struck the king, so that he was a leper until the day of his death; so he dwelt in an isolated house. And Jotham the king's son *was* over the *royal* house, judging the people of the land. Now the rest of the acts of Azariah, and all that he did, *are* they not written in the book of the chronicles of the kings of Judah? So Azariah rested with his fathers, and they buried him with his fathers in the City of David. Then Jotham his son reigned in his place.

a. **The LORD struck the king, so that he was a leper until the day of his death**: 2 Chronicles 26 also tells us of the downfall of Azariah, who *was marvelously helped till he became strong* (2 Chronicles 26:15). The Chronicler goes on: *But when he was strong his heart was lifted up, to his destruction, for he transgressed against the LORD his God by entering the temple of the LORD to burn incense on the altar of incense* (2 Chronicles 26:16). The priests tried to stop him, but the king insisted on forcing his way into the temple to offer incense.

i. Azariah violated what had become a general principle in God's dealing with Israel: that no king should also be a priest, and that the offices of prophet, priest, and king should not be combined in one man – *until* the Messiah, who fulfilled all three offices.

ii. "His great power fostered such pride and haughtiness that about 750 B.C. he sought to add to his vast power by usurping the prerogatives of the sacred priesthood." (Patterson and Austel)

b. **He dwelt in an isolated house**: Azariah came into the temple as an arrogant king, and he left as a humbled leper. Indeed, *he hurried to get out, because the LORD had struck him* (2 Chronicles 26:20).

i. "It was a fearful stroke from God. Death was the actual penalty enjoined by the law for his crime (Numbers 18:7), and leprosy was really that – a living death, prolonged and intensified." (Knapp)

c. **So Azariah rested with his fathers**: The death of Azariah (again, also known as *Uzziah*) contributed to the call of the prophet Isaiah: *In the year that King Uzziah died, I saw the LORD sitting on a throne* (Isaiah 6:1).

i. Considering the reign of Azariah:

- He began his reign at only 16 years of age.
- He reigned for 52 years.
- Overall, he was a good and strong king who led Israel to many military victories, he was an energetic builder and planner.
- Despite all this, Azariah had a tragic end.

ii. Therefore, when Isaiah wrote that he was called *in the year King Uzziah died*, he said a lot. It is to say, "In the year a great and wise king died." But it is also to say, "In the year a great and wise king who had a tragic end died." Isaiah had great reason to be discouraged and disillusioned at the death of King Uzziah, because a great king had passed away, and because his life ended tragically. Yet despite it all, he saw the enthroned LORD God who was greater than any earthly king.

B. Five kings over the kingdom of Israel.

This section of 2 Kings 15 begins the story of five kings over Israel. "This chapter anticipates the final overthrow of this kingdom of the tribes. It describes the corruption and disorganization that made them the easy prey of Assyria." (Meyer)

1. (8-12) The short, evil reign of Zechariah.

In the thirty-eighth year of Azariah king of Judah, Zechariah the son of Jeroboam reigned over Israel in Samaria six months. And he did evil in the sight of the LORD, as his fathers had done; he did not depart from the sins of Jeroboam the son of Nebat, who had made Israel sin. Then Shallum the son of Jabesh conspired against him, and struck and killed him in front of the people; and he reigned in his place. Now the rest of the acts of Zechariah, indeed they *are* written in the book of the

chronicles of the kings of Israel. This *was* the word of the LORD which He spoke to Jehu, saying, "Your sons shall sit on the throne of Israel to the fourth *generation.*" And so it was.

a. **Zechariah the son of Jeroboam reigned over Israel in Samaria six months**: The reign of Zechariah was both short and wicked, and he continued in the state-sponsored idolatry begun by Jeroboam.

i. "There appears to be (from a comparison of dates) a period unaccounted for, of about eleven years, between Jeroboam's death and the beginning of his son Zechariah's reign… Anarchy probably prevailed during the above-noted interregnum." (Knapp)

b. **Then Shallum the son of Jabesh conspired against him, and struck and killed him in front of the people**: Zechariah was so despised by his own **people** that Shallum was able to do this. This was the end of the dynasty of Jehu, which began with such potential but ended (as God had foretold) in great darkness.

i. "God keepeth promise with his foes: shall he fail his friends?" (Trapp)

ii. "The death of this last king of the dynasty of Jehu saw the end of the Northern Kingdom proper. In the last twenty years six rulers were to follow each other, but only one was to die naturally. Anarchy, rivalry and regicide led to terminal bloodshed which fulfilled Hosea's prophecies (Hosea 1:4)." (Wiseman)

iii. "Half a dozen 'pseudo-kings' would reign in rapid succession, one murderer replacing another on the throne, as the nation tottered on the brink of anarchy." (Dilday)

2. (13-16) The even briefer reign of Shallum.

Shallum the son of Jabesh became king in the thirty-ninth year of Uzziah king of Judah; and he reigned a full month in Samaria. For Menahem the son of Gadi went up from Tirzah, came to Samaria, and struck Shallum the son of Jabesh in Samaria and killed him; and he reigned in his place. Now the rest of the acts of Shallum, and the conspiracy which he led, indeed they *are* written in the book of the chronicles of the kings of Israel. Then from Tirzah, Menahem attacked Tiphsah, all who *were* there, and its territory. Because they did not surrender, therefore he attacked *it.* All the women there who were with child he ripped open.

a. **Shallum… reigned a full month**: The dynasty of Jehu lasted four generations; the dynasty of Shallum lasted four weeks.

i. "The great prosperity and expansion under Jeroboam II appears to have corrupted the people and caused them to give free reign to their evil desires and violence. Those in authority, instead of checking this spirit of lawlessness, found pleasure in it. 'They make the king glad with their wickedness, and the princes with their lies' (Hosea 7:3)." (Knapp)

b. **Now the rest of the acts of Shallum**: The writer of 2 Kings had no moral comment to make on the brief reign of Shallum. Perhaps he did not reign long enough to show himself either good or bad. Certainly, the violence that marked both his rise to and fall from power shows that he did not reign with the blessing of God.

i. "Israel was now practically under a military despotism, downtrodden and oppressed, and yet sinning still with a high hand against God." (Morgan)

c. **Menham attacked Tiphsah… Because they did not surrender, therefore he attacked it. All the women there who were with child he ripped open**: This act of horrible brutality was commanded by **Menham** – who became *the next* king of Israel. This shows the depths of brutality and ungodliness of the times.

i. "The action by Menahem against the inhabitants of Tiphsah is unparalleled for brutality by any Israelite. Here it may mark the increasing influence of the surrounding nations. It was a foreign practice inflicted on the Israelites themselves by Aram (2 Kings 8:12), Ammon (Amos 1:13) and Assyria (Hosea 13:8)." (Wiseman)

3. (17-22) A summary of the reign of Menahem.

In the thirty-ninth year of Azariah king of Judah, Menahem the son of Gadi became king over Israel, *and reigned* ten years in Samaria. And he did evil in the sight of the LORD; he did not depart all his days from the sins of Jeroboam the son of Nebat, who had made Israel sin. Pul king of Assyria came against the land; and Menahem gave Pul a thousand talents of silver, that his hand might be with him to strengthen the kingdom under his control. And Menahem exacted the money from Israel, from all the very wealthy, from each man fifty shekels of silver, to give to the king of Assyria. So the king of Assyria turned back, and did not stay there in the land. Now the rest of the acts of Menahem, and all that he did, *are* they not written in the book of the chronicles of the kings of Israel? So Menahem rested with his fathers. Then Pekahiah his son reigned in his place.

a. **Menahem the son of Gadi became king over Israel**: His reign was typical of the kings of Israel in that it was both **evil** and a continuation of the state-sponsored idolatry of Jeroboam.

b. Menahem gave Pul a thousand talents of silver, that his hand might be with him to strengthen the kingdom under his control: Menahem put the kingdom of Israel under tribute to the Assyrian Empire. He purchased the backing of the Assyrian King with a large amount of money raised from the wealthy in his kingdom, and therefore ruled with the strength of Assryia supporting him.

i. "The burden of the levy fell upon the rich, which needs not excite much sympathy when we learn from the prophets Amos and Micah how their riches were obtained. See Amos 4:1; 5:11,12; 8:4-6; Micah 2:2; 6:10-12." (Knapp)

ii. "The Assyrian policy was initially to leave a state on its borders independent, though requiring a substantial annual payment for this privilege. Thereafter the state might be made a vassal, which entailed having an Assyrian official at court as a watchdog on the ruler's attitudes." (Wiseman)

4. (23-26) The two-year reign of Pekahiah.

In the fiftieth year of Azariah king of Judah, Pekahiah the son of Menahem became king over Israel in Samaria, *and reigned* two years. And he did evil in the sight of the Lord; he did not depart from the sins of Jeroboam the son of Nebat, who had made Israel sin. Then Pekah the son of Remaliah, an officer of his, conspired against him and killed him in Samaria, in the citadel of the king's house, along with Argob and Arieh; and with him were fifty men of Gilead. He killed him and reigned in his place. Now the rest of the acts of Pekahiah, and all that he did, indeed they *are* written in the book of the chronicles of the kings of Israel.

a. Pekahiah the son of Menahem became king over Israel: The previous two kings of Israel (before Menahem) did not reign successfully enough to pass the kingdom on to a son or another dynastic descendant. Menahem ruled well enough to pass the kingdom to **Pekahiah**.

b. And he did evil in the sight of the Lord; he did not depart from the sins of Jeroboam the son of Nebat, who had made Israel sin: The familiar refrain of this indictment against the kings of Israel is repeated regarding Pekahiah.

i. "Why should Jeroboam so frequently be called 'the son of Nebat'? Why should the father be for ever pilloried with the son, except that he was in some way responsible for, and implicated in, his sins? There was a time when perhaps Nebat might have restrained the growing boy, or led him to the true worship of God; or perhaps his parental influence and example were deadly in their effect." (Meyer)

c. **He killed him and reigned in his place**: The blessing of God was obviously not on Pekahiah, whose reign ended with assassination after only two years. This was the end of another brief dynasty, and the start of a new one.

i. **An officer of his**: "The insurrection originated with the king's own personal bodyguard." (Patterson and Austel)

5. (27-31) The 20-year reign of Pekah.

In the fifty-second year of Azariah king of Judah, Pekah the son of Remaliah became king over Israel in Samaria, *and reigned* twenty years. And he did evil in the sight of the LORD; he did not depart from the sins of Jeroboam the son of Nebat, who had made Israel sin. In the days of Pekah king of Israel, Tiglath-Pileser king of Assyria came and took Ijon, Abel Beth Maachah, Janoah, Kedesh, Hazor, Gilead, and Galilee, all the land of Naphtali; and he carried them captive to Assyria. Then Hoshea the son of Elah led a conspiracy against Pekah the son of Remaliah, and struck and killed him; so he reigned in his place in the twentieth year of Jotham the son of Uzziah. Now the rest of the acts of Pekah, and all that he did, indeed they *are* written in the book of the chronicles of the kings of Israel.

a. **And he did evil in the sight of the LORD**: The kings, families, and dynasties ruling Israel changed quickly during this period. Yet there was an amazing continuity of evil through these dynasties. Each was evil, and each continued the state-sponsored idolatry in Israel.

i. For chronologers, the 20 year reign of Pekah is difficult to place. It perhaps includes time that Pekah ruled as an anti-government rebel in certain regions of Israel.

b. **Tiglath-Pileser king of Assyria came and took**: This Assyrian king, unlike in the days of Menahem, would not be paid off by the king of Israel. He **came and took** some of the best land of the kingdom of Israel, including much of the northern part of the kingdom.

i. "With the loss of Galilee and Gilead and with the presence of Assyrian troops all along Israel's western frontier, it seemed evident that Pekah's anti-Assyrian policy had brought Israel to the point of extinction." (Patterson and Austel)

ii. "From 1 Chronicles 5:26 we learn that *Pul* and *Tiglath-pileser*, kings of Assyria, carried away into captivity the two tribes of *Reuben*, and

Gad, and the half tribe of *Manasseh*; all that belonged to Israel on the other side of the Jordan. These were never restored to Israel." (Clarke)

iii. "These were dark days of Israel, her territory now reduced to a tiny kingdom only thirty miles wide by forty miles long." (Dilday)

c. **He carried them captive to Assyria**: This became an official state policy of the Assyrian Empire. Upon conquering a land, if necessary, they relocated by force the best and the brightest of the conquered nation, bringing them to Assyria.

i. "This first reference to the practice of removing leaders and selected experts into exile shows that the next step had now been taken towards making Israel a vassal-state." (Wiseman)

d. **Hoshea the son of Elah led a conspiracy against Pekah the son of Remaliah, and struck and killed him**: This was another king and another dynasty to end with assassination, as a powerful demonstration of the great instability in the Northern Kingdom.

i. "Josephus says that Hoshea was 'a friend' of Pekah's (Antiquities ix.13)… But watch as he might, his very friend in whom he trusted became, in the ordering of God, his slayer; so impossible it is for the wicked to escape their merited retribution." (Knapp)

ii. "He slew in his 'fierce anger' one hundred thousand Jews in one day (2 Chronicles 28:6); and God requited him in kind; for as he had so treacherously shed man's blood, by man was his blood also treacherously shed." (Knapp)

C. Jotham's reign over Judah.

1. (32-36) A summary of the reign of Jotham.

In the second year of Pekah the son of Remaliah, king of Israel, Jotham the son of Uzziah, king of Judah, began to reign. He was twenty-five years old when he became king, and he reigned sixteen years in Jerusalem. His mother's name *was* Jerusha the daughter of Zadok. And he did *what was* right in the sight of the LORD; he did according to all that his father Uzziah had done. However the high places were not removed; the people still sacrificed and burned incense on the high places. He built the Upper Gate of the house of the LORD. Now the rest of the acts of Jotham, and all that he did, *are* they not written in the book of the chronicles of the kings of Judah?

a. **And he did what was right in the sight of the LORD**: This stands in strong contrast to the *evil* done by the previously mentioned kings of Israel. Among the kings of Judah, there were good and godly kings.

b. **He did according to all that his father Uzziah had done**: The pattern is seen in both the kingdoms of Israel and Judah, where the son reigns as his father had before him. While this is not concretely predetermined, certainly this is a principle that shows us great influence that a father has on a son.

> i. "He also turned his attention to urban planning, constructing cities in the highlands of Judah that, together with a system of towers and fortification in the wooded areas, could serve both economic and military purposes." (Patterson and Austel)

c. **He built the Upper Gate of the house of the LORD**: This was always a positive sign in Judah. When kings and leaders were concerned about the **house of the LORD**, it reflected some measure of spiritual revival.

> i. In particular, it seems that Jotham rebuilt the *link* between the temple and the palace. "He wished free access from his own house to that of the Lord. He would strengthen the link between the two houses – keep his line of communication open (to use a military figure) with the source of his supplies of strength and wisdom. This is one of the secrets of his prosperity and power." (Knapp)

> ii. His father Azariah (Uzziah) misunderstood the link between the royal house and the house God, demanding priestly authority (2 Chronicles 26:16-21). Many kings before him wanted *no link* between the royal house and the house of God. Jotham understood that he was a king and not a priest, yet he wanted a good, open link between the palace and the temple.

> iii. 2 Chronicles 27:6 says, *So Jotham became mighty, because he prepared his ways before the LORD his God*. The building of this link between the palace and the temple was one of the chief ways that he prepared his way before the LORD. "That high gate between the palace and the temple was better than a Chinese wall around his kingdom. It is in communion with God that real prosperity and power is found." (Knapp)

> iv. "As Chronicles shows, Jotham strove to defend his small territory, and his increasing power was attributed to his steadfast way of life before God." (Wiseman)

> v. "Jotham is the only one of all the Hebrew kings, from Saul down, against whom God has nothing to record. In this his character is in beautiful accord with his name, *Jehovah-perfect*." (Knapp)

2. (37-38) Judah begins to be chastened for their partial obedience.

In those days the LORD began to send Rezin king of Syria and Pekah the son of Remaliah against Judah. So Jotham rested with his fathers, and was buried with his fathers in the City of David his father. Then Ahaz his son reigned in his place.

a. **In those days the LORD began to send Rezin king of Syria and Pekah the son of Remaliah**: Under the inspiration of the Holy Spirit, the writer of 2 Kings tells us that it was the hand of the LORD that sent these foreign rulers who troubled Judah.

b. **The LORD began to send**: This was the beginning. If Judah and her kings responded to these chastening events in the right way, God would take note. If they hardened their hearts and rejected the correction of God, He would take note of that as well.

i. "During Jotham's reign, the combined forces of King Rezin of Syria and King Pekah of Israel began their invasion of Judah, but the full impact of these military assaults was not felt until Jotham's son became king." (Dilday)

2 Kings 16 – The Compromise of Ahaz

A. A summary of the reign of Ahaz.

1. (1-2) The disobedience of Ahaz.

In the seventeenth year of Pekah the son of Remaliah, Ahaz the son of Jotham, king of Judah, began to reign. Ahaz *was* twenty years old when he became king, and he reigned sixteen years in Jerusalem; and he did not do *what was* right in the sight of the LORD his God, as his father David *had done*.

> a. **He did not do what was right in the sight of the LORD**: This briefly describes the reign of perhaps the worst king of Judah. Whereas many previous kings fell short in some area or another (typically, allowing sacrifices on the high places), of Ahaz it is simply said that **he did not do what was right in the sight of the LORD**.

> b. **As his father David had done**: Ahaz had plenty of good examples, both immediately in his father Jotham and historically in his ancestor **David**. Ahaz rejected these godly examples and walked in his own way.

2. (3-4) The idolatry of Ahaz.

But he walked in the way of the kings of Israel; indeed he made his son pass through the fire, according to the abominations of the nations whom the LORD had cast out from before the children of Israel. And he sacrificed and burned incense on the high places, on the hills, and under every green tree.

> a. **He walked in the way of the kings of Israel**: Ahaz not only rejected the godly heritage of David, he embraced the ungodly ways of the kings of the Northern Kingdom of Israel. The Southern Kingdom of Judah had a mixture of godly and ungodly kings; the Northern Kingdom of Judah had *only* ungodly kings, and Ahaz followed *their* pattern.

i. "This is the first instance where Judah imitates Israel's apostasy." (Wiseman)

ii. Micah 7:2-7 is a good description of the depravity of the times of Ahaz and the reaction of the godly remnant to it.

b. **Indeed, he made his son pass through the fire**: This describes Ahaz's participation in the worship of Molech. The pagan god (or *demon*, more accurately) Molech was worshipped by heating a metal statue representing the god until it was red hot, then placing a living infant on the outstretched hands of the statue, while beating drums drowned out the screams of the child until it burned to death.

i. In Leviticus 20:1-5, God pronounced the death sentence against all who worshipped Molech, saying: *I will set My face against that man, and will cut him off from his people, because he has given some of his descendants to Molech, to defile My sanctuary and profane My holy name* (Leviticus 20:3).

ii. Sadly, even a man as great as Solomon at least sanctioned the worship of Molech and built a temple to this idol (1 Kings 11:7). One of the great crimes of the northern tribes of Israel was their worship of Molech, leading to the Assyrian captivity (2 Kings 17:17). King Manasseh of Judah gave his son to Molech (2 Kings 21:6). Up to the days of King Josiah of Judah, Molech worship continued, because he destroyed a place of worship to that idol (2 Kings 23:10).

c. **According to the abominations of the nations whom the LORD had cast out from before the children of Israel**: The Canaanite nations that occupied Canaan before the time of Joshua also practiced this terrible form of human and child sacrifice. God would bring judgment upon Judah for their continued practice of these sins.

i. This reminds us that the war against the Canaanites in the Book of Joshua – as terrible and complete as it was – was *not* a racial war. God's judgment did not come upon the Canaanites through the armies of Israel because of their *race*, but because of their *sin*. If Israel insisted in walking in the same sins, God would bring similar judgment upon them.

B. Ahaz makes Judah a subject nation to Assyria.

1. (5-6) The attack of the Israeli-Syrian confederation.

Then Rezin king of Syria and Pekah the son of Remaliah, king of Israel, came up to Jerusalem to *make* war; and they besieged Ahaz but could not overcome *him*. At that time Rezin king of Syria captured Elath for

Syria, and drove the men of Judah from Elath. Then the Edomites went to Elath, and dwell there to this day.

a. Then Rezin king of Syria and Pekah the son of Remaliah, king of Israel, came up to Jerusalem to make war: This was part of Pekah's anti-Assyria policy. He thought that with Judah defeated, Syria and Israel together could more effectively resist the resurgent power of the Assyrian Empire.

i. The Isaiah 7 passage makes it clear that the goal of this attack was to dethrone Ahaz and set up a Syrian king over Judah, a certain *son of Tabeal* (Isaiah 7:6).

ii. On the whole, Judah suffered terrible losses from this attack. King Ahaz lost 120,000 Judean soldiers and 200,000 civilian hostages in these battles with Israel and Syria (2 Chronicles 28:5-8). It was a dark time for Judah, and it looked as if the dynasty of David would soon be extinguished, as so many dynasties in the Northern Kingdom of Israel had ended.

iii. When this great number of captives was taken to Samaria (the capital city of the Northern Kingdom of Israel), a strange and wonderful thing happened. A prophet named Oded rebuked the army managing the captives, and called on them to return them to Judah. These leaders in Israel responded, realizing that they had already offended the LORD and risked offending Him even further. So they clothed and fed the captives (who had before this been treated terribly), and returned them to Judah (2 Chronicles 28:8-15).

b. They besieged Ahaz but could not overcome him: The combined armies of Syria and Israel were strong enough to capture many cities of Judah, but not strong enough to defeat Jerusalem and overthrow the government of **Ahaz**.

i. The prophecy of Isaiah 7 – including the announcement of the *Immanuel* sign – came from Isaiah to King Ahaz during this joint Israel-Syrian invasion. As the following verses reveal, Ahaz refused to trust in the LORD and instead put his trust in the king of Assyria. Yet for the sake of David, God did not allow this disastrous attack on Judah to prevail. He would not allow this Satanic plot against the Messianic dynasty of David to succeed.

ii. The kings of Israel and Syria thought of themselves as burning torches, who had come to destroy Judah and the dynasty of David. God said they were just like burnt-out smoking sticks, who would not ultimately do much damage (Isaiah 7:4).

iii. Through Isaiah's message to Ahaz, he assured the wicked king – who did not really listen – "There should be a remnant left to return to the land; and the virgin should bear a son, so there should not fail to be a king upon the throne of David. The dynasty could never be destroyed, for of Immanuel's kingdom there shall be no end." (Knapp)

2. (7-9) Ahaz trusts in Assyria.

So Ahaz sent messengers to Tiglath-Pileser king of Assyria, saying, "I *am* your servant and your son. Come up and save me from the hand of the king of Syria and from the hand of the king of Israel, who rise up against me." And Ahaz took the silver and gold that was found in the house of the Lord, and in the treasuries of the king's house, and sent *it as* a present to the king of Assyria. So the king of Assyria heeded him; for the king of Assyria went up against Damascus and took it, carried *its people* captive to Kir, and killed Rezin.

a. **So Ahaz sent messengers to Tiglath-Pileser king of Assyria**: Before Ahaz did this, Isaiah offered him a sign for assurance of God's help in the struggle against the combined armies of Israel and Syria (Isaiah 7:1-12). "This was a fair offer to a foul sinner" (Trapp), but Ahaz refused under the excuse of not wanting to test God, when instead he really wanted to trust in the king of Assyria.

b. **I am your servant and your son. Come up and save me**: Ahaz surrendered to one enemy in order to defeat another. He refused to trust in the God of Israel and instead submitted himself and his kingdom to an enemy of Israel.

i. "The address 'I am your servant and your son' clearly places Ahaz as the petitioning vassal and shows he was trusting in Assyria rather than in the Lord, against the advice of Isaiah (Isaiah 7:10-16; *cf.* Exodus 23:22)." (Wiseman)

c. **Ahaz took the silver and gold that was found in the house of the Lord, and in the treasuries of the king's house, and sent it as a present to the king of Assyria**: Essentially, Ahaz made Judah a subject kingdom to Assyria. Ahaz now took his orders from the Assyrian king, sacrificing the independence of the kingdom of Judah.

i. We can only wonder what blessing might have come if Ahaz would have surrendered and sacrificed to the Lord with the same energy and whole heart that he surrendered to the Assyrian king.

ii. When anyone appeals to God saying, "**I am your servant and your son. Come up and save me**," then God answers. It is true that the Assyrian king answered and delivered Ahaz; but it was short-lived deliverance. He could have really secured his kingdom by surrendering and sacrificing to God in the same way.

iii. "How different was his great ancestor David! 'In my distress,' he says, 'I called upon the Lord, and cried unto my God' (Psalm 18:6). Even his wicked grandson Manasseh sought the Lord his God 'when he was in affliction.' But Ahaz seemed determined to fill up the measure of his sins." (Knapp)

C. Ahaz perverts worship at the temple.

1. (10-11) He has a heathen altar made and set up in the temple court.

Now King Ahaz went to Damascus to meet Tiglath-Pileser king of Assyria, and saw an altar that *was* at Damascus; and King Ahaz sent to Urijah the priest the design of the altar and its pattern, according to all its workmanship. Then Urijah the priest built an altar according to all that King Ahaz had sent from Damascus. So Urijah the priest made *it* before King Ahaz came back from Damascus.

a. **Now King Ahaz went to Damascus**: It was unusual for the kings of Judah to make official visits to other kingdoms; they generally stayed within the borders of the Promised Land. Yet this was much more than a visit – this was an official act of submission from Ahaz unto **Tiglath-Pileser**, king of Assyria.

b. **King Ahaz sent to Urijah the priest the design of the altar and its pattern**: Using the plans sent from Ahaz, Urijah imitated the pagan altar at Damascus and had it ready by the time Ahaz returned from the Syrian capital. He did this both to please his new lord, Tiglath-Pileser, and to incorporate the latest trends in altar design into the national worship of Judah.

i. 2 Chronicles 28:23 explains why King Ahaz was attracted to the worship he saw in Damascus: *For he sacrificed to the gods of Damascus which had defeated him, saying, "Because the gods of the kings of Syria help them, I will sacrifice to them that they may help me." But they were the ruin of him and of all Israel.*

ii. This explains why many churches today put their trust in the tools, techniques, and principles of worldly success: They think the gods of Damascus will give them victory. "This introduction of the altar of a heathen shrine into the holy temple of Jerusalem reminds us of the many rites in modern religious observances which have been borrowed from paganism, and warns us that the Church has no right to go to the world for its methods and principles." (Meyer)

c. **Then Urijah the priest built an altar**: Of course, Ahaz bears the greater blame in this matter; but the high priest Urijah also bore significant blame in the replacement of the LORD's altar with this one of pagan design.

i. This Urijah is likely the same as Uriah in Isaiah 8. Curiously, Isaiah 8:1-2 says he was a "faithful witness." Apparently, he was a good and faithful man who later compromised. The corruption of King Ahaz spread to other leaders in Judah.

2. (12-20) Ahaz directs the renovation of the temple court, giving preference to the new altar.

And when the king came back from Damascus, the king saw the altar; and the king approached the altar and made offerings on it. So he burned his burnt offering and his grain offering; and he poured his drink offering and sprinkled the blood of his peace offerings on the altar. He also brought the bronze altar which *was* before the LORD, from the front of the temple—from between the *new* altar and the house of the LORD—and put it on the north side of the *new* altar. Then King Ahaz commanded Urijah the priest, saying, "On the great *new* altar burn the morning burnt offering, the evening grain offering, the king's burnt sacrifice, and his grain offering, with the burnt offering of all the people of the land, their grain offering, and their drink offerings; and sprinkle on it all the blood of the burnt offering and all the blood of the sacrifice. And the bronze altar shall be for me to inquire *by*." Thus did Urijah the priest, according to all that King Ahaz commanded. And King Ahaz cut off the panels of the carts, and removed the lavers from them; and he took down the Sea from the bronze oxen that *were* under it, and put it on a pavement of stones. Also he removed the Sabbath pavilion which they had built in the temple, and he removed the king's outer entrance from the house of the LORD, on account of the king of Assyria. Now the rest of the acts of Ahaz which he did, *are* they not written in the book of the chronicles of the kings of Judah? So Ahaz rested with his fathers, and was buried with his fathers in the City of David. Then Hezekiah his son reigned in his place.

a. **So he burned his burnt offering and his grain offering; and he poured his drink offering and sprinkled the blood of his peace offerings on the altar**: Ahaz served as a priest at the altar of his own design. Since he created his own place of worship, it also made sense that he would disregard God's command that a king must not serve as a priest (Numbers 18:7).

i. Ahaz's grandfather Azariah (Uzziah) dared to enter the temple and serve God as a priest (2 Chronicles 26). Yet at least Azariah *falsely* worshipped the *true God*. Ahaz *falsely* worshipped a *false god* of his own creation. "Uzziah for so doing was smitten with leprosy; but Ahaz of a far worse disease, an incurable hardness of heart." (Trapp)

ii. "Ahaz wildly experimented, trying to inject the religion of Judah with new life. He seemed to be drawn to the most lurid elements in the pagan religions around him. Like the Athenians in Acts 17 who 'spent their time in nothing else but either to tell or to hear some new thing,' Ahaz was addicted to the lure of the sensational." (Dilday)

b. **Thus did Urijah the priest, according to all that King Ahaz commanded**: Urijah not only *allowed* Ahaz to do this; he participated in his evil and idolatrous plans. This was in dramatic contrast to the priests in the days of King Uzziah, who did all they could to restrain the madness of the king (2 Chronicles 26:17-18).

i. Corrupt political leaders have almost always been able to find corrupt religious leaders to help them.

ii. Wiseman on the phrase, **on account of the king of Assyria**: "All these changes are said to have been made 'from before the face of the king of Assyria' (MT), perhaps 'because of' (RSV) the installation of an alien royal statue. Most interpret these actions as carried out by a vassal *in deference* to the king of Assyria, but that is not the only interpretation possible."

c. **And King Ahaz cut off the panels of the carts, and removed the lavers… he removed the Sabbath pavilion… he removed the king's outer entrance**: Ahaz could not bring in his pagan, corrupt innovations without *also* removing what had stood before at the temple. This was an ungodly exchange, taking away the good and putting in the bad – including **the king's outer entrance** built in the days of his father, King Jotham. Collectively, all these things served to *discourage* the worship of the true God at the temple of God.

i. During these changes, Ahaz shut down the operation of the temple and established small pagan altars all around Judah (2 Chronicles 28:24-25).

ii. "Ahaz's appropriation of the panels and bases from the sacred furniture does not seem to be for the purpose of sending a further gift to Tiglath-pileser but rather for de-emphasizing their importance in the worship services. Perhaps he planned to reuse them in some other decorative way. At any rate death overtook him before his attention could be turned to them. They are mentioned among the several items that were carried away in the later Babylonian despoiling of Jerusalem (25:13-14; Jeremiah 27:19-20; 52:17-23)." (Patterson and Austel)

iii. "The plain brazen altar seems to have offended his aesthetic eye; so it was relegated to a place of relative obscurity on the north side of his own foreign substitute." (Knapp)

iv. We remember that *all this took place at the temple Solomon built unto the* LORD. The mere *location* did not make it true worship. Sometimes idols are worshipped at a house that was once dedicated to the true God.

v. "It would seem as though the light of truth were absolutely extinguished. It was not so, however, for it is likely that throughout the whole reigns of Jotham and Ahaz, Isaiah was uttering his message, and that during the reign of Ahaz, Micah also was delivering the word of God." (Morgan)

d. **Now the rest of the acts of Ahaz which he did**: So ended the reign of perhaps the worst king of Judah. Micah – who prophesied during the reign of Ahaz – describes the man who works to *successfully do evil with both hands* (Micah 7:3). The idea is that the man pursues evil with all his effort, *with both hands*. He may very well have had King Ahaz in mind.

i. Yet in many ways, Ahaz is a warning to our generation. He could be considered a church leader from the 21st century in many ways.

- Based on his admiration of the altar of Damascus, we can say that Ahaz was a man with an artistic sense of style.
- Ahaz also seemed to be impressed with technology, apparently introducing the Babylonian innovation of the sundial to Jerusalem (2 Kings 20:11).
- He was in love with innovation and new things, and didn't hesitate to bring these innovations into worship.
- At the same time, he seemed to be a *nice* man. He did not have the persecuting spirit of his grandson Manasseh, who persecuted the prophets and people of God (2 Kings 21:16).
- Ahaz had the advantage of many great prophets and messengers (such as Isaiah and Micah).
- Ahaz had the blessing of a great deliverance of God. God spared Jerusalem and Judah from total defeat when the armies of Israel and Syria came against them.
- Ahaz had the influence of a godly father and a godly heritage from the line of David.

ii. The key was that Ahaz had no relationship with God. He was interested in spiritual things, and would even make great spiritual sacrifices (such as sacrificing his own sons to Molech). Yet he destroyed the link that his father Jotham made between the palace and the temple, and this was an illustration of his destroyed relationship with God. For Ahaz, it wasn't enough to have a spiritual interest and all the aforementioned advantages.

iii. Despite all this, he put his trust in himself and in man – instead of in the living God who reigns from heaven. Therefore his reign was a disaster, probably the worst among the kings of Judah. "He was possessed (Ahaz – *possessor*) of much that men admire and magnify today; but all this, without godliness, is of absolutely no worth." (Knapp)

2 Kings 17 – The Fall of Israel

A. The fall of Samaria.

1. (1-2) The evil reign of Hoshea.

In the twelfth year of Ahaz king of Judah, Hoshea the son of Elah became king of Israel in Samaria, *and he reigned* nine years. And he did evil in the sight of the Lord, but not as the kings of Israel who were before him.

> a. **Hoshea the son of Elah**: We last saw **Hoshea** in 2 Kings 15:30, as the man who led a conspiracy against Pekah, the king of Israel. After the successful assassination, Hoshea took the throne and started his own brief dynasty.
>
> b. **And he did evil in the sight of the Lord, but not as the kings of Israel who were before him**: Hoshea was an **evil** man, but by no means the worst of the kings of Israel. Sadly, his bloody overthrow of the preceding king and violent ascent to power did not make him unusually evil among the kings of Israel.
>
>> i. "He seems not to have inaugurated or continued the anti-Yahwistic practices for which Israel itself is condemned." (Wiseman)
>>
>> ii. This reminds us that *judgment may not come at the height of sin*. When God judges a nation or a culture, He has the big picture in view. For that reason, the actual events of judgment may come when things are not as bad in a relative sense.
>>
>> iii. "It is not the last sand that exhausteth the hour-glass, nor the last stroke of the axe that felleth the tree; so here." (Trapp)

2. (3-4) Hoshea's futile resistance against Assyria.

Shalmaneser king of Assyria came up against him; and Hoshea became his vassal, and paid him tribute money. And the king of Assyria uncovered a conspiracy by Hoshea; for he had sent messengers to So,

king of Egypt, and brought no tribute to the king of Assyria, as *he had done* year by year. Therefore the king of Assyria shut him up, and bound him in prison.

a. **Hoshea became his vassal, and paid him tribute money**: In the pattern of Menaham before him (2 Kings 15:17-22), Hoshea accepted the status of vassal unto the **king of Assyria**. If he paid his money and did as the king of Assyria pleased, he would be allowed to continue on the throne of Israel.

i. Hoshea thought he had a strategic opportunity when a new king came to the Assyrian throne, but he was wrong. "When Tiglath-pileser III died in 727 B.C. and was succeeded by his own son Shalmaneser V (727-722), the time seemed ripe for certain western states to renounce their vassal status. Moreover, a seemingly important ally lay southward in the delta of Egypt." (Patterson and Austel)

b. **And the king of Assyria uncovered a conspiracy by Hoshea**: King Hoshea hoped to find help among the Egyptians, who were in a constant power struggle with the Assyrian Empire. On account of this **conspiracy**, and the failure to pay the yearly **tribute** money, Hoshea was imprisoned by the king of Assyria.

i. As we might expect among the kings of Israel, Hoshea did not look to the LORD for help – he looked to Egypt. Therefore, Hosea said of him: *As for Samaria, her king is cut off like a twig on the water.* (Hosea 10:7)

ii. The reference to **So, king of Egypt**, is probably better understood as a reference to a place – *Sais*, which was at that time the capital of Egypt. "Thus understood, v. 4 would read 'he had sent envoys to Sais (even unto) the king of Egypt.' " (Patterson and Austel)

3. (5-6) The Northern Kingdom of Israel is finally conquered by the Assyrians.

Now the king of Assyria went throughout all the land, and went up to Samaria and besieged it for three years. In the ninth year of Hoshea, the king of Assyria took Samaria and carried Israel away to Assyria, and placed them in Halah and by the Habor, the River of Gozan, and in the cities of the Medes.

a. **The king of Assyria went throughout all the land, and went up to Samaria and besieged it for three years**: This was a long, dedicated campaign to finally crush the rebellious kingdom of Israel, who had defied the power of the Assyrian Empire. Though it took a three-year siege, it was worth it to the Assyrians.

i. **Three years**: "The fact that it took Assyria that long to break Samaria's resistance is a testimony to the good wall Omri and Ahab had built around the capital city." (Dilday)

ii. This shows us that when God brings His judgment, He *may use human instruments* to do it.

b. **The king of Assyria took Samaria and carried Israel away to Assyria**: When Samaria finally fell and the Northern Kingdom was conquered, the Assyrians implemented their policy towards conquered nations. They deported all but the very lowest classes back to the key cities of their empire, either to train and utilize the talented or to enslave the able.

i. Two hundred years and 19 kings after the time of Solomon (the last king over a united Israel), the Northern Kingdom of Israel fell. It was not because the God of Israel was unable to help them, but because they had so forsaken God and ignored His guidance and correction that He finally stopped actively protecting them and let them rot and degrade according to their desire.

ii. As they **carried Israel away to Assyria**, they followed their typical custom. When the Assyrians depopulated and exiled a conquered community, they led the captives away on journeys of hundreds of miles, with the captives naked and attached together with a system of strings and fishhooks pierced through their lower lips. God would make sure they were led in this humiliating manner through the broken walls of their conquered cities (Amos 4:2-3).

iii. This shows another principle of God's judgment: When it comes, it is often humiliating and degrading.

iv. It seems that Sargon II, the brother and successor of Shalmaneser, *finished* this siege or at least took credit for it: "The men of Samaria with their king were hostile to me and consorted together not to carry out their vassal obligations and bring tribute to me, so they fought me… I clashed with them and took as booty 27,280 people with their chariots and their gods in whom they trusted. I incorporated 200 chariots into my army. The rest of the people I made to dwell within Assyria. I restored the city of Samaria and made it greater than before." (*Inscribed Prisms of Sargon II from Nimrud*, cited in Wiseman)

B. The reasons for the fall of the Northern Kingdom of Israel.

"The rest of this chapter is spent in vindicating the Divine providence and justice, showing the reason why God permitted such a desolation to fall on a people who had been so long his peculiar children." (Clarke)

1. (7) They disregarded the God of their redemption.

For so it was that the children of Israel had sinned against the Lord their God, who had brought them up out of the land of Egypt, from under the hand of Pharaoh king of Egypt; and they had feared other gods,

> a. **For so it was that the children of Israel had sinned against the Lord**: In the following verses, the divine historian explains the fundamental reasons for the conquering and captivity of the Northern Kingdom. At the root, it was a problem with *sin*. It wasn't geopolitical changes or social causes – it was *sin*.
>
> b. **They had feared other gods**: In the central act of redemption in Old Testament history, God **brought** Israel **up out of the land of Egypt**. Remembrance of this act alone should prompt Israel to a single-hearted commitment to the Lord. Yet they did not remember this and instead they **feared other gods**, breaking the covenant God made with His people.
>
>> i. However, the kingdom of Israel had **feared other gods** since their founding some 200 years before this. This shows us another principle of God's judgment: It is often a long time in coming, because God holds back His judgment as long as possible.

2. (8) They conformed themselves to the godless nations around them.

And had walked in the statutes of the nations whom the Lord had cast out from before the children of Israel, and of the kings of Israel, which they had made.

> a. **And had walked in the statutes of the nations whom the Lord had cast out from before the children of Israel**: Before Israel occupied Canaan in the days of Joshua, the Promised Land was populated by degenerate, pagan peoples who practiced the worst kinds of idolatry and human sacrifice. One of the fundamental sins of Israel was that they followed in these ancient Canaanite ways.
>
>> i. **Whom the Lord had cast out**: God **cast out** the Canaanite nations in the days of Joshua because of these sins. Now He had **cast out** the Northern Kingdom of Israel for the same sins. God's judgment was not against the ancient Canaanites because of race or ethnicity; it was because of their *conduct*. As Israel shared the same conduct, they would share the same judgment.
>
> b. **Which they had made**: It is a little difficult to say if what they **made** refers to the *other gods* mentioned in the previous verse or to the **statutes** mentioned in this verse. Either is valid or true. Men make both their laws and their idols after their own ingenuity and desire.

3. (9-12) Their secret and openly practiced idolatry.

Also the children of Israel secretly did against the Lord their God things that *were* not right, and they built for themselves high places in all their cities, from watchtower to fortified city. They set up for themselves *sacred* pillars and wooden images on every high hill and under every green tree. There they burned incense on all the high places, like the nations whom the Lord had carried away before them; and they did wicked things to provoke the Lord to anger, for they served idols, of which the Lord had said to them, "You shall not do this thing."

> a. **Also the children of Israel secretly did against the Lord their God things that were not right**: Rebellion and sin cloud the judgment of men, and clearly the judgment of Israel was affected. Their judgment was impaired enough to think they could sin **secretly** against the God who sees everything.
>
> b. **They built for themselves high places in all their cities**: These were places of unauthorized and idolatrous sacrifice, as were the **sacred pillars**.
>
> c. **Like the nations whom the Lord had carried away before them**: The divine historian repeats this theme. The same sins that brought judgment upon the Canaanites also brought judgment on the Northern Kingdom of Israel.

4. (13-15) They rejected the repeated warnings from God.

Yet the Lord testified against Israel and against Judah, by all of His prophets, every seer, saying, "Turn from your evil ways, and keep My commandments *and* My statutes, according to all the law which I commanded your fathers, and which I sent to you by My servants the prophets." Nevertheless they would not hear, but stiffened their necks, like the necks of their fathers, who did not believe in the Lord their God. And they rejected His statutes and His covenant that He had made with their fathers, and His testimonies which He had testified against them; they followed idols, became idolaters, and *went* after the nations who *were* all around them, *concerning* whom the Lord had charged them that they should not do like them.

> a. **Yet the Lord testified against Israel and against Judah, by all of His prophets**: In love, God sent **prophets** to the Northern and Southern Kingdoms. Their message was a warning against the sins that corrupted God's people and separated them from their God. They invited God's people with the theme, **"Turn from your evil ways."**
>
> b. **Nevertheless they would not hear**: God sent these messengers to help Israel and to spare them the judgment that would come if they did not

turn from their **evil ways**. Yet God's people became more stubborn when God brought this call to repentance, and they sank deeper into sin.

i. When God brings judgment, He first brings warning – and often many warnings over a long period. It is only after these warnings are rejected that the judgment comes.

ii. "Their sin was first against law, but finally it was against patient love." (Morgan)

iii. **But stiffened their necks**: "Refused to submit their neck to the yoke of God's precepts; a metaphor from stubborn oxen, that make their necks hard, or stiff, and will not bow to the yoke." (Poole)

c. **They followed idols, became idolaters**: The NIV translates this, "*They followed worthless idols and themselves became worthless.*" The NASB has it, "*They followed vanity and became vain.*"

i. "The original is more accurate at this point: 'They worshipped emptiness and became empty.' The word here is *hebel* meaning 'air,' 'delusion,' or 'vanity.' The idea is that they became like the gods they worshipped. They bowed down to nothingness and became nothing." (Dilday)

5. (16-23) They forsook God and served idols – until judgment finally came.

So they left all the commandments of the LORD **their God, made for themselves a molded image *and* two calves, made a wooden image and worshiped all the host of heaven, and served Baal. And they caused their sons and daughters to pass through the fire, practiced witchcraft and soothsaying, and sold themselves to do evil in the sight of the L**ORD**, to provoke Him to anger. Therefore the L**ORD **was very angry with Israel, and removed them from His sight; there was none left but the tribe of Judah alone. Also Judah did not keep the commandments of the L**ORD **their God, but walked in the statutes of Israel which they made. And the L**ORD **rejected all the descendants of Israel, afflicted them, and delivered them into the hand of plunderers, until He had cast them from His sight. For He tore Israel from the house of David, and they made Jeroboam the son of Nebat king. Then Jeroboam drove Israel from following the L**ORD**, and made them commit a great sin. For the children of Israel walked in all the sins of Jeroboam which he did; they did not depart from them, until the L**ORD **removed Israel out of His sight, as He had said by all His servants the prophets. So Israel was carried away from their own land to Assyria, *as it is* to this day.**

a. **Made for themselves a molded image and two calves**: This refers to the infamous sin of Jeroboam (1 Kings 12:26-29). This state-sponsored idolatry did not *immediately* ruin the kingdom – the Northern Kingdom of Israel lasted as an independent nation for another 200 years following the time of Jeroboam. Yet it certainly was the *beginning* of the end.

b. And they caused their sons and daughters to pass through the fire: This refers to the abominable worship of the idol Molech, to whom children were burned in sacrifice.

c. Practiced witchcraft and soothsaying: The northern tribes embraced the same occult practices that the Canaanite tribes before them had embraced. Collectively, these great sins of idolatry provoked God to anger.

d. Therefore the LORD was very angry with Israel, and removed them from His sight; there was none left but the tribe of Judah alone: This was the end of the ten northern tribes as an independent kingdom. When they were dispersed by the Assyrians, some assimilated into other cultures, but others kept their Jewish identity as exiles in other lands.

i. Yet, it is a mistake to think of these ten northern tribes as *lost*. Far back in the days of Jeroboam and his original break with the Southern Kingdom of Judah, the legitimate priests and Levites who lived in the northern ten tribes did not like Jeroboam's idolatry. They, along with others who *set their hearts to seek the* LORD *God of Israel*, then moved from the Northern Kingdom of Israel to the Southern Kingdom of Judah (2 Chronicles 11:13-16). So actually, the *Southern Kingdom of Judah* contained Israelites from all of the ten tribes.

ii. Considering all this, we can say that the ten northern tribes were not lost, and they certainly did not migrate to Britain in accord with some British-Israelite theories.

- Some (in particular, the godly of that day) migrated to the Southern Kingdom of Judah in the days of Jeroboam I.
- Some assimilated into other cultures.
- Some kept their Jewish culture and identity in the lands of their exile.

e. Judah did not keep the commandments of the LORD their God, but walked in the statutes of Israel which they made: Spiritually speaking, Judah was more faithful to God than the Northern Kingdom of Israel. Yet they also began to imitate their sinful neighbors to the north.

i. Judah had the lesson right in front of them – the conquered nation of Israel was evidence of what happened when hearts turned from God. Yet they ignored these plain lessons and imitated the sins of Israel.

f. **For the children of Israel walked in all the sins of Jeroboam which he did; they did not depart from them, until the LORD removed Israel out of His sight**: The summary of Israel's sin is simply that they were given over to *idolatry*. They worshipped the true God in a false way and then began to also worship false gods.

C. The resettlement of Samaria.

1. (24-26) God warns the foreigners who are resettled in Samaria.

Then the king of Assyria brought *people* from Babylon, Cuthah, Ava, Hamath, and from Sepharvaim, and placed *them* in the cities of Samaria instead of the children of Israel; and they took possession of Samaria and dwelt in its cities. And it was so, at the beginning of their dwelling there, *that* they did not fear the LORD; therefore the LORD sent lions among them, which killed *some* of them. So they spoke to the king of Assyria, saying, "The nations whom you have removed and placed in the cities of Samaria do not know the rituals of the God of the land; therefore He has sent lions among them, and indeed, they are killing them because they do not know the rituals of the God of the land."

a. **Then the king of Assyria brought people**: The policy of the Assyrian Empire was to *remove* rebellious, resistant people and to *resettle* their former lands with people from other parts of the empire.

i. "Not only did the Assyrian monarchs hope to make the repopulated and reconstituted districts more manageable, but they hoped to train and encourage the citizenry to transfer their loyalties to the Assyrian Empire." (Patterson and Austel)

b. **They did not fear the LORD; therefore the LORD sent lions among them**: This shows that there was not only something special about the *kingdom* of Israel, but also something special about the *land* of Israel. God demanded to be feared among the people of the land, even if they came from other nations.

i. "Perhaps because many unburied bodies still remained after the bloody warfare and due to the depopulating of the land, voracious lions began to roam freely through the area." (Patterson and Austel)

ii. Zechariah 2:12 tells us that the land of Israel is the *Holy Land*. God regards it as something special, and will hold accountable those who live there and do not fear Him.

iii. "Hereby also God asserted his own right and sovereignty over that land, and made them to understand that neither the Israelites were cast out nor they brought into that land by their valour or strength, but by God's providence." (Poole)

c. **Because they do not know the rituals of the God of the land**: These Assyrian officials seemed to know what the recently-conquered kingdom of Israel *did not know* – that they had to honor the God of Israel. Yet, any faith in God among these resettled people was founded in simple fear of the lions – leading to an inadequate relationship with God.

> i. "He did send lions among them, and it was these lions that converted them. Their teeth and fangs and fiery eyes and the thunders of their roars converted them. They must have a god to deliver them: they could not bear the lions, therefore they must fear the Lord who could send lions, and who perhaps would cease to send them. Now, dear friends, always be somewhat diffident of your own conversion if you can trace it only and solely to motives of terror." (Spurgeon)

2. (27-33) A religion for Samaria is established.

Then the king of Assyria commanded, saying, "Send there one of the priests whom you brought from there; let him go and dwell there, and let him teach them the rituals of the God of the land." Then one of the priests whom they had carried away from Samaria came and dwelt in Bethel, and taught them how they should fear the Lord. However every nation continued to make gods of its own, and put *them* in the shrines on the high places which the Samaritans had made, *every* nation in the cities where they dwelt. The men of Babylon made Succoth Benoth, the men of Cuth made Nergal, the men of Hamath made Ashima, and the Avites made Nibhaz and Tartak; and the Sepharvites burned their children in fire to Adrammelech and Anammelech, the gods of Sepharvaim. So they feared the Lord, and from every class they appointed for themselves priests of the high places, who sacrificed for them in the shrines of the high places. They feared the Lord, yet served their own gods—according to the rituals of the nations from among whom they were carried away.

a. **Taught them how they should fear the Lord**: The priesthood of the kingdom of Israel was corrupt, but the king of Assyria did not know and was not interested in the pure religion of Israel. Therefore this nameless, corrupt priest taught the new inhabitants of the land a corrupt religion.

> i. Certainly, it had *elements* of the true faith in it; but at the same time it was corrupted by the centuries of state-sponsored idolatry that reigned in Israel.

b. **Every nation continued to make gods of its own**: The priest-for-hire brought in by the Assyrians did not tell the new inhabitants of the land that they must *only* worship the Lord God of Israel. He did not teach it because, coming from Israel, he did not believe it.

c. **They feared the LORD, yet served their own gods**: This described the *pagan* peoples that the Assyrians brought in to populate the area of the Northern Kingdom of Israel. They gave a measure of respect to the God of Israel – after all, they did not want to be eaten by lions. Yet they also served their own gods and picked and chose among religious and spiritual beliefs as it pleased them.

- This accurately described the pagan peoples who re-populated Israel.
- This accurately described the Northern Kingdom of *Israel* before they were conquered and exiled.
- This accurately describes *common religious belief* in the modern world.

i. "Are you sure this is not a true description of your own position? You pay an outward deference to God by attending his house, and acknowledging his day, whilst you are really prostrating yourself before other shrines." (Meyer)

ii. "Is not worldly piety, or pious worldliness, the current religion of England? They live among godly people, and God chastens them, and they therefore fear him, but not enough to give their hearts to him. They seek out a trimming teacher who is not too precise and plain-spoken, and they settle down comfortably to a mongrel faith, half truth, half error, and a mongrel worship, half-dead form, and half orthodoxy." (Spurgeon)

iii. "Let me be right, and let there be no mistake about it; but do not let me try to be both right and wrong, washed and filthy, white and black, a child of God and a child of Satan." (Spurgeon)

3. (34-41) The continuance of this false religion.

To this day they continue practicing the former rituals; they do not fear the LORD, nor do they follow their statutes or their ordinances, or the law and commandment which the LORD had commanded the children of Jacob, whom He named Israel, with whom the LORD had made a covenant and charged them, saying: "You shall not fear other gods, nor bow down to them nor serve them nor sacrifice to them; but the LORD, who brought you up from the land of Egypt with great power and an outstretched arm, Him you shall fear, Him you shall worship, and to Him you shall offer sacrifice. And the statutes, the ordinances, the law, and the commandment which He wrote for you, you shall be careful to observe forever; you shall not fear other gods. And the covenant that I have made with you, you shall not forget, nor shall you fear other gods. But the LORD your God you shall fear; and He will deliver you from the hand of all your enemies." However they did not obey, but they followed

their former rituals. So these nations feared the LORD, yet served their carved images; also their children and their children's children have continued doing as their fathers did, even to this day.

a. **To this day they continue practicing the former rituals**: The area of the Northern Kingdom of Israel was not re-occupied by Judah before their own subjugation and conquest by the Babylonian empire. This mixed religion first promoted by the Assyrians continued for many centuries in Samaria, existing even until New Testament times.

i. It seems that God was more lenient with these Samaritans of corrupt belief than He was with disobedient Israel. This teaches us that those with more revelation from God are held to stricter account before Him.

ii. Yet, 2 Chronicles 30:10-19 shows us that in the days of King Hezekiah of Judah, there were some worshippers of the true God among the area that was formerly the Northern Kingdom of Israel. Some responded to his invitation to celebrate Passover in Jerusalem.

b. **But the LORD your God you shall fear; and He will deliver you from the hand of all your enemies**: The writer states this to remind us that if Israel had been faithful – even *moderately faithful* – to their covenant with God, they would still stand. God would have delivered them from all of their enemies. Instead, they were conquered by the Assyrian Empire after their own self-destruction in sin and rebellion.

2 Kings 18 – Hezekiah's Reign; Assyria's Threat

A. The righteous reign of Hezekiah.

1. (1-2) Hezekiah reigns over Judah for 29 years.

Now it came to pass in the third year of Hoshea the son of Elah, king of Israel, *that* **Hezekiah the son of Ahaz, king of Judah, began to reign. He was twenty-five years old when he became king, and he reigned twenty-nine years in Jerusalem. His mother's name** *was* **Abi the daughter of Zechariah.**

> a. **In the third year of Hoshea**: Hezekiah came to the throne of Judah at the very end of the kingdom of Israel. Three years after the start of his reign, the Assyrian armies laid siege to Samaria, and three years after that the Northern Kingdom was conquered.
>
>> i. The sad fate of the Northern Kingdom was a valuable lesson to Hezekiah. He saw first hand what happened when the people of God rejected their God and His word, and worshipped other gods.
>>
>> ii. "Perhaps the knottiest of all scriptural chronological problems occurs in this chapter… Despite the many ingenious attempts to resolve these difficulties, the harmonization of these data remains a thorny problem." (Patterson and Austel)
>>
>> iii. **In the third year of Hoshea**: "…729/8 B.C. in which year Hezekiah became co-regent with Ahaz. His sole reign began in 716/5 B.C. Compare this with verse 13 where his *fourteenth year* as sole ruler (716/5-687/6 B.C.) is a date (701 B.C.) verifiable from Sennacherib's annals." (Wiseman)
>
> b. **He reigned twenty-nine years in Jerusalem**: Hezekiah was one of the better kings of Judah, and thus had a long and mostly blessed reign.

2. (3-6) Hezekiah's righteousness.

And he did *what was* right in the sight of the LORD, according to all that his father David had done. He removed the high places and broke the *sacred* pillars, cut down the wooden image and broke in pieces the bronze serpent that Moses had made; for until those days the children of Israel burned incense to it, and called it Nehushtan. He trusted in the LORD God of Israel, so that after him was none like him among all the kings of Judah, nor who were before him. For he held fast to the LORD; he did not depart from following Him, but kept His commandments, which the LORD had commanded Moses.

a. **He did what was right in the sight of the LORD… He removed the high places**: Hezekiah was one of Judah's most zealous reformers, even prohibiting worship on **the high places**. These were popular altars for sacrifice set up as the worshipper desired, not according to God's direction.

i. "God was never happy about this practice, but none of the other good kings ever found the courage to forbid it. Hezekiah did." (Dilday)

b. **And broke in pieces the bronze serpent that Moses had made**: Numbers 21:1-9 describes how during a time of a plague of fiery serpents upon the whole nation, Moses made a bronze serpent for the nation to look upon and be spared death from the snake bites. This statement in 2 Kings tells us that this particular **bronze serpent** had been preserved for more than 800 years and had come to be worshipped as **Nehushtan**. Hezekiah, in his zeal, **broke in pieces** this bronze artifact and put an end to the idolatrous worship of this object.

i. This **bronze serpent** was a wonderful thing – when the afflicted people of Israel looked upon it, they were saved. It was even a representation of Jesus Christ, as Jesus Himself said in John 3:14-15. At the same time, man could take something so good and so used by God and make a destructive idol out of it.

ii. In the same way, sometimes *good things* become idols and therefore must be destroyed. For example, if the true cross of Jesus or His actual burial cloth were to be discovered, and these objects became idolatrous distractions, then it would be better for those objects to be destroyed. "Although it was an interesting memorial, it must be utterly destroyed, because it presented a temptation to idolatry. Here if ever in this world was a relic of high antiquity, of undoubted authenticity, a relic which had seen its hundreds of years, about which there was no question as to its being indisputably the very serpent which Moses made; and it was moreover a relic which had formerly possessed miraculous power – for in the wilderness the looking at it had saved the dying. Yet it must be broken in pieces, because Israel burned incense to it." (Spurgeon)

iii. God's people must likewise be on guard against idolatry today. There are many dangers of idolatry in the modern church:

- Making leaders idols.
- Making education an idol.
- Making human eloquence an idol.
- Making customs and habits of ministry an idol.
- Making forms of worship an idol.

iv. The name **Nehushtan** means "piece of brass" and is a way to *make less* of this object that was made an idol. "So Hezekiah had it turned from an object of false worship into scrap-metal." (Wiseman)

v. "Such was the venom of the Israelitish idolatry, that the brazen serpent stung worse than the fiery." (Trapp)

c. **He trusted in the LORD God of Israel, so that after him was none like him among all the kings of Judah**: Hezekiah was unique in his passion and energy of his personal trust in God and for promoting the true worship of God. This is even more remarkable when we consider that his father Ahaz was one of the *worst* kings Judah had (2 Kings 16:10-20).

i. "It is remarkable that such a man as Hezekiah could be the son of Ahaz. Yet we must remember that all his life he was under the influence of Isaiah." (Morgan)

3. (7-8) Hezekiah's political achievements.

The LORD was with him; he prospered wherever he went. And he rebelled against the king of Assyria and did not serve him. He subdued the Philistines, as far as Gaza and its territory, from watchtower to fortified city.

a. **The LORD was with him; he prospered wherever he went**: Because of Hezekiah's faithful trust in the LORD, God blessed him thoroughly. It fulfilled a long-standing promise to David and his descendants: if they obeyed God, their reign would always be secure (1 Kings 2:1-4).

b. **He rebelled against the king of Assyria and did not serve him**: At this time Assyria was mighty enough to completely conquer the Northern Kingdom of Israel. Yet the kingdom of Judah stood strong, because God blessed the trusting and obedient king.

i. "He shook off that yoke of subjugation and tribute to which his father had wickedly submitted, and reassumed that full independent sovereignty which God had settled in the house of David." (Poole)

ii. Later, Zedekiah was rebuked for his rebellion against the king of Babylon. But that was a different case, and shows that sometimes rebellion is justified and sometimes it is not.

c. **He subdued the Philistines**: Hezekiah also found success in subjugating Judah's aggressive neighbors. He worked for a strong, free, and independent Judah.

4. (9-12) Israel falls into exile during his reign.

Now it came to pass in the fourth year of King Hezekiah, which *was* the seventh year of Hoshea the son of Elah, king of Israel, *that* Shalmaneser king of Assyria came up against Samaria and besieged it. And at the end of three years they took it. In the sixth year of Hezekiah, that *is,* the ninth year of Hoshea king of Israel, Samaria was taken. Then the king of Assyria carried Israel away captive to Assyria, and put them in Halah and by the Habor, the River of Gozan, and in the cities of the Medes, because they did not obey the voice of the LORD their God, but transgressed His covenant *and* all that Moses the servant of the LORD had commanded; and they would neither hear nor do *them.*

a. **Samaria was taken**: This was – and should have been – a sobering experience for the Southern Kingdom of Judah to see. The cruel devastation brought by the Assyrians showed what calamities could come upon the disobedient people of God.

i. "From this time on, the Southern Kingdom would be known not only by the name 'Judah' but also by the ancient name 'Israel.'" (Dilday)

b. **They would neither hear nor do them**: The people of the Northern Kingdom were not any less Israelites and descendants of Abraham by blood than were the people of the Southern Kingdom. Therefore, this clearly showed Judah that when they also stopped hearing and doing the commandments of God, they would also face judgment.

B. The Assyrian threat during the reign of Hezekiah.

1. (13-16) Hezekiah tries to buy peace from the Assyrians.

And in the fourteenth year of King Hezekiah, Sennacherib king of Assyria came up against all the fortified cities of Judah and took them. Then Hezekiah king of Judah sent to the king of Assyria at Lachish, saying, "I have done wrong; turn away from me; whatever you impose on me I will pay." And the king of Assyria assessed Hezekiah king of Judah three hundred talents of silver and thirty talents of gold. So Hezekiah gave *him* all the silver that was found in the house of the LORD and in the treasuries of the king's house. At that time Hezekiah stripped

the gold from **the doors of the temple of the L**ORD**, and *from* the pillars which Hezekiah king of Judah had overlaid, and gave it to the king of Assyria.**

a. **In the fourteenth year of King Hezekiah, Sennacherib king of Assyria came up against all the fortified cities of Judah and took them**: This was approximately five years after the fall of Samaria. Now the king of Assyria brought his force against Judah, who had successfully resisted him before (2 Kings 18:7). He captured all of the **fortified cities of Judah** and needed to only take Jerusalem itself to completely conquer Judah.

i. The mention of **Lachish** is important to historians and archaeologists. The British Museum displays the Assyrian carvings depicting the siege of the city of Lachish, which was an important fortress city of Judah. Lachish was thirty miles southwest of Jerusalem.

ii. "An interesting wall relief taken from the excavation of Sennacherib's royal palace in Nineveh is persevered in the British Museum. It portrays the Assyrian king on a portable throne in his military camp outside Lachish. Prisoners of war are marching by on foot, and all the booty from the city is being displayed on ox-wagons." (Dilday)

iii. Archaeologists also discovered a pit at Lachish with the remains of about 1,500 casualties that probably came from the later attack of Nebuchadnezzar more than 100 years after this attack of the Assyrians.

b. **I have done wrong; turn away from me; whatever you impose on me I will pay**: This was a clear – though understandable – lack of faith on the part of Hezekiah. He felt it was wiser to pay off the Assyrian king and become his subject than it was to trust God to defend Judah against this mighty king.

i. We can suppose that Hezekiah thought that since the Northern Kingdom had been recently conquered and that all the **fortified cities of Judah** had been captured, God had demonstrated that He *would not* intervene on behalf of Judah. Therefore Hezekiah felt he had to do something *himself*.

ii. Perhaps this idea was strengthened in Hezekiah when he remembered the wickedness of his own father Ahaz, and when he considered that because of their prior sin, Judah *deserved* such judgment.

c. **So Hezekiah gave him all the silver that was found in the house of the L**ORD **and in the treasuries of the king's house**: Hezekiah hoped that this policy of appeasement would make Judah safe. He was wrong, and his policy only impoverished Judah and the temple and made the king of Assyria more bold than ever against Judah.

2. (17-20) The Rabshakeh tries to convince Judah to surrender.

Then the king of Assyria sent *the* Tartan, *the* Rabsaris, *and the* Rabshakeh from Lachish, with a great army against Jerusalem, to King Hezekiah. And they went up and came to Jerusalem. When they had come up, they went and stood by the aqueduct from the upper pool, which *was* on the highway to the Fuller's Field. And when they had called to the king, Eliakim the son of Hilkiah, who *was* over the household, Shebna the scribe, and Joah the son of Asaph, the recorder, came out to them. Then *the* Rabshakeh said to them, "Say now to Hezekiah, 'Thus says the great king, the king of Assyria: "What confidence *is* this in which you trust? You speak of *having* plans and power for war; but *they are* mere words. And in whom do you trust, that you rebel against me?"'"

a. **The Rabshakeh**: This actually is not a name, but a title. It describes the "field commander" for the Assyrian army, who represented the Assyrian King Sennacherib. "Rab-shakeh, an Assyrian title, possibly originally 'chief cup-bearer' but by this time some high officer of state." (Motyer, cited in his commentary on Isaiah)

b. **Stood by the aqueduct from the upper pool… Eliakim… Shebna… Joah… came out to them**: The Rabshakeh seemed to be in complete command of the situation. He could walk right into the city of Jerusalem, and stand at the crucial water supply – which was Jerusalem's life-line in a siege attack. As he stood there, three officials from Hezekiah's government came to meet him.

c. **What confidence is this in which you trust**: We might wish that Hezekiah trusted in the LORD, and that this is what the Rabshakeh mocked. Instead, Hezekiah put his hope in an alliance with Egypt, and the Rabshakeh wanted him to lose confidence in that alliance.

i. It was a great temptation for Hezekiah during this time to make a defensive alliance with Egypt, which seemed to be the only nation strong enough to protect Judah against the mighty Assyrians. As a prophet, Isaiah did everything he could to discourage Hezekiah and the leaders of Judah from putting their trust in Egypt (Isaiah 19:11-17, 20:1-6, 30:1-7). The LORD wanted Judah to trust Him instead of Egypt.

ii. In this sense, the Rabshakeh spoke the truth. God wanted Judah to have no **confidence** in Egypt at all. But the Rabshakeh did not do it to bring Judah to a firm trust in the LORD God, who can and will deliver them from the Assyrians. He did it to completely demoralize Judah and drive them to despair.

iii. Satan often attacks us the same way. Often, even when he tells the truth ("You are such a rotten sinner!"), he never does it to lead us to a firm trust in the LORD our God ("Jesus died for sinners, so if I am a rotten sinner, Jesus died to forgive and free me!"). Instead, Satan's strategy – even if he tells us the truth – is always to demoralize us and drive us to despair.

iv. From the perspective of the unbeliever, Sennacherib asked a valid question: **And in whom do you trust, that you rebel against me?** "Our life must to a large extent be a mystery, our peace pass understanding, and our motives be hidden. The sources of our supply, the ground of our confidence, the reasons for our actions, must evade the most searching scrutiny of those who stand outside the charmed circle of the face of God... We must be prepared to be criticized, because our behavior is determined by facts which the princes of this world know not." (Meyer)

3. (21-25) The demoralizing arguments of the Rabshakeh.

"Now look! You are trusting in the staff of this broken reed, Egypt, on which if a man leans, it will go into his hand and pierce it. So *is* Pharaoh king of Egypt to all who trust in him. But if you say to me, 'We trust in the LORD our God,' *is* it not He whose high places and whose altars Hezekiah has taken away, and said to Judah and Jerusalem, 'You shall worship before this altar in Jerusalem'? Now therefore, I urge you, give a pledge to my master the king of Assyria, and I will give you two thousand horses—if you are able on your part to put riders on them! How then will you repel one captain of the least of my master's servants, and put your trust in Egypt for chariots and horsemen? Have I now come up without the LORD against this place to destroy it? The LORD said to me, 'Go up against this land, and destroy it.'"

a. **You are trusting in the staff of this broken reed, Egypt**: Strangely, the Rabshakeh could see the truth of Egypt's weakness better than many of the leaders of Judah could. Hezekiah's trust-in-Egypt policy would indeed be trouble for Judah.

i. "*Egypt* had made its one attempt to redeem its promises (Isaiah 28:14) and its army had been beaten at El Tekeh. The Rab-shakeh had himself seen this, but his words are more far-reaching and damaging, exposing the criminal stupidity of Judah's leaders: surely, he said, they knew that anyone who ever trusted Egypt suffered for it." (Motyer, Isaiah Commentary)

ii. "Since this is the same terminology Isaiah used to symbolize Egypt (Isaiah 42:3), some have suggested that Sennacherib was familiar with Isaiah's prophecies and quoted here to imply he was carrying out Yahweh's will. Further support for this idea is found in verse 25 where Sennacherib seemed to be aware of Isaiah's statement that Assyria was a rod which Yahweh would use to punish Judah (Isaiah 10:5)." (Dilday)

b. **If you say to me, "We trust in the LORD our God"**: The Rabshakeh anticipated the response of the leaders of Judah. "Rabshakeh, you say that we can't trust in Egypt. All right, we won't. But we can trust in the LORD our God."

c. **Is it not He whose high places and whose altars Hezekiah has taken away**: The Rabshakeh knew that King Hezekiah had implemented broad reforms in Judah, including the removal of the **high places** (2 Kings 18:3-4). Yet in the Rabshakeh's thinking, Hezekiah's reforms had really *displeased* God, so he should not expect help from the LORD God of Israel. The Rabshakeh would say, "Look at all the places there used to be where people would worship the LORD God of Israel. Now, since Hezekiah came in, there is only one place. More is always better, so the LORD God of Israel must be pretty sore at Hezekiah!"

i. The enemy of our souls has an amazing way of discouraging our disobedience. If Hezekiah were not careful, this argument of the Rabshakeh would start to make sense, when really it was demonic logic through and through.

ii. "The theological misunderstanding shown by the field commander at this point argues for the authenticity of the speech, which many critics have dubbed a free creation by the author of the narrative." (Grogan, Isaiah Commentary)

d. **Give a pledge to my master the king of Assyria**: This reminds us of the Rabshakeh's whole strategy, which was to *make Judah give up*. This was the *entire reason* the Rabshakeh was at the aqueduct, speaking to these leaders of Hezekiah's government. He had the vastly superior armies; he could have just attacked Jerusalem without this little speech. But the Rabshekah would prefer it if Judah would simply *give up*, out of fear, discouragement, or despair.

i. The enemy of our soul uses the exact same approach. Many of us picture Satan as "itching for a fight" with us. Really, Satan doesn't want to do battle with you. First of all, there is the strong chance you will win. Second of all, win or lose, the battle can draw you closer to the LORD. Thirdly, what the LORD does in your life through the battle can be a great blessing for other people. No, Satan would much rather not fight you at all! He would much rather try to *talk you into giving up!*

ii. We see this exact strategy used against Jesus during His temptation in the wilderness. When Satan promised Jesus all the kingdoms of the world in exchange for Jesus' worship, Satan was trying to *avoid* the fight, and trying to *talk Jesus into giving up* (Luke 4:5-8). It didn't work with Jesus, and it shouldn't work with us.

e. **I will give you two thousand horses – if you are able on your part to put riders on them**: Here, the Rabshakeh mocked Judah's weak army. He said, "Even if we helped you with 2,000 horses, it wouldn't do you any good." His basic message is, "We could beat you with one hand tied behind our backs!" (**How then will you repel one captain of the least of my master's servants?**).

f. **Have I now come up without the LORD against this land to destroy it**: The Rabshakeh saved his best thrust for last: "Admit it, Hezekiah. You know that *your* God is on *my* side."

i. Like all good deception, it would have been easy for Hezekiah and his men to believe this one. After all, hadn't the Assyrians been *wildly successful*? Surely, God must be on their side. Didn't they have the *most powerful army*? Surely, God must be on their side.

g. **The LORD said to me, "Go up against this land, and destroy it"**: This was the finishing blow of a brilliant attack. "Hezekiah, *God told me* to destroy you. I'm just doing His will, and there is nothing you can do to stop it, so you may as well surrender."

i. Significantly, we can say that *the Rabshekah was partially correct!* God was with him, and his attack on Judah fulfilled God's prophesied plan. In conquering Syria, in conquering Israel, and in bringing Judah to the brink, the Assyrians *did the will of God*. God prophesied that all this would happen (Isaiah 8:3-4, 7:16-17 and many other passages in Isaiah). He allowed it to happen so His prophesied plan would be fulfilled.

ii. However, we should never think that God tempted an *innocent man* with an *evil plan*. In fact, even though God predicted and planned this invasion of the Assyrians, the Rabshakeh may have been lying indeed when he said, **"The LORD said to me…"** God did not have to do *anything special* to direct the bloodthirsty, conquest-hungry Assyrians to attack Syria, Israel, and Judah. He simply allowed the Assyrians to carry out the corrupt desires of their evil hearts. Therefore, the Assyrians could *never* excuse themselves by saying, "We were doing the LORD's will," even as Judas could never legitimately make that excuse regarding his wicked betrayal of Jesus.

4. (26-27) Hezekiah's men ask Rabshakeh to speak only to them.

Then Eliakim the son of Hilkiah, Shebna, and Joah said to *the* Rabshakeh, "Please speak to your servants in Aramaic, for we understand *it;* and do not speak to us in Hebrew in the hearing of the people who *are* on the wall." But *the* Rabshakeh said to them, "Has my master sent me to your master and to you to speak these words, and not to the men who sit on the wall, who will eat and drink their own waste with you?"

> a. **Please speak to your servants in the Aramaic language, for we understand it**: We can just imagine how difficult this was for these leaders in Hezekiah's government. They must have thought, "It's bad enough we have to hear this. But since he is speaking in Hebrew, *everyone* will hear, and soon the people will become so discouraged they will rise up against us and make us surrender!"
>
>> i. "Aramaic became the diplomatic lingua franca of the Near East in the neo-Assyrian period. That a well-educated member of Sennacherib's staff could speak both Hebrew and Aramaic as well as Akkadian need no longer be doubted." (Patterson and Austel)
>
> b. **Has my master sent me to your master and to you to speak these words, and not to the men who sit on the wall**: The Rabshakeh didn't care if the common citizens of Jerusalem could hear him. That was one of his goals. The more fear, discouragement, and despair he could spread, the better he liked it.
>
> c. **Who will eat and drink their own waste with you**: The Rabshakeh pointed forward to what conditions would be like in Jerusalem after an extended siege. He wanted this to offend and frighten everyone who heard it, and magnify their sense of fear, discouragement, and despair.

5. (28-35) The Rabshakeh appeals to the people directly.

Then *the* Rabshakeh stood and called out with a loud voice in Hebrew, and spoke, saying, "Hear the word of the great king, the king of Assyria! Thus says the king: 'Do not let Hezekiah deceive you, for he shall not be able to deliver you from his hand; nor let Hezekiah make you trust in the LORD, saying, "The LORD will surely deliver us; this city shall not be given into the hand of the king of Assyria."' Do not listen to Hezekiah; for thus says the king of Assyria: 'Make *peace* with me by a present and come out to me; and every one of you eat from his own vine and every one from his own fig tree, and every one of you drink the waters of his own cistern; until I come and take you away to a land like your own land, a land of grain and new wine, a land of bread and vineyards, a land of olive groves and honey, that you may live and not die. But do not

listen to Hezekiah, lest he persuade you, saying, "The LORD will deliver us." Has any of the gods of the nations at all delivered its land from the hand of the king of Assyria? Where *are* the gods of Hamath and Arpad? Where *are* the gods of Sepharvaim and Hena and Ivah? Indeed, have they delivered Samaria from my hand? Who among all the gods of the lands have delivered their countries from my hand, that the LORD should deliver Jerusalem from my hand?'"

> a. **Then the Rabshakeh stood and called out with a loud voice in Hebrew**: Saying "don't do that" to the Rabshakeh was like saying it to a naughty child. He *couldn't wait* to speak to the people of Jerusalem.
>
> b. **Hear the words of the great king**: The Rabshakeh's speech was intended to *glorify the enemy facing God's people*.
>
> c. **Do not let Hezekiah deceive you**: The Rabshakeh's speech was intended to *make God's people doubt their leaders*.
>
> d. **Nor let Hezekiah make you trust in the LORD**: The Rabshakeh's speech was intended to *build fear and unbelief in God's people*.
>
> e. **For thus says the king of Assyria: "Make peace with me by a present and come out to me, and every one of you will eat from his own vine"**: The Rabshakeh's speech was intended to make *surrender an attractive option*.
>
> f. **Until I come and take you away to a land like your own land**: Here, the Rabshakeh referred to the policies of ethnic cleansing and forced resettlement practiced by the Assyrians. When they conquered a people, they forcibly resettled them in faraway places, to keep their spirits broken and their power weak. The Rabshakeh's speech was intended to make this terrible fate *seem attractive*.
>
> g. **Has any one of the gods of the nations delivered its land from the hand of the king of Assyria**: The Rabshakeh's speech was intended to *destroy their trust in God*. His message was simple, and brilliant in its Satanic logic: "The gods of other nations have not been able to protect them against us. Your God is just like one of them, and can't protect you either."
>
>> i. For anyone who had the spiritual understanding to see it, Judah could have started planning the victory party right then. It is one thing to speak against Judah, its people and leaders. It was another thing altogether to mock the LORD God of Israel this way, and count Him as "just another god."
>>
>> ii. Typical of the work of the enemy of our souls, the Rabshakeh was going well until he simply overstepped his bounds. There was no way

God would let him off the hook for this one. He had offended the LORD God in a way he would soon regret.

6. (36-37) The response from the officials and the people.

But the people held their peace and answered him not a word; for the king's commandment was, "Do not answer him." Then Eliakim the son of Hilkiah, who *was* over the household, Shebna the scribe, and Joah the son of Asaph, the recorder, came to Hezekiah with *their* clothes torn, and told him the words of *the* Rabshakeh.

a. **But they held their peace and answered him not a word**: They didn't try to argue with the Rabshakeh. Often, it is useless – if not dangerous – to try and match wits with this demonic logic. It is almost always better to keep silent and trust God, instead of trying to win an argument with Satan or his servants.

i. "Silence is our best reply to the allegations and taunts of our foes. Be still, O persecuted soul! Hand over thy cause to God. It is useless to argue, even in many cases to give explanations. Be still, and commit thy cause to God." (Meyer, on Isaiah)

b. **For the king's commandment was, "Do not answer him"**: King Hezekiah was wise enough to make this command, and his officials and the people were wise enough to obey him.

c. **Came to Hezekiah with their clothes torn**: Though they were silent, they were still deeply affected by this attack. They had the same experience Paul described in 2 Corinthians 4:8-9: *We are hard pressed on every side, yet not crushed; we are perplexed, but not in despair; persecuted, but not forsaken; struck down, but not destroyed.* Things were hard, but the battle was not yet lost.

2 Kings 19 – God Delivers Jerusalem from Assyria

A. Hezekiah's prayers and Sennacherib's threats.

1. (1-5) Hezekiah seeks Isaiah in the time of great distress.

And so it was, when King Hezekiah heard *it*, that he tore his clothes, covered himself with sackcloth, and went into the house of the LORD. Then he sent Eliakim, who *was* over the household, Shebna the scribe, and the elders of the priests, covered with sackcloth, to Isaiah the prophet, the son of Amoz. And they said to him, "Thus says Hezekiah: 'This day *is* a day of trouble, and rebuke, and blasphemy; for the children have come to birth, but *there is* no strength to bring them forth. It may be that the LORD your God will hear all the words of *the* Rabshakeh, whom his master the king of Assyria has sent to reproach the living God, and will rebuke the words which the LORD your God has heard. Therefore lift up *your* prayer for the remnant that is left.'" So the servants of King Hezekiah came to Isaiah.

a. **When King Hezekiah heard it, that he tore his clothes, covered himself with sackcloth**: The tearing of clothes and the wearing of **sackcloth** (a rough, burlap-type material) were expressions of deep mourning, usually for the death of a loved one. Hezekiah received this report regarding Rabshakeh seriously, knowing how dedicated this enemy was to completely conquering Jerusalem.

i. Hezekiah's initial reaction was good. *He saw the situation for what it really was*. Often, when we are in some kind of trial or difficulty, we handle it poorly because we never see the situation accurately. Jerusalem's situation was desperate and Hezekiah knew it.

ii. There was good reason for Hezekiah to be so humble before the LORD. "City after city has fallen to Sennacherib and long lines of deportees are already snaking their bitter way into exile – and it is all Hezekiah's fault! He followed the lunatic policy of rebellion and was bewitched by Egyptian promises. He might as well have sold his people himself. But even when a matter is our own fault we can still pray about it. And the Lord can always be trusted to pity his people." (Motyer, commentary on Isaiah)

b. **And went into the house of the Lord**: Hezekiah's second reaction was even better. He did not allow his mourning and grief to spin him into a rejection of the Lord's power and help. He knew this was a more necessary time than ever to seek the Lord.

  i. When it says, **went into the house of the Lord**, we should not think that it means that King Hezekiah went into the holy place itself, which was forbidden for all except priests. It simply means that Hezekiah went to the courts of the house of the Lord, to seek God in the place which was open to him as a man of Israel.

  ii. A previous king of Judah, King Uzziah, saw his reign tragically ended when he broke this command of the Lord to stay out of the holy place of the temple. 2 Chronicles 26:16 says, *But when he was strong his heart was lifted up, to his destruction, for he transgressed against the Lord his God by entering the temple of the Lord to burn incense on the altar of incense*. In response, God struck Uzziah with leprosy and he was an isolated leper until his death.

c. **Then he sent Eliakim… Shebna… and the elders of the priests… to Isaiah the prophet**: The third thing Hezekiah did was also good. The king sought out the word of the Lord, given through the prophet of the Lord.

d. **The children have come to birth, but there is no strength to bring them forth**: Hezekiah put these words in the mouth of his messengers to Isaiah to express the total calamity of the situation. This was a proverbial expression for a disaster – a woman so exhausted by labor that she could not complete the birth, so it was likely that both mother and child would die.

e. **It may be that the Lord your God will hear the words of the Rabshakeh**: Hezekiah knew that their only hope was that God would take offense at the blasphemies of Rabshakeh and rise up against him.

  i. "The impudent blasphemy of this speech is without parallel. Hezekiah treated it as he ought: it was not properly against *him*, but against the Lord; therefore he refers the matter to Jehovah himself, who punishes this blasphemy in the most signal manner." (Clarke)

f. **Therefore lift up your prayer for the remnant that is left**: "Isaiah, pray for us. Our nation is devastated by this Assyrian invasion, and Jerusalem alone is left standing. Pray **for the remnant that is left**."

2. (6-7) God's word of assurance to Hezekiah.

And Isaiah said to them, "Thus you shall say to your master, 'Thus says the Lord: "Do not be afraid of the words which you have heard, with which the servants of the king of Assyria have blasphemed Me. Surely I will send a spirit upon him, and he shall hear a rumor and return to his own land; and I will cause him to fall by the sword in his own land."'"

a. **Thus says the Lord**: Isaiah was aware that he spoke as a prophet of the Lord. Without hesitation, he spoke as if he were speaking for the Lord God of heaven. We can be sure that Isaiah did not take this lightly. The fate of the nation, and his entire credibility as a prophet, were riding on what he said.

i. Isaiah, speaking for the Lord, was about to make a bold prediction. His prophecy would be entirely "provable." It would either happen or it would not happen; Isaiah would be known as a true prophet or a false prophet shortly.

b. **Do not be afraid of the words which you have heard**: Perhaps we can sense a gentle rebuke in these words from the Lord. "Hezekiah, it is good for you to seek Me so passionately. But the **words** of the Rabshakeh are only **words**. **Do not be afraid of** them."

c. **With which the servants of the king of Assyria have blasphemed Me**: How these words must have cheered Hezekiah! Before, he had hoped *it may be that the Lord your God will hear the words of the Rabshakeh… to reproach the living God* (2 Kings 19:4). Now, the Lord spoke through the prophet Isaiah, saying He had indeed heard those words. It was evident that God took this offense personally.

i. **The servants of the king of Assyria**: **Servants** is "a deliberately belittling expression, 'the king of Assyria's lads/flunkies'." (Motyer, commentary on Isaiah) "He calls Rabshakeh and the other officers of the army the *slaves* or *servant boys* – we could say the *errand boys* – of the king of Assyria." (Bultema, commentary on Isaiah)

d. **Surely I will send a spirit upon him, and he shall hear a rumor and return to his own land; and I will cause him to fall by the sword in his own land**: Here, the Lord God assured Hezekiah that He would indeed deal with the Rabshakeh. He had heard his blasphemy and would bring judgment against him.

i. Significantly, in this initial word from the prophet Isaiah, there was no mention of Jerusalem's deliverance or the defeat of the Assyrian army. God focused this word against the Rabshakeh *personally*.

ii. "The *rumour* was, that Tirhakah had invaded Assyria. The *blast* was that which slew *one hundred and eighty-five thousand* of them in one night, see verse 35." (Clarke)

3. (8-13) The response of Rabshakeh to King Hezekiah and Jerusalem.

Then *the* Rabshakeh returned and found the king of Assyria warring against Libnah, for he heard that he had departed from Lachish. And the king heard concerning Tirhakah king of Ethiopia, "Look, he has come out to make war with you." So he again sent messengers to Hezekiah, saying, "Thus you shall speak to Hezekiah king of Judah, saying: 'Do not let your God in whom you trust deceive you, saying, "Jerusalem shall not be given into the hand of the king of Assyria." Look! You have heard what the kings of Assyria have done to all lands by utterly destroying them; and shall you be delivered? Have the gods of the nations delivered those whom my fathers have destroyed, Gozan and Haran and Rezeph, and the people of Eden who *were* in Telassar? Where *is* the king of Hamath, the king of Arpad, and the king of the city of Sepharvaim, Hena, and Ivah?'"

a. **So the Rabshakeh returned, and found the king of Assyria warring against Libnah**: This must have seemed to Hezekiah to be the fulfillment of the Lord's promise through the prophet Isaiah. The Rabshakeh left Jerusalem and Hezekiah must have thought, "Now he'll go back to his own land and be killed, just like the Lord promised. Good riddance! Thank You, Lord!"

b. **The king heard concerning Tirhakah king of Ethiopia, "He has come out to make war with you"**: While the Rabshakeh was away, the Assyrians learned that Egyptian troops (under an Ethiopian king) were advancing from the south. This would be the Egyptian intervention Assyria feared, and that many in Judah trusted in. As Isaiah prophesied, it would come to nothing (Isaiah 20:1-6 and 30:1-7).

i. "Actually Tirhakah was only a prince at the time, but because he assumed the throne in 690 B.C., the title 'king' is used proleptically." (Wolf, commentary on Isaiah)

c. **Do not let your God in whom you trust deceive you**: The Rabshakeh was not in Jerusalem, but that didn't stop him from trying to build fear, discouragement, and despair in Hezekiah. He sent a letter to the king of Judah to attack him from a distance.

d. **Have the gods of the nations**: If read with an eye of faith, these must have been trust-building words of the Rabshakeh to Hezekiah. In counting the LORD God of Israel among the gods of the nations, the Rabshakeh blasphemed the LORD and invited judgment.

i. The Rabshakeh listed many cities that the Assyrian army conquered, **utterly destroying them**: "The list of city-states put to the ban (Hebrew *herem*; 'exterminated' or destroyed completely, RSV) reminds the reader that it was not only Israel who used this method in warfare (see Numbers 21:2-3; Joshua 6:21)." (Wiseman)

4. (14-19) Hezekiah's prayer.

And Hezekiah received the letter from the hand of the messengers, and read it; and Hezekiah went up to the house of the LORD, and spread it before the LORD. Then Hezekiah prayed before the LORD, and said: "O LORD God of Israel, *the One* **who dwells** *between* **the cherubim, You are God, You alone, of all the kingdoms of the earth. You have made heaven and earth. Incline Your ear, O LORD, and hear; open Your eyes, O LORD, and see; and hear the words of Sennacherib, which he has sent to reproach the living God. Truly, LORD, the kings of Assyria have laid waste the nations and their lands, and have cast their gods into the fire; for they** *were* **not gods, but the work of men's hands—wood and stone. Therefore they destroyed them. Now therefore, O LORD our God, I pray, save us from his hand, that all the kingdoms of the earth may know that You** *are* **the LORD God, You alone."**

a. **Hezekiah went up to the house of the LORD, and spread it before the LORD**: Hezekiah did exactly what any child of God should do with such a letter. He took it **to the house of the LORD** (to the outer courts, not the holy place), and he **spread it out before the LORD**. In this, Hezekiah boldly and effectively fulfilled the later command of 1 Peter 5:7: *casting all your care upon Him, for He cares for you.*

i. "As a child bringing his broken toy to his father for repair, so Hezekiah laid the issues in God's sight for resolution." (Patterson and Austel)

ii. "In verse 14, Hezekiah reacted to the second letter in a different manner. He didn't go to Isaiah. He went to the temple and prayed alone, taking his plea directly to the Lord. Both kinds of prayer are appropriate for a believer who is facing a crisis." (Dilday)

iii. "When therefore letters come to you, anonymous or otherwise, full of bitter reproach; when unkind and malignant stories are set on foot with respect to you; when all hope from man has perished, then take your complaint – the letter, the article, the speech, the rumour – and lay it before God. Let your requests be known unto Him." (Meyer)

iv. One old preacher received a letter with no sender or return address on the envelope. When he opened it, he saw a single piece of paper with only one word: "Fool!" He took it to the pulpit the next Sunday, and said: "I received an unusual letter this week. Never before have I received a letter where the writer signed his name, but forgot to write anything else!"

b. **God of Israel**: This title for God reminded Hezekiah – and the LORD also, in our human way of understanding – that the LORD God was the covenant God of Israel, and that He should not forsake His people.

i. As recorded in Isaiah 37:16, Hezekiah also used another title when he addressed God, crying out "*O LORD of hosts*." This title for our God essentially means, "LORD of armies." Hezekiah was in a crisis that was primarily *military* in nature, so it made sense for him to address the LORD first according to the aspect of God's nature that was most needful for him. "LORD of armies, send some troops to help us!"

c. **The One who dwells between the cherubim**: Here, Hezekiah saw the great majesty of God. Surely, **the One who dwells between the cherubim** would never allow the Rabshakeh's blasphemies to go unpunished.

i. "He is our Judge, Lawgiver, and King, and is therefore bound by the most solemn obligation to save us, or his name will be tarnished." (Meyer)

d. **You are God, You alone**: **God** is a simple title for our Master, but perhaps the most powerful. If He is **God**, then what can He *not* do? If He is **God**, then what is *beyond* His control? Hezekiah realized the most fundamental fact of all theology: God is **God**, and we *are not!* God is **God**, and the Rabshakeh or the Assyrians *were not!*

e. **You have made heaven and earth**: In recognizing the LORD God as Creator, Hezekiah saw that the LORD had all *power* and all *rights* over every created thing. We can almost feel Hezekiah's faith rising as he prayed this!

f. **Incline Your ear, O LORD, and hear; open Your eyes, O LORD, and see**: Hezekiah knew very well that the LORD did in fact hear and see the blasphemies of Rabshakeh. This is a poetic way of asking God to *act upon* what He has seen and heard, assuming that if God *has seen* such things, He will certainly act!

g. **Hear the words of Sennacherib, which he has sent to reproach the living God**: In his prayer, King Hezekiah drew the contrast between **the living God** and the false gods of the nations the Assyrians had already conquered. Those false gods were **not gods, but the work of men's hands – wood and stone**, so they were not able to save them from the Assyrians.

But Hezekiah prayed confidently that the **living God** would save them, **that all the kingdoms of the earth may know that You are the** LORD **God, You alone**.

B. God speaks concerning the situation.

1. (20-21) Sennacherib is worthy of scorn - not fear and trembling.

Then Isaiah the son of Amoz sent to Hezekiah, saying, "Thus says the LORD **God of Israel: 'Because you have prayed to Me against Sennacherib king of Assyria, I have heard.' This *is* the word which the** LORD **has spoken concerning him:**

'The virgin, the daughter of Zion,
Has despised you, laughed you to scorn;
The daughter of Jerusalem
Has shaken *her* head behind your back!

a. **Because you have prayed to Me**: The glorious answer which fills the rest of the chapter came because Hezekiah prayed. What if he had not prayed? Then we are to think that no answer would have come, and Jerusalem would have been conquered. Hezekiah's prayer really mattered.

i. We should ask: How many blessings, how many victories, how many souls saved for Jesus' glory, lie unclaimed in heaven until the LORD can say, "**because you have prayed to Me**"?

b. **The virgin, the daughter of Zion, has despised you, laughed you to scorn**: The idea is that the Assyrians had come to ravish the **daughter of Zion**, the city of Jerusalem. But God would not allow it. "Jerusalem is represented as a young girl rebuffing with contempt the unwelcome advances of a churl." (Grogan, commentary on Isaiah)

i. Jerusalem could be called **the virgin, the daughter of Zion** for several reasons:

- She was unpolluted with the gross idolatry of the pagans.
- God would defend her from the intended rape by Sennacherib and the Assyrians.
- She had never been invaded or conquered by another since the days of David.

2. (22-28) God's word to the King of Assyria and his representatives.

'Whom have you reproached and blasphemed?
Against whom have you raised *your* voice,
And lifted up your eyes on high?
Against the Holy *One* of Israel.

By your messengers you have reproached the Lord,
And said: "By the multitude of my chariots
I have come up to the height of the mountains,
To the limits of Lebanon;
I will cut down its tall cedars
And its choice cypress trees;
I will enter the extremity of its borders,
To its fruitful forest.
I have dug and drunk strange water,
And with the soles of my feet I have dried up
All the brooks of defense."

'Did you not hear long ago
How I made it,
*F*rom ancient times that I formed it?
Now I have brought it to pass,
That you should be
For crushing fortified cities *into* heaps of ruins.
Therefore their inhabitants had little power;
They were dismayed and confounded;
They were *as* the grass of the field
And the green herb,
As the grass on the housetops
And *grain* blighted before it is grown.

'But I know your dwelling place,
Your going out and your coming in,
And your rage against Me.
Because your rage against Me and your tumult
Have come up to My ears,
Therefore I will put My hook in your nose
And My bridle in your lips,
And I will turn you back By the way which you came.

> a. **Whom have you reproached and blasphemed? Against whom have you raised your voice, and lifted up your eyes on high? Against the Holy One of Israel**: The Lord, speaking through Isaiah, simply said to the Rabshakeh, "Do you know whom you are dealing with?" The Rabshakeh obviously did not know.
>
>> i. Curiously, this prophecy may have never reached the ears of the Rabshakeh. After all, Isaiah didn't exactly have free access to him. But perhaps before his terrible end, God found a way to get this prophecy to him. Or, perhaps God had it for this blasphemer as a

special message in hell. At the very least, this prophecy would have been hugely encouraging to Hezekiah and all of Judah, even if the Rabshakeh never heard it on this earth.

ii. Sometimes God speaks to the enemy more for the sake of His people than for the sake of the enemy himself.

b. **By the multitude of my chariots, I have come up to the height of the mountains**: Here, the LORD described the great pride the Assyrians had in their own conquests. But they forgot that the LORD was really in charge (**Now I have brought it to pass, that you should be for crushing fortified cites into heaps of ruins. Therefore the inhabitants had little power**). Even if the Assyrians didn't know it, they owed their success to the LORD.

i. "God then confronted Sennacherib with that which he had apparently not considered: Sennacherib's successes were foreordained by God… Sennacherib should not boast as though what he had done was either self-generated or self-accomplished." (Patterson and Austel)

ii. This was humbling for the Assyrians. All along, they thought it was because of their mighty power they had accomplished so much. Here, God made it plain that it was His power that did it.

iii. "*With the soles of my feet* was Sennacherib's boast that he commanded so many soldiers that when they marched across riverbeds, they literally dried up the rivers." (Dilday)

c. **I know your dwelling place, your going out and your coming in**: God knew how to find the Assyrians. And because Assyria went too far in blaspheming the One who made all their success possible, **therefore I will put My hook in your nose… and I will turn you back by the way which you came**. This was an especially dramatic statement, because this is exactly how the Assryians cruelly marched those whom they forced to relocate out of their conquered lands. They lined up the captives and drove a large fishhook through the lip or the nose of each captive, strung them all together and marched them. God said, "I'm going to do the same thing to you."

i. "The Assyrian practice of leading foreign princes captive with a ring or *hook* in the *nose* is depicted on Esarhaddon's stela at Zenjirli showing him holding Tirhakah of Egypt and Ba'alu of Tyre." (Wiseman)

3. (29-31) God will prosper wounded Judah.

'**This *shall be* a sign to you:**

You shall eat this year such as grows of itself,
And in the second year what springs from the same;
Also in the third year sow and reap,
Plant vineyards and eat the fruit of them.
And the remnant who have escaped of the house of Judah
Shall again take root downward,
And bear fruit upward.
For out of Jerusalem shall go a remnant,
And those who escape from Mount Zion.
The zeal of the LORD of hosts will do this.'

> a. **You shall eat this year such as grows of itself**: "The invasion prevented sowing in 702 B.C., but when the threat lifted in 701 they would find sufficient growth to preserve life; in 701 the withdrawing Assyrians still inhibited agriculture, yet in 700 there would still be enough through 'chance growth'. Thus the Lord would confirm retrospectively that it was his hand that dispersed the threat." (Motyer, commentary on Isaiah)
>
>> i. "When in the harvest of the third year the people ate in abundance, they would know assuredly that God had been in the entire crisis." (Patterson and Austel)
>
> b. **For out of Jerusalem shall go a remnant**: As much as the Assyrians would like to crush Jerusalem and Judah, they would not be able to. God would preserve His remnant.
>
>> i. "The doctrine of *the remnant* (vv. 4, 30) left by God's grace through times of trial was demonstrated by Isaiah, whose son was named Shear-Jashub, 'remnant will return' (Isaiah 7:3; 37:30-32). Israelites fled to Judah so that in one sense Judah also included the remnant of Israel to carry on God's name and work." (Wiseman)

4. (32-34) God will defend Judah for His sake.

"Therefore thus says the LORD concerning the king of Assyria:
'He shall not come into this city,
Nor shoot an arrow there,
Nor come before it with shield,
Nor build a siege mound against it.
By the way that he came,
By the same shall he return;
And he shall not come into this city,'
Says the LORD.
'For I will defend this city, to save it
For My own sake and for My servant David's sake.'"

a. **He shall not come into this city, nor shoot an arrow there… for I will defend this city, to save it**: God plainly and clearly drew a line. Although the Assyrian military machine was poised to lay siege to Jerusalem and ultimately crush them, they won't. The king of Assyria would not come into this city because God promised to defend it.

i. It is hard for modern people to understand the ancient horror of the siege, when a city was surrounded by a hostile army and trapped into a slow, suffering starvation. King Hezekiah and the people of Jerusalem lived under the shadow of this threat, but God's promise through Isaiah assured them that Sennacherib and the Assyrian army would not only fail to capture the city, but would not even shoot an arrow or build a siege mound against Jerusalem. God promised that they wouldn't even *begin* a siege.

b. **For My own sake and for My servant David's sake**: This explains why God promised to defend Jerusalem. God would defend His own glory. Often, we unnecessarily think that we must defend the glory of the LORD. But that isn't really the case. God is more than able to defend His own glory.

i. God also does it "**For My servant David's sake.**" King David had died almost 300 years before this, but God still honored His promise to David (2 Samuel 7:10-17). God defended Jerusalem, not for the city's sake at all – Jerusalem *deserved* judgment! But He did it for His own sake and for the sake of David. In the same way, God the Father defends and blesses us, not for our own sake – we often *deserve* His judgment – but He often does it for His own sake, and for the sake of Jesus Christ our Lord.

ii. **For I will defend this city, to save it For My own sake and for My servant David's sake**: "Jeremiah later argued that those who traded on this prophecy as meaning that the temple in Jerusalem would never be taken were superstitious and presumptuous (Jeremiah 7:1-15)." (Wiseman)

C. God defends Jerusalem.

1. (35) God strikes down the mighty army of Assyria.

And it came to pass on a certain night that the angel of the LORD went out, and killed in the camp of the Assyrians one hundred and eighty-five thousand; and when *people* arose early in the morning, there were the corpses—all dead.

a. **The angel of the LORD went out**: Simply and powerfully, God destroyed this mighty army in one night; 185,000 died at the hand of **the angel** of the LORD. Against all odds, and against every expectation except the expectation of faith, the Assyrian army was turned back without having even shot an arrow into Jerusalem. The unstoppable was stopped, the undefeated was defeated.

> i. The prophet Hosea made this same prediction: *Yet I will have mercy on the house of Judah, will save them by the LORD their God, and will not save them by bow, nor by sword or battle, by horses or horsemen.* (Hosea 1:7)
>
> ii. "Herodotus, the Greek historian, recorded that one night Sennacherib's army camp was infested with mice (or rats) that destroyed the arrows and shield-thongs of the soldiers. He probably got this tradition from Egyptian sources, and it could well be a somewhat garbled version of the event recorded here." (Grogan)

b. **There were the corpses – all dead**: This was not difficult for God to do. In a manner of speaking, it was far harder for the LORD to get the heart and minds of His people in the right place. Once they were there, it was nothing for God to dispatch *one angel* to do this.

> i. Some have speculated that there was a natural means that the angel used. "This has been thought to be a bacillary dysentery which had a three-day incubation period." (Wiseman)

2. (36-37) The defeated Sennacherib is judged in Nineveh.

So Sennacherib king of Assyria departed and went away, returned *home*, and remained at Nineveh. Now it came to pass, as he was worshiping in the temple of Nisroch his god, that his sons Adrammelech and Sharezer struck him down with the sword; and they escaped into the land of Ararat. Then Esarhaddon his son reigned in his place.

a. **Departed and went away**: This happened exactly as God said it would. But he left still full of pride. After this retreat from Judah, Sennacherib commissioned a record, which is preserved in the spectacular Annals of Sennacherib (the Taylor Prism), which can be seen in the British Museum. It shows how full of pride Sennacherib's heart still was, even if he could not even claim he conquered Jerusalem.

> i. "I attacked Hezekiah of Judah who had not subjected himself to me, and took forty-six fortresses, forts and small cities. I carried away captive 200,150 people, big and small, both male and female, a multitude of horses, young bulls, asses, camels, and oxen. Hezekiah himself I locked up in Jerusalem like a bird in its cage. I put up banks against the city. I separated his cities whose inhabitants I had taken prisoners from his realm and gave them to Mitiniti, king of Ashdod,

Padi, king of Ekron, and Zilbel, king of Gaza and thus diminished his country. And I added another tax to the one imposed on him earlier." (Cited in Bultema, commentary on Isaiah)

ii. "The Biblical account concludes with the much debated statement that the Assyrian army was struck down in some way during the night with considerable loss of life, following which the siege was called off… The Assyrian Annals tacitly agree with the Biblical version by making no claim that Jerusalem was taken, only describing tribute from Hezekiah." (T.C. Mitchell, *The Bible in the British Museum*)

iii. "God spared *Sennacherib*, not in mercy, but in wrath, reserving to him a more dreadful and shameful death by the hands of his own children." (Poole)

b. **Now it came to pass**: Between 2 Kings 19:36 and 2 Kings 19:37, 20 years passed. Perhaps Sennacherib thought he had escaped the judgment of God, but he hadn't. He met the bitter end of death at the end of swords held by his own sons.

i. An old Jewish legend – and nothing more than a legend – says how it was that Sennacherib's sons came to kill him. Sennacherib was troubled at how God seemed to bless the Jews so much, and tried to find out why. Someone told him it was because Abraham had loved God so much that he was willing to sacrifice his son unto the LORD. Sennacherib thought he would be even more favored by God, and decided to kill two of his sons in sacrifice to the LORD, becoming even more blessed than Abraham and his descendants. But his two sons learned of the plan, and killed him before he could kill them, thus fulfilling the word of the LORD.

2 Kings 20 – God Extends Hezekiah's Life

A. Hezekiah's recovery.

1. (1) Isaiah's announcement to Hezekiah.

In those days Hezekiah was sick and near death. And Isaiah the prophet, the son of Amoz, went to him and said to him, "Thus says the LORD: 'Set your house in order, for you shall die, and not live.'"

> a. **In those days**: This happened at the time of the Assyrian invasion of Judah, because Jerusalem had not been delivered from the Assyrian threat yet (2 Kings 20:6). The events of this chapter are also recorded in Isaiah 38.
>
>> i. "Interpreters agree that the events described in chapters 38 and 39 preceded the invasion of 701 B.C.... Many date these events in 703 B.C., but the evidence more strongly suggests a date of about 712 B.C." (Wolf, commentary on Isaiah)
>
> b. **Was sick and near death**: We are not told how Hezekiah became sick. It may have been through something obvious to all, or it may have been through something known only to God. However Hezekiah became sick, it was certainly permitted by the LORD.
>
> c. **Set your house in order, for you shall die and not live**: God was remarkably kind to Hezekiah, telling him that his death was near. Not all people are given the time to set your house in order.
>
>> i. We know from comparing 2 Kings 18:2 with 2 Kings 20:6 that Hezekiah was 39 years old when he learned he would soon die.
>>
>> ii. "Such threatenings, though absolutely expressed, have ofttimes secret conditions, which God reserves in his own breast." (Poole)

2. (2-3) Hezekiah's prayer.

Then he turned his face toward the wall, and prayed to the LORD, saying, "Remember now, O LORD, I pray, how I have walked before You

in truth and with a loyal heart, and have done *what was* good in Your sight." And Hezekiah wept bitterly.

> a. **He turned his face toward the wall**: This shows how earnest Hezekiah was in his prayer. He directed his prayer in privacy to God, and not to any man.
>
>> i. "Turning his face to the wall, thereby both dismissing Isaiah and entering into solitary confinement with God, Hezekiah poured out his heart to the Lord." (Patterson and Austel)
>
> b. **Remember now, O LORD**: To our ears, Hezekiah's prayer might almost sound ungodly. In it, his focus is on self-justification and his own merits. It is pretty much as if Hezekiah prayed, "LORD, I've been such a good boy and You aren't being fair to me. Remember what a good boy I've been and rescue me."
>
>> i. But under the Old Covenant, this was a valid principle on which to approach God. Passages like Leviticus 26 and Deuteronomy 28 show that under the Old Covenant, blessing or cursing was sent by God on the basis of obedience or disobedience. On that principle, David could write in Psalm 15: *LORD, who may abide in Your tabernacle? Who may dwell in Your holy hill? He who walks uprightly, and works righteousness, and speaks the truth in his heart.* (Psalm 15:1-2)
>>
>> ii. But under the New Covenant, we are blessed on the principle of faith in Jesus (Galatians 3:13-14). Hezekiah's principle of prayer isn't fitting for a Christian today. We pray in the name of Jesus (John 16:23-24), not in the name of who we are or what we have done.
>>
>> iii. "We come across similar pleas again and again in the prayers of God's children of old. The Psalms abound with them. But we do not find them in the New Testament. The Church bases its pleas on Christ's righteousness." (Bultema)
>
> c. **And Hezekiah wept bitterly**: Hezekiah lived under the Old Covenant, and at that time there was not a confident assurance of the glory in the life beyond. Instead, Jesus brought life, and immortality came to light through the gospel (2 Timothy 1:10). Also, under the Old Covenant, Hezekiah would have regarded this as evidence that God was very displeased with him.
>
>> i. "But why should a saint be fond of life, or afraid of death, since to him it is as his father's horse, to carry him to his father's house?" (Trapp)

3. (4-7) Isaiah brings God's answer to Hezekiah's prayer.

And it happened, before Isaiah had gone out into the middle court, that the word of the LORD came to him, saying, "Return and tell Hezekiah the leader of My people, 'Thus says the LORD, the God of David your father: "I have heard your prayer, I have seen your tears; surely I will heal you. On the third day you shall go up to the house of the LORD. And I will add to your days fifteen years. I will deliver you and this city from the hand of the king of Assyria; and I will defend this city for My own sake, and for the sake of My servant David."'" Then Isaiah said, "Take a lump of figs." So they took and laid *it* **on the boil, and he recovered.**

a. **I will add to your days fifteen years**: In response to Hezekiah's prayer, God granted Hezekiah **fifteen years** more.

i. "Hezekiah was granted an added *fifteen years*; since he died c. 686 B.C. this promise can be dated from about the time of the siege of Jerusalem. His recovery was also symbolic of the recovery of Jerusalem." (Wiseman)

ii. Because Hezekiah recovered, was God's word (*You shall die and not live*, 2 Kings 20:1) proved false? No; first, Hezekiah did in fact die – just not as soon as God first announced. Second, when God announces judgment it is almost always an invitation to repent and to receive mercy.

iii. "Hezekiah, though but a little prince, suddenly found himself a wealthy man, having moreover one thing in his treasury which could not have been discovered among the riches of any other living man, namely, a writ from the Court of Heaven, that he should live fifteen years… This great prosperity was a great temptation, far more difficult to endure than Rabshakeh's letter, and all the ills which invasion brought upon the land." (Spurgeon)

b. **I have heard your prayer**: Hezekiah's prayer was important. By all indications, if Hezekiah had not made his passionate prayer, his life would not have been extended. This is another demonstration of the principle that prayer matters.

i. In fact, God gave two gifts to Hezekiah. First, He gave the gift of an extended life. Second, He gave the gift of knowing he only had fifteen years left. If he were wise, this would still give King Hezekiah the motivation to walk right with God and to set his house in order.

c. **I will defend this city for My own sake, and for the sake of My servant David**: This promise was in accord with the LORD's previous prophecies of deliverance, and dates this chapter as being before God destroyed the Assyrian army (Isaiah 37:36-37).

i. The connection of the two promises indicates that one would confirm the other. When Hezekiah recovered his health, he could know that God would also deliver him from the Assyrians.

d. **Take a lump of figs**: Apparently, God used this medical treatment to bring Hezekiah's healing. God can, and often does, bring healing through medical treatments, and apart from an unusual direction from God, medical treatment should never be rejected in the name of faith.

3. (8-11) God's sign to Hezekiah: the retreating shadow.

And Hezekiah said to Isaiah, "What *is* the sign that the LORD will heal me, and that I shall go up to the house of the LORD the third day?" Then Isaiah said, "This is the sign to you from the LORD, that the LORD will do the thing which He has spoken: *shall* the shadow go forward ten degrees or go backward ten degrees?" And Hezekiah answered, "It is an easy thing for the shadow to go down ten degrees; no, but let the shadow go backward ten degrees." So Isaiah the prophet cried out to the LORD, and He brought the shadow ten degrees backward, by which it had gone down on the sundial of Ahaz.

a. **What is the sign that the LORD will heal me**: Hezekiah wanted a sign, and a sign that would allow him to **go up to the house of the LORD**. This was because he could not, and would not **go up to the house of the LORD** until he was healed, so the two were connected.

i. "Hezekiah quite properly asks for a sign to assure himself of his recovery. His hypocritical father, in mock modesty, refused to ask for a sign." (Knapp)

b. **This is the sign… that the LORD will do this thing which He has spoken**: God showed even more mercy to Hezekiah. God was under no obligation to give this sign. In fact, God would have been justified in saying, "I said it and you believe it. How dare you not take My word for true?" But in real love, God gave Hezekiah more than he needed or deserved.

i. God shows the same mercy to us. It should be enough for God to simply say to us, "I love you." But God did so much to *demonstrate* His love to us (John 3:16, Romans 5:8).

c. **Shall the shadow go forward ten degrees or go backward ten degrees**: God promised to do something completely miraculous for the confirming sign. He promised to make the shadow on the sundial move *backward* instead of *forward*.

i. This was a wonderfully appropriate sign for Hezekiah. By having the shadow of the sundial move backward, it gave *more time* in a day – just as God gave Hezekiah *more time*.

ii. "It was a miracle, whatever way we take it. God could have reversed the revolution of the earth, had He seen fit to do so – for he is a poor clockmaker even, who cannot turn the hands of his own workmanship backward; or He could have caused the phenomenon by the ordinary law of refraction." (Knapp)

iii. "Certainly there is no need to postulate any reversal of the earth's rotation or receding of the sun. The fact that the miracle was felt only 'in the land' (i.e. Judah; cf. 2 Chronicles 32:31) makes such solutions most dubious." (Patterson and Austel)

iv. No matter how the miracle happened, 2 Chronicles 32:24-26 tells us that Hezekiah did not respond rightly to this gift of healing: *In those days Hezekiah was sick and near death, and he prayed to the LORD; and He spoke to him and gave him a sign. But Hezekiah did not repay according to the favor shown him, for his heart was lifted up; therefore wrath was looming over him and over Judah and Jerusalem. Then Hezekiah humbled himself for the pride of his heart, he and the inhabitants of Jerusalem, so that the wrath of the LORD did not come upon them in the days of Hezekiah.*

B. Hezekiah's reception of the Babylonian envoys.

1. (12-13) Hezekiah bares the riches of his kingdom – out of pride.

At that time Berodach-Baladan the son of Baladan, king of Babylon, sent letters and a present to Hezekiah, for he heard that Hezekiah had been sick. And Hezekiah was attentive to them, and showed them all the house of his treasures—the silver and gold, the spices and precious ointment, and all his armory—all that was found among his treasures. There was nothing in his house or in all his dominion that Hezekiah did not show them.

a. **At that time**: This was after the miraculous recovery of Hezekiah. The LORD was good enough to give King Hezekiah 15 years more of life; but it was up to Hezekiah if those years would be lived in wisdom and to the glory of God.

b. **King of Babylon sent letters and a present to Hezekiah, for he heard that he had been sick and had recovered**: Apparently this was a gesture of kindness from the king of Babylon, showing concern to Hezekiah as fellow royalty.

i. "The sun – which was their god – had honoured Hezekiah; therefore they were sent to honour him too with a visit and a present." (Trapp)

ii. "Sending *letters and a gift* by envoys was the normal Babylonian diplomatic procedure." (Wiseman)

c. **Berodach-Baladan**: His presence shows that this was more than a courtesy call. This was an attempt to bring the kingdom of Judah on to the side of the Babylonians against the Assyrians.

> i. "According to Josephus (*Ant.* X.2.2.) the purpose of the visit was to secure Hezekiah as an ally against an anti-Assyrian coalition." (Wiseman)
>
> ii. "The real reason of the visit was political; Babylon desired to throw off the yoke of Assyria. What nation was more likely to help them than the one at the hands of which Assyria had been so completely defeated? Babylon sought alliance with Judah against Assyria." (Morgan)

d. **And Hezekiah was pleased with them**: We can imagine that this was flattering for King Hezekiah. After all, Judah was a lowly nation with little power, and Babylon was a junior superpower. To receive this notice and recognition from the king of Babylon must have really made Hezekiah feel he was important.

e. **Showed them the house of his treasures**: We can imagine Hezekiah wanting to please these envoys from Babylon, and wanting to show them that they had good reason to be impressed with him and his kingdom. So he did everything he could to impress them, and showed them the very best riches of the royal household – and he showed them everything (**There was nothing in his house or in all his dominion that Hezekiah did not show them**).

> i. As the coming rebuke from Isaiah will demonstrate, this was nothing but proud foolishness on Hezekiah's part. He was in the dangerous place of wanting to please and impress men, especially ungodly men.
>
> ii. "It was not *spiritual* pride, as with his great-grandfather Uzziah; but *worldly* pride – 'the pride of life,' we might say. It was *his* precious things, *his* armor, *his* treasures, *his* house, *his* dominion, etc., that he showed the ambassadors from Babylon." (Knapp)
>
> iii. Hezekiah faced – and failed under – a temptation common to many, especially those in ministry – the temptation of success. Many men who stand strong against the temptations of failure and weakness fail under the temptations of success and strength. Think about the extent of Hezekiah's success:
>
> - He was godly.
> - He was victorious.
> - He was healed.
> - He had experienced a miracle.

- He had been promised a long life.
- He had connection to a great prophet.
- He had seen a remarkable sign.
- He was wealthy.
- He was famous.
- He was praised and honored.
- He was honored by God.

iv. Nevertheless, he sinned greatly after this great gift of fifteen more years of life and the deliverance of Jerusalem. We might say that Hezekiah sinned in at least five ways:

- *Pride*, in that he was proud of the honors the Babylonians brought.
- *Ingratitude*, in that he took honor to himself that really belonged to God.
- *Abusing the gifts given to him*, where he took the gifts and favors to his own honor and gratification of his lusts (2 Chronicles 32:25-26).
- *Carnal confidence*, in that he trusted in the coalition he had made with the king of Babylon.
- *Missing opportunity*, in that he had a great opportunity to testify to the Babylonian envoys about the greatness of God and the LORD's blessing on Judah. Instead, he glorified himself.

v. "Why did he not show these learned heathen *God's* house? 'Every whit' of which showeth '*His*' glory' (Psalm 29:9, margin). There he could have explained to them the meaning of the brazen altar, and the sacrifices offered thereon; and who can tell what the results might not have been in the souls of these idolaters?" (Knapp)

2. (14-18) Isaiah brings a rebuke from God to Hezekiah.

Then Isaiah the prophet went to King Hezekiah, and said to him, "What did these men say, and from where did they come to you?" So Hezekiah said, "They came from a far country, from Babylon." And he said, "What have they seen in your house?" So Hezekiah answered, "They have seen all that *is* in my house; there is nothing among my treasures that I have not shown them." Then Isaiah said to Hezekiah, "Hear the word of the LORD: 'Behold, the days are coming when all that *is* in your house, and what your fathers have accumulated until this day, shall be carried to Babylon; nothing shall be left,' says the LORD. And they shall

take away some of your sons who will descend from you, whom you will beget; and they shall be eunuchs in the palace of the king of Babylon.'"

a. **What did these men say, and from where did they come to you**: Isaiah probably already knew the answer to these questions. It was likely that his questions were guided by God to allow Hezekiah the opportunity to answer honestly (which he did) and to see his error himself (which he apparently did not).

b. **They have seen all that is in my house**: There is the flavor that Hezekiah was *proud* to tell Isaiah this. He was like a small-town boy who was awed by the attention of a big-city man. "Isaiah, you should have seen how impressed those Babylonians were by all I have. They really know we are something here in Judah!" Hezekiah's pride and inflated ego seemed to make him *blind*.

c. **All that is in your house… shall be carried to Babylon**: Hezekiah thought that this display of wealth would impress the Babylonians. All it did was show them what the kings of Judah had and what they could get from them. One day the kings of Babylon would come and take it all away. This was fulfilled in 2 Kings 24:10-13 and 2 Kings 25:11-17, under the Babylonian king Nebuchadnezzar.

i. "This was proudly and foolishly done; for now gold-thirsty Babylon knew where to have her draught, where to fetch a fat and fit booty." (Trapp)

ii. It would be more than a hundred years before Babylon carried away the royal treasures of Judah, but they did come, just as Isaiah prophesied. This prophecy is so remarkably accurate that many skeptics insist – without grounds other than unbelief – a later "Isaiah" must have written it after the fact.

d. **And they shall take away some of your sons… and they shall be eunuchs in the palace of the king of Babylon**: Worse than taking the material **riches** of the kings of Judah, the king of Babylon would take the **sons** of the king of Judah – his true riches!

i. One fulfillment of this was the taking of Daniel and his companions into captivity. Daniel was one *of the king's descendants* taken into the **palace of the king of Babylon** (Daniel 1:1-4). Because of this promise of God through Isaiah, many think that Daniel and his companions were made **eunuchs** when they were taken to serve in the palace.

ii. Clarke on the word **eunuchs**: "Perhaps this means no more than that they should become *household servants* to the kings of Babylon. See the fulfillment, 2 Kings 24:13-15, and Daniel 1:1-3."

3. (19-21) Hezekiah's curious reaction and the end of his reign.

So Hezekiah said to Isaiah, "The word of the Lord which you have spoken *is* good!" For he said, "Will there not be peace and truth at least in my days?" Now the rest of the acts of Hezekiah—all his might, and how he made a pool and a tunnel and brought water into the city—*are* they not written in the book of the chronicles of the kings of Judah? So Hezekiah rested with his fathers. Then Manasseh his son reigned in his place.

a. **The word of the Lord which you have spoken is good**: This was a sad state of heart in the king of Judah. God announced coming judgment, and all he could respond with was relief that it would not happen in his lifetime.

i. In this, Hezekiah showed himself to be almost the exact opposite of an "others-centered" person. He was almost totally self-centered. All he cared about was his own personal comfort and success.

b. **How he made a pool and a tunnel and brought water into the city**: This was an amazing engineering feat. He built an aqueduct to insure fresh water inside the city walls even during sieges. It was more than 650 yards long through solid rock, begun on each end and meeting in the middle. It can still be seen today and it empties into the pool of Siloam.

i. "This tunnel, found in 1880, was cut for 643 metres to cover a direct distance of 332 metres to enable the defenders to fetch water within the protective walls even during a siege." (Wiseman)

ii. "An inscription in cursive Hebrew of the early eighth century B.C. details the work: 'When (the tunnel) was driven through while (the quarrymen were swinging their) axes, each man towards the other and, while there was still 3 cubits to be cut through (there was heard) the voice of a man calling to his fellow, for there was a crevice (?) on the right... and when the tunnel was (finally) driven through, the quarrymen hewed each towards the others, axe against axe. Then the waters flowed from the Spring to the Pool for 1,200 cubits and the height of the rock above the head(s) of the quarrymen was 100 cubits.'" (Wiseman)

c. **So Hezekiah rested with his fathers**: There is no doubt that Hezekiah started out as a godly king, and overall his reign was one of outstanding godliness (2 Kings 18:3-7). Yet his beginning was much better than his end; Hezekiah did not finish well. God gave Hezekiah the gift of 15 more years of life, but the added years did not make him a better or a more godly man.

i. Time or age doesn't necessarily make us any better. Consider that time does nothing but pass away. We sometimes say, "Time will tell," "Time will heal," or "Time will bring out the potential in me." But time will do nothing of the sort! Time will only come and go. It is only how we *use* time that matters. Hezekiah didn't make good use of the extra time the Lord gave him.

ii. "Hezekiah was buried on the sloping hill where the tombs of David's descendants were cut (2 Chronicles 32:33). This was because the royal Iron Age burial caves north of the city were full by this time and hereafter no Judean king was buried in the rock-hewn caves there." (Wiseman)

2 Kings 21 – The Wicked Reigns of Manasseh and Amon

A. The reign of Manasseh, son of Hezekiah.

1. (1-2) A summary of the reign of Manasseh, a 55-year rule of evil.

Manasseh *was* twelve years old when he became king, and he reigned fifty-five years in Jerusalem. His mother's name *was* Hephzibah. And he did evil in the sight of the LORD, according to the abominations of the nations whom the LORD had cast out before the children of Israel.

a. **Manasseh was twelve years old when he became king**: This means that he was born in the *last fifteen years* of Hezekiah's life, the *additional* fifteen years that Hezekiah prayed for. Those additional fifteen years brought Judah one of its worst kings.

i. "Had this good king been able to foresee the wickedness of his unworthy son, he would doubtless have no desire to recover from his sickness. Better by far die childless than beget a son such as Manasseh proved to be." (Knapp)

b. **And he reigned fifty-five years in Jerusalem**: This was both a remarkably long and a remarkably evil reign. A long career or longevity is not necessarily evidence of the blessing and approval of God.

i. "A degenerate plant of so noble a vine." (Trapp)

ii. "Manasseh is named in Assyrian annals (*Menasi* or *Minse*, King of Yaudi) among twelve rulers of Palestine who brought tribute in kind to their overlord." (Wiseman)

c. **According to the abominations of the nations whom the LORD had cast out before**: Manasseh imitated the sins of both the Canaanites and the Israelites of the Northern Kingdom (2 Kings 16:3). Since God brought judgment on these groups for their sin, casting them out of their land, similar judgment against an unrepentant Judah should be expected.

2. (3-9) The specific sins of Manasseh.

For he rebuilt the high places which Hezekiah his father had destroyed; he raised up altars for Baal, and made a wooden image, as Ahab king of Israel had done; and he worshiped all the host of heaven and served them. He also built altars in the house of the LORD, of which the LORD had said, "In Jerusalem I will put My name." And he built altars for all the host of heaven in the two courts of the house of the LORD. Also he made his son pass through the fire, practiced soothsaying, used witchcraft, and consulted spiritists and mediums. He did much evil in the sight of the LORD, to provoke *Him* to anger. He even set a carved image of Asherah that he had made, in the house of which the LORD had said to David and to Solomon his son, "In this house and in Jerusalem, which I have chosen out of all the tribes of Israel, I will put My name forever; and I will not make the feet of Israel wander anymore from the land which I gave their fathers—only if they are careful to do according to all that I have commanded them, and according to all the law that My servant Moses commanded them." But they paid no attention, and Manasseh seduced them to do more evil than the nations whom the LORD had destroyed before the children of Israel.

a. **He rebuilt the high places which Hezekiah his father had destroyed**: Manasseh opposed the reforms of his father Hezekiah and he brought Judah back into terrible idolatry.

i. This shows us that repentance, reform, and revival are not permanent standing conditions. What is accomplished at one time can be opposed and turned back at another time.

b. **He raised up altars for Baal, and made a wooden image**: Manasseh did not want to imitate his godly father. Instead, he imitated one of the very worst kings of Israel: Ahab. He embraced the same state-sponsored worship of Baal and Asherah (honored with **a wooden image**) that marked the reign of Ahab.

c. **He worshiped all the host of heaven and served them**: Manasseh did not only bring back old forms of idolatry; he also brought new forms of idolatry to Judah. At this time the Babylonian Empire was rising in influence, and they had a special attraction to astrological worship. Manasseh probably imitated this.

d. **He also built altars in the house of the LORD**: It was bad enough for Manasseh to allow this idol worship into Judah. Worse, he corrupted the worship of the true God at the temple, and made the temple a place of idol altars, including those dedicated to his cult of astrological worship (**he built altars for all the host of heaven**).

e. **He made his son pass through the fire**: Manasseh sacrificed his own son to the Canaanite god Molech, who was worshipped with the burning of children.

f. **Practiced soothsaying, used witchcraft, and consulted spiritists and mediums**: Manasseh invited direct Satanic influence by his approval and introduction of these occult arts.

g. **He even set a carved image of Asherah that he had made, in the house of… the LORD**: Asherah was the Canaanite goddess of fertility, and worshipped through ritual prostitution. This means that Manasseh made the temple into an idolatrous brothel, dedicated to Asherah.

> i. "From the whole it is evident that Asherah was no other than *Venus*; the nature of whose worship is plain enough from the mention of *whoremongers* and *prostitutes*." (Clarke)

h. **But they paid no attention, and Manasseh seduced them to do more evil**: This describes the basic attitude of the people of Judah during the 55-year reign of Manasseh. They **paid no attention** to the generous promises of God, promising protection to His obedient people. In addition, they were willingly **seduced** by Manasseh's wickedness and were attracted **to do more evil**.

> i. He was indeed a wicked king, but perhaps the greater sin was on the part of the people who accepted this seduction willingly. 2 Chronicles 33:10 says, *And the LORD spoke to Manasseh and his people, but they would not listen*. God spoke to both the people and the leader, but they rejected His word.
>
> ii. "He did all he could to pervert the national character, and totally destroy the worship of the true God; and he succeeded." (Clarke)
>
> iii. "How superficial had been the nation's compliance with Hezekiah's reforms! Without a strong spiritual leader, the sinful people quickly turned to their own evil machinations. The judgment of God could not be far away." (Patterson and Austel)
>
> iv. This was a transformation of the culture from something generally God-honoring to a culture that glorified idolatry and immorality. In general, we can say this happened because the people *wanted* it to happen. They didn't care about the direction of their culture.

3. (10-15) God promises judgment against Judah.

And the LORD spoke by His servants the prophets, saying, "Because Manasseh king of Judah has done these abominations (he has acted more wickedly than all the Amorites who *were* before him, and has also made Judah sin with his idols), therefore thus says the LORD God of Israel: 'Behold, *I* am bringing *such* calamity upon Jerusalem and Judah, that whoever hears of it, both his ears will tingle. And I will stretch over Jerusalem the measuring line of Samaria and the plummet of the house of Ahab; I will wipe Jerusalem as *one* wipes a dish, wiping *it* and turning *it* upside down. So I will forsake the remnant of My inheritance and deliver them into the hand of their enemies; and they shall become victims of plunder to all their enemies, because they have done evil in My sight, and have provoked Me to anger since the day their fathers came out of Egypt, even to this day.' "

a. **The LORD spoke by His servants the prophets**: When the leaders and the popular culture had abandoned God, the LORD still had a voice to Judah. He spoke by **the prophets** to His disobedient people.

i. "The prophets were Hosea, Joel, Nahum, Habakkuk, and Isaiah. These five following verses contain the sum of what these prophets spoke." (Clarke)

b. **He has acted more wickedly than all the Amorites who were before him**: This was a remarkable achievement of evil. The Amorites were among the Canaanite tribes who populated the Promised Land before Israel captured it, and they were infamous for their violent, immoral, and depraved culture.

c. **Both his ears will tingle**: In other places in the Old Testament, *tingling ears* are a sign that an especially severe judgment was coming (1 Samuel 3:11, Jeremiah 19:3).

d. **The measuring line of Samaria**: God's logic is simple. If Judah insisted on imitating the sins of the Northern Kingdom, then God would answer their similar sins with a similar judgment. God would cleanse Jerusalem **as one wipes a dish, wiping it and turning it upside down**, subjecting them to their enemies.

i. "To wipe a dish and turn it *upside-down* to drain signified the depopulation of the land (*cf.* Jeremiah 51:34)." (Wiseman)

ii. **So I will forsake**: "*Forsake* is a strong, forceful word used to describe the skinning of an animal. It is sometimes translated *cast off*." (Dilday)

4. (16) Manasseh persecutes the people of God.

Moreover Manasseh shed very much innocent blood, till he had filled Jerusalem from one end to another, besides his sin by which he made Judah sin, in doing evil in the sight of the LORD.

    a. **Manasseh shed very much innocent blood**: This puts Manasseh, king of Judah, in the same spiritual family as Ahab, king of Israel. Under both of these kings – among others – the people of God were persecuted by the religion of state-sponsored idolatry. The extent of it was so great that it could be metaphorically said, **he had filled Jerusalem from one end to another** with the blood of his victims.

        i. We see the tragic progression in Manasseh's sin.

- First, idolatry is *tolerated* among God's people.
- Then idolatry is *promoted*.
- Then idolatry is *supported and funded*.
- Then the worship of the true God is *undermined*.
- Then the worshippers of the true God are *persecuted and murdered*.
- Then the judgment of God *soon comes*.

    b. **In doing evil in the sight of the LORD**: By tradition, one of the evils done by Manasseh was the murder of Isaiah the prophet. Many think that Hebrews 11:37 (*they were sawn in two*) is a reference to the martyrdom of Isaiah.

        i. "To *shed innocent blood* implies oppression against the young, innocent and godly (*cf.* 2 Kings 24:3-4). The uncorroborated Jewish tradition (*The Ascension of Isaiah*) says that Isaiah was sawn in half during the reign of Manasseh (*cf.* Hebrews 11:37)." (Wiseman)

5. (17-18) Conclusion of Manasseh's reign.

Now the rest of the acts of Manasseh—all that he did, and the sin that he committed—*are* they not written in the book of the chronicles of the kings of Judah? So Manasseh rested with his fathers, and was buried in the garden of his own house, in the garden of Uzza. Then his son Amon reigned in his place.

    a. **All that he did, and the sin that he committed**: This was the terrible legacy of Manasseh, who was born of one of the better kings of Judah (Hezekiah).

    b. **Are they not written in the book of the chronicles of the kings of Judah**: 2 Chronicles 33:11-19 describes a remarkable repentance on the part of Manasseh. Because he and his people would not listen to the warnings of

God, the LORD allowed the Babylonians to bind King Manasseh and take him as a captive to Babylon. There, *when he was in affliction, he implored the LORD his God, and humbled himself greatly before the God of his fathers* (2 Chronicles 33:12) and God answered his prayer and restored him to the throne. Manasseh then proved that his repentance was genuine by taking away the idols and the foreign gods from Jerusalem, and he *commanded Judah to serve the LORD God of Israel* (2 Chronicles 33:16).

i. This is a wonderful example of the principle, *Train up a child in the way he should go, and when he is old he will not depart from it* (Proverbs 22:6). Manasseh was raised by a godly father, yet he lived in defiance of his father's faith for most of his life. Nevertheless, at the end of his days he truly repented and served God. In this way, we can say that it was very true that **Manasseh rested with his fathers**.

ii. Yet, his repentance was too late to change the nation. "The widespread revolts during the reign of Ashurbanipal, which occurred from 652-648 B.C., may provide the occasion for Manasseh's summons to Babylon and imprisonment. If so, his subsequent release and reform were apparently far too late to have much of an effect on the obdurately backslidden people." (Patterson and Austel)

iii. It was also not soon enough to change the *destiny* of the kingdom. "Years later, when Jerusalem fell to the Babylonians, the writer would blame Judah's punishment on the sins of Manasseh (2 Kings 24:3-4)." (Dilday)

B. The reign of Amon, son of Manasseh.

1. (19-22) A two-year, evil reign.

Amon *was* twenty-two years old when he became king, and he reigned two years in Jerusalem. His mother's name *was* Meshullemeth the daughter of Haruz of Jotbah. And he did evil in the sight of the LORD, as his father Manasseh had done. So he walked in all the ways that his father had walked; and he served the idols that his father had served, and worshiped them. He forsook the LORD God of his fathers, and did not walk in the way of the LORD.

a. **He reigned two years in Jerusalem**: This unusually short reign is an indication that the blessing of God was *not* upon the reign of Amon.

b. **And he did evil in the sight of the LORD, as his father Manasseh had done**: Amon sinned as Manasseh had sinned, without having the repentance that Manasseh repented. It is likely that one of the greatest sorrows to the repentant Manasseh was that his sons and others who were influenced by his sin did not also repent.

i. "There is not one bright spot in this king's character to relieve the darkness of his life's brief record." (Knapp)

ii. 2 Chronicles 33:23 says: *And he did not humble himself before the LORD, as his father Manasseh had humbled himself; but Amon trespassed more and more.*

iii. "Glycas saith that Amon hardened himself in sin by his father's example, who took his swing in sin, and yet at length repented. So, thought he, will I do; wherefore he was soon sent out of the world for his presumption, dying in his sins, as 2 Chronicles 33:23." (Trapp)

2. (23-26) The assassination of Amon.

Then the servants of Amon conspired against him, and killed the king in his own house. But the people of the land executed all those who had conspired against King Amon. Then the people of the land made his son Josiah king in his place. Now the rest of the acts of Amon which he did, *are* they not written in the book of the chronicles of the kings of Judah? And he was buried in his tomb in the garden of Uzza. Then Josiah his son reigned in his place.

a. **The servants of Amon conspired against him, and killed the king in his own house**: This story of conspiracy and assassination seems to belong among the kings of *Israel*, not Judah. Yet when the kings and people of Judah began to imitate the sins of their conquered northern neighbors, they slipped into the same chaos and anarchy that marked the last period of Israel's history.

i. "Although the Scriptures give no reason for the conspiracy, its cause may lie within the tangled web of revolts that Asurbanipal suppressed from 642-639 and that caused him to turn his attention to the west… Amnon's death may thus reflect a power struggle between those who wished to remain loyal to the Assyrian crown and those who aspired to link Judah's fortunes to the rising star of Psammetik I (664-609) of Egypt's Twenty-Sixth Dynasty." (Patterson and Austel)

b. **But the people of the land executed all those who had conspired against King Amon**: This was a hopeful sign. Up to this point, the people of Judah had largely tolerated some 57 years of utterly wicked kings who led the nation in evil. Now it seems that they wanted righteousness and justice instead of the evil they had lived with for so long.

i. In some way, it could be said that the people of Judah had these wicked kings for more than 50 years because *that is what they wanted*. God gave them the leaders they wanted and deserved. Now, as the people of the kingdom turned towards godliness, God will give them a better king.

c. Then the people of the land made his son Josiah king in his place: Though King Amon was assassinated, God did not yet allow Judah to slip into the same pit of anarchy that Israel had sunk into. Because of the righteous action of **the people of the land**, there was no change of *dynasty*, and the rightful heir to the throne of David received the throne.

i. "The only positive contribution Amon made to the history of Judah was to produce one of the best kings to reign on the throne of Jerusalem." (Dilday)

2 Kings 22 – King Josiah Finds the Book of the Law

A. The beginnings of Josiah's reforms.

1. (1-2) A summary of the reign of Josiah, the son of Amon.

Josiah *was* eight years old when he became king, and he reigned thirty-one years in Jerusalem. His mother's name *was* Jedidah the daughter of Adaiah of Bozkath. And he did *what was* right in the sight of the LORD, and walked in all the ways of his father David; he did not turn aside to the right hand or to the left.

> a. **Josiah was eight years old when he became king**: Unusually, this young boy came to the throne at **eight years** of age. This was because of the assassination of his father.
>
> > i. "At last, after more than three hundred years, the prophecy of 'the man of God out of Judah' is fulfilled (1 Kings 13:2)." (Knapp)
>
> b. **He did what was right in the sight of the LORD**: This was true of Josiah at this young age; but it is really more intended as a general description of his reign rather than a description of him at eight years of age.

2. (3-7) Josiah tells Hilkiah to repair the temple.

Now it came to pass, in the eighteenth year of King Josiah, *that* the king sent Shaphan the scribe, the son of Azaliah, the son of Meshullam, to the house of the LORD, saying: "Go up to Hilkiah the high priest, that he may count the money which has been brought into the house of the LORD, which the doorkeepers have gathered from the people. And let them deliver it into the hand of those doing the work, who are the overseers in the house of the LORD; let them give it to those who *are* in the house of the LORD doing the work, to repair the damages of the house—to carpenters and builders and masons—and to buy timber and hewn stone to repair the house. However there need be no accounting

made with them of the money delivered into their hand, because they deal faithfully."

a. **In the eighteenth year of King Josiah**: According to 2 Chronicles 34, this repair of the temple was preceded by a definite commitment to God when Josiah was 16, and then some four years later by an iconoclastic purge attacking idolatry in Judah.

i. "The Chronicler (2 Chronicles 34-35) appears to present a two-stage sequence of events: (i) the purification of religious practices in Judah, Jerusalem and Naphtali in Josiah's twelfth year, and (ii) a continuing reformation stimulated by the discovery of the Book of the Law in the eighteenth year. But this may be a presentation to fit in with the Chroniciler's particular emphases." (Wiseman)

ii. "If Josiah had not yet seen a copy of this book, (which is not impossible,) yet there was so much of the law left in the minds and memories of the people, as might easily persuade and direct him to all that he did till this time." (Poole)

iii. It is possible that Josiah was motivated to rebuild the temple after hearing (or remembering) that this was what King Jehoash did many years before (2 Kings 12).

b. **Let them give it to those who are in the house of the LORD doing the work, to repair the damages of the house**: Josiah understood that the work of repair and rebuilding the temple needed organization and funding. He paid attention to both of these needs when he commanded **Hilkiah** to begin the work on the temple.

i. According to Jeremiah 1:1-2, the prophet Jeremiah was the son of this particular priest **Hilkiah**. Jeremiah began his ministry during the reign of King Josiah.

3. (8-10) The **Book of the Law** is found and read.

Then Hilkiah the high priest said to Shaphan the scribe, "I have found the Book of the Law in the house of the LORD." And Hilkiah gave the book to Shaphan, and he read it. So Shaphan the scribe went to the king, bringing the king word, saying, "Your servants have gathered the money that was found in the house, and have delivered it into the hand of those who do the work, who oversee the house of the LORD." Then Shaphan the scribe showed the king, saying, "Hilkiah the priest has given me a book." And Shaphan read it before the king.

a. **I have found the Book of the Law in the house of the LORD**: According to Deuteronomy 31:24-27, there was to be a copy of *this Book of the Law* beside the ark of the covenant, beginning in the days of Moses. The word of God was *with* Israel, but it was greatly *neglected* in those days.

i. This neglect could only happen because Judah was in prolonged disobedience to God.

- Deuteronomy 17:18-20 tells us that each king was to have a personal copy of the law, and he was to read it.
- Deuteronomy 31:9-13 tells us that the entire law was to be read to an assembly of the nation once every 7 years at the Feast of Tabernacles to keep the law before the people.
- The Levites, scattered among the country, also had the implied responsibility to teach the law to the people of Israel.

ii. The first we know of a public reading of the law is in Joshua 8:30. The next we hear of it is during the reign of Jehoshaphat (2 Chronicles 17:7), more than 500 years later. Then, in the reign of Josiah there was another public reading of the law (2 Chronicles 34:30), more than 250 years after Jehoshaphat. Of course, there might have been public readings of the law as commanded here which are not recorded; but the fact that some are recorded probably means they were unusual, not typical.

iii. Some believe that the particular portion of the law that was found and read before King Josiah was the Book of Deuteronomy. "The identification with Deuteronomy rests on the dependence of some of Josiah's actions on the book (*e.g.* 23:9, *cf.* Deuteronomy 18:6-8; and the impact of the prophecies predicting exile; the support Deuteronomy 17:14 gives to nationalistic aspirations, *etc.*)." (Wiseman)

iv. "Was this the *autograph* of Moses? It is very probable that it was; for in the parallel place, 2 Chronicles 34:14, it is said to be the book of *the law of the Lord by Moses*. It is supposed to be that part of Deuteronomy (28, 29, 30, and 31,) which contains the renewing of the covenant in the plains of Moab, and which contains the most terrible invectives against the corrupters of God's word and worship." (Clarke)

b. **And he read it**: It seems remarkable that this was even worthy of mention – that the high priest found the word of God and a scribe read it. Yet the word of God was so neglected in those days that this was worthy of mention.

i. Shaphan simply told the king, "**Hilkiah the priest has given me a book**." "Shaphan did not despise the book, but he had not yet, like many a modern scribe, realized the importance of that blessed volume. Then – after 'money,' and 'overseers,' and 'workmen,' have all been mentioned – 'then Shaphan the scribe told the king, saying, "Hilkiah the priest hath given me a book' – only *a* book!" (Knapp)

c. **Shaphan read it before the king**: Here the word of God spreads. It had been forgotten and regarded as nothing more than an old, dusty book. Now it was found, read, and spread. We should expect some measure of spiritual revival and renewal to follow.

i. Throughout the history of God's people, when the word of God is recovered and spread, spiritual revival follows. It can begin as simply as it did in the days of Josiah, with one man finding and reading and believing and spreading the Book.

ii. Another example of this in history is the story of Peter Waldo and his followers, sometimes known as Waldenses. Waldo was a rich merchant living in the 12th century who gave up his business to radically follow Jesus. He hired two priests to translate the New Testament into the common language and using this, he began to teach others. He taught in the streets or wherever he could find someone to listen. Many common people came to hear him and started to radically follow Jesus Christ. He taught them the text of the New Testament in the common language and was rebuked by church officials for doing so. He ignored the rebuke and continued to teach, eventually sending his followers out two by two into villages and market places, to teach and explain the scriptures. The scriptures were memorized by the Waldenses, and it was not unusual for their ministers to memorize the entire New Testament and large sections of the Old Testament. The word of God – when found, read, believed, and spread – has this kind of transforming power.

iii. "It is interesting to note the popularity of animal names for persons in this period. 'Shaphan' means 'rock badger' and 'Achbor' means 'mouse.' 'Huldah' the name of the prophetess introduced in the next section, means 'mole.'" (Dilday)

B. King Josiah is confronted with the Book of the Law.

1. (11) The initial reaction to the discovery of the Book of the Law.

Now it happened, when the king heard the words of the Book of the Law, that he tore his clothes.

a. **When the king heard the words of the Book of the Law**: The hearing of God's word did a spiritual work in King Josiah. It was not merely the transmission of information; the hearing of God's word had an impact of spiritual power on Josiah.

b. **He tore his clothes**: The tearing of clothing was a traditional expression of horror and astonishment. In the strongest possible way, Josiah showed his grief on his own account and on account of the nation. This was an expression of deep conviction of sin, and a good thing.

i. Revival and spiritual awakening are marked by such expressions of the conviction of sin. Dr. J. Edwin Orr, in *The Second Evangelical Awakening in Britain*, recounted some examples from the great movement that impacted Britain and the world in 1859-1861:

- "At the commencement of the prayer-meeting, a sturdy looking man (who had been coming to the chapel every night but going away hardening his heart) jumped on to a form, and speaking out before all the people, said, 'Do you know me?' The praying men answered, 'Yes.' 'What am I then?' he said. They replied, 'A backslider.' 'Well, then,' said he, 'I will be a backslider no longer; all of you come to Jesus with me,' and he fell in an agony of prayer for God to have mercy on him; indeed the anguish and desire of his soul was too much for him, for he swooned away on the floor before us all. His wife was one of the first converted the previous week, and only that evening had sent up a request that God would save her husband, who was a poor miserable backslider. About thirty that night professed to obtain mercy…"

- In the town of Coleraine, Northern Ireland, a schoolboy was under so much conviction of sin that he couldn't continue on in class. The teacher sent him home in the company of another boy, who was already converted. On the way home the two boys noticed an empty house and stopped there to pray. The unhappy boy found peace and returned to the classroom immediately to tell the teacher: "I am so happy: I have the Lord Jesus in my heart!" His testimony had a striking effect on the class, and boy after boy slipped outside the classroom. The teacher peeked out the window and saw boys kneeling in prayer all around the schoolyard. The teacher was so convicted that he asked the first converted boy to minister to him. Finally the whole school was in such a state that the administrators sent for pastors to come and minister to the students, teachers, and parents, and people received ministry at the school until 11:00 that night.

- A high-ranking army officer described the conviction of sin in his Scottish town: "Those of you who are at ease have little conception of how terrifying a sight it is when the Holy Spirit is pleased to open a man's eyes to see the real state of heart…

Men who were thought to be, and who thought themselves to be good, religious people… have been led to search into the foundation upon which they were resting, and have found all rotten, that they were self-satisfied, resting on their own goodness, and not upon Christ. Many turned from open sin to lives of holiness, some weeping for joy for sins forgiven."

ii. This conviction of sin is the special work of the Holy Spirit, even as Jesus said in John 16:8: "And when He has come, He will convict the world of sin."

2. (12-13) King Josiah seeks the LORD.

Then the king commanded Hilkiah the priest, Ahikam the son of Shaphan, Achbor the son of Michaiah, Shaphan the scribe, and Asaiah a servant of the king, saying, "Go, inquire of the LORD for me, for the people and for all Judah, concerning the words of this book that has been found; for great is the wrath of the LORD that is aroused against us, because our fathers have not obeyed the words of this book, to do according to all that is written concerning us."

a. **Go, inquire of the LORD for me**: It wasn't that King Josiah knew nothing of God or how to seek him. It was that he was so under the conviction of sin that he did not know what to do next.

b. **For great is the wrath of the LORD that is aroused against us**: Josiah knew that the kingdom of Judah deserved *judgment* from God. He could not hear the word of God and respond to the Spirit of God without seriously confronting the sin of his kingdom.

3. (14-17) God's word to the kingdom of Judah: Judgment is coming.

So Hilkiah the priest, Ahikam, Achbor, Shaphan, and Asaiah went to Huldah the prophetess, the wife of Shallum the son of Tikvah, the son of Harhas, keeper of the wardrobe. (She dwelt in Jerusalem in the Second Quarter.) And they spoke with her. Then she said to them, "Thus says the LORD God of Israel, 'Tell the man who sent you to Me, "Thus says the LORD: 'Behold, I will bring calamity on this place and on its inhabitants—all the words of the book which the king of Judah has read—because they have forsaken Me and burned incense to other gods, that they might provoke Me to anger with all the works of their hands. Therefore My wrath shall be aroused against this place and shall not be quenched.'"'"

a. **Huldah the prophetess**: We know little of this woman other than this mention here (and the similar account recorded in 2 Chronicles 34:22). With the apparent approval of King Josiah, Hilkiah the priest consulted this woman for spiritual guidance. It wasn't because of her own wisdom and spirituality, but that she was recognized as a **prophetess** and could reveal the heart and mind of God.

> i. There were certainly other prophets in Judah. "Though the contemporary prophet Jeremiah is not mentioned, he commended Josiah (Jeremiah 22:15-16), and the prophet Zephaniah (1:1) was at work in this reign." (Wiseman) Yet for some reason – perhaps spiritual, perhaps practical – they chose to consult **Huldah the prophetess**.
>
> ii. "We find from this, and we have many facts in all ages to corroborate it, that a pontiff, a pope, a bishop, or a priest, may, in some cases, not possess the true knowledge of God; and that a simple *woman*, possessing the life of God in her soul, may have more knowledge of the divine testimonies than many of those whose office it is to explain and enforce them." (Clarke)

b. **I will bring calamity on this place and on its inhabitants**: Josiah knew that Judah deserved judgment, and that judgment would indeed come. Judah and its leaders had walked against the LORD for too long, and would not genuinely repent so as to avoid eventual judgment.

c. **All the words of the book**: God's word was true, even in its promises of judgment. God's faithfulness is demonstrated as much by His judgment upon the wicked as it is by His mercy upon the repentant.

4. (18-20) God's word to King Josiah: The judgment will not come in your day.

"But as for the king of Judah, who sent you to inquire of the LORD, in this manner you shall speak to him, 'Thus says the LORD God of Israel: "*Concerning* the words which you have heard— because your heart was tender, and you humbled yourself before the LORD when you heard what I spoke against this place and against its inhabitants, that they would become a desolation and a curse, and you tore your clothes and wept before Me, I also have heard *you*," says the LORD. Surely, therefore, I will gather you to your fathers, and you shall be gathered to your grave in peace; and your eyes shall not see all the calamity which I will bring on this place."'" So they brought back word to the king.

a. **Because your heart was tender**: Josiah's heart was tender in two ways. First, it was **tender** to the word of God and was able to receive the convicting voice of the Holy Spirit. Second, it was **tender** to the message of judgment from Huldah in the previous verses.

b. **You shall be gathered to your grave in peace**: Though Josiah died in battle, there are at least three ways that this was true.

- He died before the great spiritual disaster and exile came to Judah.

- He was gathered to the spirits of his fathers, who were in peace.
- He died in God's favor, though by the hand of an enemy.

c. **Your eyes shall not see all the calamity which I will bring on this place**: This was God's mercy to Josiah. His own godliness and tender heart could not stop the eventual judgment of God, but it could delay it. Inevitable judgment is sometimes delayed because of the tender hearts of the people of God.

i. God delayed judgment even in the case of Ahab, who responded to a word of warning with a kind of repentance (1 Kings 21:25-29).

2 Kings 23 – The Reforms of Josiah

A. The covenant and the reforms of King Josiah.

1. (1-3) The covenant is renewed.

Now the king sent them to gather all the elders of Judah and Jerusalem to him. The king went up to the house of the LORD with all the men of Judah, and with him all the inhabitants of Jerusalem—the priests and the prophets and all the people, both small and great. And he read in their hearing all the words of the Book of the Covenant which had been found in the house of the LORD. Then the king stood by a pillar and made a covenant before the LORD, to follow the LORD and to keep His commandments and His testimonies and His statutes, with all *his* heart and all *his* soul, to perform the words of this covenant that were written in this book. And all the people took a stand for the covenant.

> a. **The king sent them to gather all the elders of Judah**: Josiah heard the promise of both eventual judgment and the immediate delay of judgment. He did not respond with indifference or simple contentment that he would not see the judgment in his day. He wanted to get the kingdom right with God, and he knew that he could not do it all by himself – he needed **all the elders of Judah** to join in broken repentance with him.

> b. **And he read in their hearing all the words of the Book**: The king did this himself. He was so concerned that the nation would hear the word of God that **he read** it to them himself.

> c. **The king stood by a pillar and made a covenant before the LORD, to follow the LORD**: King Josiah stood before the people and publicly declared his commitment to obey the word of God to the very best of his ability (**with all his heart and all his soul**).

>> i. "*[He] made a covenant* is literally '[he] cut a covenant,' which goes back to the practice of cutting the carcass of an animal and separating

the parts so the contracting parties could seal their agreement by walking between them (cf. Genesis 15:17; Jeremiah 34:18)." (Dilday)

d. **And all the people took a stand for the covenant**: They did this in response to the example and leadership of King Josiah. We do not read of any *command* for the people to do this; they did it spontaneously as they followed the king's example and leadership.

i. This kind of mass response and commitment to the LORD cannot be commanded, but that does not mean that there is no part for man to play. It was clearly the work of God among the people, but God worked through the example and leadership of King Josiah.

ii. The fact that this happened among **all the people** means that this was a special work of the Holy Spirit. The Bible tells us that there are times when the Holy Spirit comes upon people as a *group*, which is a different work than the individual filling of the Spirit. There are times when the Holy Spirit seems to work on a group, and we should pray for such moving of the Holy Spirit today.

- Acts 2:4: *And they were all filled with the Holy Spirit and began to speak with other tongues, as the Spirit gave them utterance.*
- Acts 4:31: *And when they had prayed, the place where they were assembled together was shaken; and they were all filled with the Holy Spirit, and they spoke the word of God with boldness.*
- Acts 10:44: *While Peter was still speaking these words, the Holy Spirit fell upon all those who heard the word.*

iii. "The ceremony compares with the basic Mizpah covenant (1 Samuel 8:11-17; 10:25) and the renewal of the covenant at Shechem (Joshua 24), both of which marked turning points in Jewish history." (Wiseman)

2. (4-14) The extent of King Josiah's reformation in Judah.

And the king commanded Hilkiah the high priest, the priests of the second order, and the doorkeepers, to bring out of the temple of the LORD all the articles that were made for Baal, for Asherah, and for all the host of heaven; and he burned them outside Jerusalem in the fields of Kidron, and carried their ashes to Bethel. Then he removed the idolatrous priests whom the kings of Judah had ordained to burn incense on the high places in the cities of Judah and in the places all around Jerusalem, and those who burned incense to Baal, to the sun, to the moon, to the constellations, and to all the host of heaven. And he brought out the wooden image from the house of the LORD, to the Brook Kidron outside Jerusalem, burned it at the Brook Kidron and

ground *it* to ashes, and threw its ashes on the graves of the common people. Then he tore down the *ritual* booths of the perverted persons that *were* in the house of the LORD, where the women wove hangings for the wooden image. And he brought all the priests from the cities of Judah, and defiled the high places where the priests had burned incense, from Geba to Beersheba; also he broke down the high places at the gates which *were* at the entrance of the Gate of Joshua the governor of the city, which *were* to the left of the city gate. Nevertheless the priests of the high places did not come up to the altar of the LORD in Jerusalem, but they ate unleavened bread among their brethren. And he defiled Topheth, which *is* in the Valley of the Son of Hinnom, that no man might make his son or his daughter pass through the fire to Molech. Then he removed the horses that the kings of Judah had dedicated to the sun, at the entrance to the house of the LORD, by the chamber of Nathan-Melech, the officer who *was* in the court; and he burned the chariots of the sun with fire. The altars that *were* on the roof, the upper chamber of Ahaz, which the kings of Judah had made, and the altars which Manasseh had made in the two courts of the house of the LORD, the king broke down and pulverized there, and threw their dust into the Brook Kidron. Then the king defiled the high places that *were* east of Jerusalem, which *were* on the south of the Mount of Corruption, which Solomon king of Israel had built for Ashtoreth the abomination of the Sidonians, for Chemosh the abomination of the Moabites, and for Milcom the abomination of the people of Ammon. And he broke in pieces the *sacred* pillars and cut down the wooden images, and filled their places with the bones of men.

a. **To bring out of the temple of the LORD all of the articles that were made for Baal, for Asherah, and for all the host of heaven**: This shows us *how deep* idolatry was in Judah. There were idols dedicated to **Baal**, to **Asherah**, and to **all the host of heaven** in the *very temple itself*. From this account, it seems that Josiah began the cleansing reforms at the center and worked outwards.

> i. **Threw its ashes on the graves of the common people**: "Throwing the ashes of the idol on the graves of the common people outside the city was not intended to defile their graves, but the very opposite. Any contact with death was believed to be an act of defilement, so scattering the dust on the graves served to defile the idols." (Dilday)

b. **Then he removed the idolatrous priests**: Josiah's reforms did not only remove sinful *things*, but also the sinful *people* that promoted and permitted these sinful things. The idols that filled the temple did not get there or stay there on their own – there were **idolatrous priests** who were responsible for these sinful practices.

i. Any thorough reformation can not only deal with sinful things; it must also deal with sinful people. If sinful people are not dealt with, they will quickly bring back the sinful things that were righteously removed.

ii. **The idolatrous priests**: "Probably they were an *order* made by the idolatrous kings of Judah, and called *kemarim*, from *camar*, which signifies to be *scorched*, *shriveled together*, *made dark*, or *black*, because their business was constantly to attend *sacrificial fires*, and probably they wore *black garments*." (Clarke)

c. **Then he tore down the ritual booths of the perverted persons**: Supposedly sacred prostitution was an integral part of the worship of many of these pagan idols. The temple had become a brothel and King Josiah corrected this disgraceful perversion.

i. **Perverted persons**: "The Hebrew word basically denotes 'holy, set apart', here clearly for non-Yahwistic purposes." (Wiseman) "We have already often met with these *kedeshim* or *consecrated persons*." (Clarke)

ii. "The word translated '*hangings*' likely refers to a fabric woven by idol worshippers for curtains behind which the ritual obscenities were practiced." (Dilday)

d. **He defiled Topheth… he removed the horses that the kings of Judah had dedicated to the sun… he burned the chariots of the sun… the king broke down and pulverized… he broke in pieces the sacred pillars**: This passage reveals something of the *extent* of official idolatry in Judah. It was widespread, elaborate, and heavily invested in. Previous kings of Judah had spent a lot of time and money to honor these pagan idols. It took a long, dedicated commitment on the part of King Josiah to do this work.

i. "The utilization of the horse in the solar cultus was widespread in the ancient Near East, being attested particularly in Assyrian and Aramean inscriptional and artifactual sources." (Patterson and Austel)

ii. "Since the symbolic wooden pole could be burned and pulverized, the scattering of the ashes over peoples' graves served to despise both the god and its worshippers (*cf.* Jeremiah 26:23)." (Wiseman)

iii. **And he defiled Topheth, which is in the Valley of the Son of Hinnom**: "Here it appears the sacred rites of Molech were performed, and to this all the filth of the city was carried, and perpetual fires were kept up in order to consume it. Hence, it has been considered a *type* of *hell*; and in this sense it is used in the New Testament." (Clarke)

iv. "The rabbins say that Topheth had its name from *toph*, a *drum*, because instruments of this kind were used to drown the cries of the children that were put into the burning arms of Molech, to be scorched to death." (Clarke)

3. (15-20) Josiah extends his reformation to Bethel and Samaria.

Moreover the altar that *was* at Bethel, *and* the high place which Jeroboam the son of Nebat, who made Israel sin, had made, both that altar and the high place he broke down; and he burned the high place *and* crushed *it* to powder, and burned the wooden image. As Josiah turned, he saw the tombs that *were* there on the mountain. And he sent and took the bones out of the tombs and burned *them* on the altar, and defiled it according to the word of the LORD which the man of God proclaimed, who proclaimed these words. Then he said, "What gravestone *is* this that I see?" So the men of the city told him, "*It is* the tomb of the man of God who came from Judah and proclaimed these things which you have done against the altar of Bethel." And he said, "Let him alone; let no one move his bones." So they let his bones alone, with the bones of the prophet who came from Samaria. Now Josiah also took away all the shrines of the high places that *were* in the cities of Samaria, which the kings of Israel had made to provoke the LORD to anger; and he did to them according to all the deeds he had done in Bethel. He executed all the priests of the high places who *were* there, on the altars, and burned men's bones on them; and he returned to Jerusalem.

a. **Moreover the altar that was at Bethel**: King Josiah was so diligent in his reforms that he took down altars located in the former kingdom of Israel. He removed the pagan altar at Bethel that Jeroboam set up hundreds of years earlier.

i. Politically speaking, this was possible because the Assyrian Empire was weak in the days of Josiah. Josiah could intervene in this area that was subject to the Assyrian Empire because they were concerned with other things and could not stop him.

ii. "The altar at Bethel, which Josiah's reform also reached, had been established by Jeroboam at Solomon's death; but in the course of time a purely Canaanite worship had apparently replaced the earlier worship of the golden calf." (Patterson and Austel)

b. **What gravestone is this that I see**: This is the remarkable fulfillment of a prophecy made hundreds of years earlier. The words of this anonymous prophet are recorded in 1 Kings 13:1-2: *Behold, a child, Josiah by name, shall be born to the house of David; and on you he shall sacrifice the priests* *of the high places who burn incense on you.* Josiah was careful to honor the gravestone of this anonymous prophet.

4. (21-23) Josiah keeps the Passover on a national basis.

Then the king commanded all the people, saying, "Keep the Passover to the LORD **your God, as** *it is* **written in this Book of the Covenant." Such a Passover surely had never been held since the days of the judges who judged Israel, nor in all the days of the kings of Israel and the kings of Judah. But in the eighteenth year of King Josiah this Passover was held before the L**ORD **in Jerusalem.**

a. **Keep the Passover to the L**ORD **your God, as it is written in this Book of the Covenant**: Josiah could not command heart obedience to the word of God, but he could establish a national holiday to observe the Passover.

b. **Such a Passover surely had never been held**: The celebration of the Passover had become so neglected that this was a remarkable observance.

i. The Passover remembered the central act of redemption in the Old Testament: God's deliverance of Israel from Egypt in the days of Moses. Their neglect of the Passover proved that they had neglected to remember the LORD's work of redemption for them. It was as if a group of modern Christians had completely forgotten communion or the celebration of the Lord's Supper, which remembers Jesus' work of redemption for us.

5. (24-25) The vast extent of Josiah's reforms.

Moreover Josiah put away those who consulted mediums and spiritists, the household gods and idols, all the abominations that were seen in the land of Judah and in Jerusalem, that he might perform the words of the law which were written in the book that Hilkiah the priest found in the house of the LORD**. Now before him there was no king like him, who turned to the L**ORD **with all his heart, with all his soul, and with all his might, according to all the Law of Moses; nor after him did** *any* **arise like him.**

a. **Moreover Josiah put away**: King Josiah also fulfilled the commandment of God to **put away** those who practiced the occult and spiritism. His passion was to **perform the words of the law which were written in the book**.

i. The great reformation in the days of Josiah is an example of simply going back to the word of God and seeking to base all thought and practice on what God has revealed in His word. It was an Old Testament example of the Reformation principle of *sola scriptura*.

b. **There was no king like him**: Josiah was one of the most remarkable kings of Judah, unique in the strength of his obedience and commitment. He stands as a wonderful example of what a leader can and should be.

i. There were other great kings of Judah and the united kingdom of Israel – such as David and Hezekiah. Yet one thing that made Josiah unique was his godliness *in his day*. He lived in a remarkably wicked time, so his godliness was remarkable against the backdrop of his times. "David was a *greater* but not a *better* man than Josiah." (Clarke)

ii. Nevertheless, not long after his reign, Judah was severely judged by the Lord. This shows that despite all Josiah's efforts, there was an *outward* conformity among the people of Judah, yet their *hearts* were not really turned towards the Lord. "They pretended and professed to do so; but most of them dissembled and dealt deceitfully, not turning to God with their whole hearts, as good Jeremiah complaineth." (Trapp)

iii. Jeremiah ministered in the days of Josiah, and his message to the people of Israel shows this. Through Jeremiah, God promised that if the people genuinely turned to Him that they would dwell in the land securely (Jeremiah 7:5-7). Nevertheless, God looked at the people of Judah and said: *Judah has not turned to Me with her whole heart, but in pretense.* (Jeremiah 3:10)

6. (26-27) God's promise of judgment.

Nevertheless the Lord did not turn from the fierceness of His great wrath, with which His anger was aroused against Judah, because of all the provocations with which Manasseh had provoked Him. And the Lord said, "I will also remove Judah from My sight, as I have removed Israel, and will cast off this city Jerusalem which I have chosen, and the house of which I said, 'My name shall be there.'"

a. **Nevertheless the Lord did not turn from the fierceness of His great wrath**: God did not turn from His wrath because despite Josiah's personal godliness, and his righteous example and leadership, the people of Judah still **provoked Him**, loving the sins introduced during the wicked days of Manasseh, Josiah's grandfather.

i. "From consultation with Huldah he knew that there would be no deep note or lasting value in their reformation. That fact, however, did not give him the right to refuse to follow the light which had come to him." (Morgan)

b. **I will also remove Judah from My sight**: God promised to bring Judah down, conquering by another and sending them into exile.

B. Josiah's end and his successors.

1. (28-30) Josiah dies in battle against Egypt.

Now the rest of the acts of Josiah, and all that he did, *are* they not written in the book of the chronicles of the kings of Judah? In his days Pharaoh Necho king of Egypt went to the aid of the king of Assyria, to the River Euphrates; and King Josiah went against him. And *Pharaoh Necho* killed him at Megiddo when he confronted him. Then his servants moved his body in a chariot from Megiddo, brought him to Jerusalem, and buried him in his own tomb. And the people of the land took Jehoahaz the son of Josiah, anointed him, and made him king in his father's place.

> a. **In his days Pharaoh Necho king of Egypt went to the aid of the king of Assyria**: This was part of the geopolitical struggle between the declining Assyrian Empire and the emerging Babylonian Empire. The Assyrians made an alliance with the Egyptians to protect against the growing power of the Babylonians.
>
> b. **King Josiah went against him… Pharaoh Necho killed him**: 2 Chronicles 35:20-25 tells us more about this. Pharaoh warned Josiah against battling against him saying, *What have I to do with you, king of Judah? I have not come against you this day*. Josiah stubbornly refused to hear this warning (which was actually from God) and disguised himself in battle – yet he was still shot by archers and died. This was a sad end to one of the great kings of Judah.
>
>> i. "It was not of faith, else why 'disguise' himself? There is no record of any prayer before the battle, as in the case of so many of his godly ancestors; and this rash act of Josiah seems unaccountable." (Knapp)
>>
>> ii. "The exact place of the battle seems to have been *Hadadrimmon*, in the valley of Megiddo, for there Zechariah tells us, chapter 12:11, was the great mourning for Josiah." (Clarke)
>
> c. **And the people of the land took Jehoahaz the son of Josiah, anointed him, and made him king in his father's place**: "The regular succession to the throne of Judah ceased with the lamented Josiah. Jehoahaz was not the eldest son of the late king. Johanan and Jehoiakim were both older than he (1 Chronicles 3:15). He was made king by popular choice: it was the preference of the multitude, not the appointment of God." (Knapp)
>
>> i. "Thus the people's sins were the true cause why God gave them wicked kings, whom he suffered to do wickedly, that they might bring the long deserved and threatened punishment upon themselves and their people." (Poole)

2. (31-34) The evil reign of Jehoahaz and his captivity to Egypt.

Jehoahaz *was* twenty-three years old when he became king, and he reigned three months in Jerusalem. His mother's name *was* Hamutal the daughter of Jeremiah of Libnah. And he did evil in the sight of the LORD, according to all that his fathers had done. Now Pharaoh Necho put him in prison at Riblah in the land of Hamath, that he might not reign in Jerusalem; and he imposed on the land a tribute of one hundred talents of silver and a talent of gold. Then Pharaoh Necho made Eliakim the son of Josiah king in place of his father Josiah, and changed his name to Jehoiakim. And *Pharaoh* took Jehoahaz and went to Egypt, and he died there.

a. **He did evil in the sight of the LORD**: The reforms of King Josiah were wonderful, but they were not a long-lasting revival. His own son Jehoahaz did not follow in his godly ways.

i. "*Jehoahaz* ('Yahweh has seized') was probably a throne name, for his personal name was Shallum (Jeremiah 22:11; 1 Chronicles 3:15). The practice of primogeniture was overridden in view of his older brother (Eliakim) showing anti-Egyptian tendencies." (Wiseman)

ii. "His name is omitted from among those of our Lord's ancestors in Matthew 1… which may imply that God did not recognize Jehoahaz, the people's choice, as being in a true sense the successor." (Knapp)

b. **How Pharaoh Necho put him in prison**: After the defeat of King Josiah in battle, Pharaoh was able to dominate Judah and make it effectively a vassal kingdom and a buffer against the growing Babylonian Empire. He **imposed on the land a tribute** and put on the throne of Judah a puppet king, a brother of Jehoahaz (**Eliakim**, renamed **Jehoiakim**).

3. (35-37) The reign of Jehoiakim over Judah.

So Jehoiakim gave the silver and gold to Pharaoh; but he taxed the land to give money according to the command of Pharaoh; he exacted the silver and gold from the people of the land, from every one according to his assessment, to give *it* to Pharaoh Necho. Jehoiakim *was* twenty-five years old when he became king, and he reigned eleven years in Jerusalem. His mother's name *was* Zebudah the daughter of Pedaiah of Rumah. And he did evil in the sight of the LORD, according to all that his fathers had done.

a. **He taxed the land according to the command of Pharaoh**: Jehoiakim was nothing more than a puppet king presiding over a vassal kingdom under the Egyptians. He imposed heavy taxes on the people and paid the money to the Egyptians, as required.

i. "Nechoh had placed him there as a viceroy, simply to *raise* and *collect his taxes*." (Clarke)

ii. "Yet at the same time Jehoiakim was wasting resources on the construction of a new palace by forced labour (Jeremiah 22:13-19)." (Wiseman)

b. **He did evil in the sight of the LORD**: Jehoiakim, like his brother Jehoahaz, did not follow the godly example of his father Josiah.

i. Jeremiah 36:22-24 describes the great ungodliness of Jehoiakim – how he even burned a scroll of God's word. In response to this, Jeremiah received this message from God: *And you shall say to Jehoiakim king of Judah, "Thus says the LORD: 'You have burned this scroll, saying, "Why have you written in it that the king of Babylon will certainly come and destroy this land, and cause man and beast to cease from here?"' Therefore thus says the LORD concerning Jehoiakim king of Judah: 'He shall have no one to sit on the throne of David, and his dead body shall be cast out to the heat of the day and the frost of the night.'"* (Jeremiah 36:29-30)

ii. "To all his former evils he added this, that he slew Urijah the prophet (Jeremiah 26:20, 23)." (Trapp)

2 Kings 24 – Judah Subjected Under Babylon

A. The reign of King Jehoiakim of Judah.

1. (1) Nebuchadnezzar makes Judah a vassal kingdom.

In his days Nebuchadnezzar king of Babylon came up, and Jehoiakim became his vassal *for* three years. Then he turned and rebelled against him.

> a. **Nebuchadnezzar king of Babylon came up**: Nebuchadnezzar, king of the Babylonian Empire, was concerned with Judah because of its strategic position in relation to the empires of Egypt and Assyria. Therefore it was important to him to conquer Judah and make it a subject kingdom (**his vassal**), securely loyal to Babylon.
>
>> i. Nebuchadnezzar came against Jerusalem because the Pharaoh of Egypt invaded Babylon. In response the young prince Nebuchadnezzar defeated the Egyptians at Charchemish, and then he pursued their fleeing army all the way down to the Sinai. Along the way (or on the way back), he subdued Jerusalem, who had been loyal to the Pharaoh of Egypt.
>>
>> ii. This happened in 605 B.C. and it was the first (but not the last) encounter between Nebuchadnezzar and Jehoiakim. There would be two later invasions (597 and 587 B.C.).
>>
>> iii. This specific attack is documented by the Babylonian Chronicles, a collection of tablets discovered as early as 1887, held in the British Museum. In them, Nebuchadnezzar's 605 B.C. presence in Judah is documented and clarified. When the Babylonian chronicles were finally published in 1956, they gave us first-rate, detailed political and military information about the first 10 years of Nebuchadnezzar's reign. L.W. King prepared these tablets in 1919; he then died, and they were neglected for four decades.

iv. Excavations also document the victory of Nebuchadnezzar over the Egyptians at Carchemish in May or June of 605 B.C. Archaeologists found evidences of battle, vast quantities of arrowheads, layers of ash, and a shield of a Greek mercenary fighting for the Egyptians.

v. This campaign of Nebuchadnezzar was interrupted suddenly when he heard of his father's death and raced back to Babylon to secure his succession to the throne. He traveled about 500 miles in two weeks – remarkable speed for travel in that day. Nebuchadnezzar only had the time to take a few choice captives (such as Daniel), a few treasures and a promise of submission from Jehoiakim.

b. **Then he turned and rebelled against him**: When Nebuchadnezzar had to make a hurried return to Babylon, Jehoiakim took advantage of his absence and **rebelled against him**.

2. (2-4) The troubled reign of Jehoiakim.

And the LORD sent against him *raiding* bands of Chaldeans, bands of Syrians, bands of Moabites, and bands of the people of Ammon; He sent them against Judah to destroy it, according to the word of the LORD which He had spoken by His servants the prophets. Surely at the commandment of the LORD *this* came upon Judah, to remove *them* from His sight because of the sins of Manasseh, according to all that he had done, and also because of the innocent blood that he had shed; for he had filled Jerusalem with innocent blood, which the LORD would not pardon.

a. **The LORD sent against him**: We might think that God would honor the Judean independence movement of Jehoiakim, but He did not bless it. God **sent against him** many adversaries because Jehoiakim was a patriot of the kingdom of Judah, but not a man submitted to God.

i. **Bands of Syrians, bands of Moabites, and bands of the people of Ammon**: "Nebuchadnezzar's army was made up of several nations, who were willing to fight under the banner of such a puissant and victorious emperor." (Poole)

b. **Surely at the commandment of the LORD this came upon Judah**: Many in the days of Jehoiakim believed that God's will was to deliver them from their enemies and to preserve an independent Judah. Yet that was not God's will; it was His will to bring Judah into judgment (knowing they had not genuinely repented and would not). The best thing for Judah to do was to *submit* to this will of God, as Jeremiah told them to do – despite great opposition.

c. **Also because of the innocent blood that he had shed**: This tells us that one of the great sins of Manasseh was that he persecuted the godly in his day, and **he had filled Jerusalem with innocent blood.**

i. "His name, like that of his brother, is omitted from the royal genealogy of Matthew 1." (Knapp)

3. (5-7) The passing of Jehoiakim.

Now the rest of the acts of Jehoiakim, and all that he did, *are* they not written in the book of the chronicles of the kings of Judah? So Jehoiakim rested with his fathers. Then Jehoiachin his son reigned in his place. And the king of Egypt did not come out of his land anymore, for the king of Babylon had taken all that belonged to the king of Egypt from the Brook of Egypt to the River Euphrates.

a. **Now the rest of the acts of Jehoiakim**: 2 Chronicles 36:6 tells us that Nebuchadnezzar intended to take Jehoiakim to Babylon, bound in bronze fetters. Yet Jeremiah 22:19 tells us that he would be disgracefully buried outside of Jerusalem.

i. "The closing formulae make no reference to the burial of Jehoiakim, whose death occurred about December 598 before the first capture of Jerusalem by Nebuchadnezzar. 2 Chronicles 36:7 implies that he was taken to Babylon, but Jeremiah 22:19 tells how he was thrown unmourned outside Jerusalem, perhaps by a pro-Babylonian group who gave him the unceremonial burial of 'an ass'." (Wiseman)

ii. "2 Chronicles 36:6 states that Nebuchadnezzar 'bound him in fetters, to carry him to Babylon.' It does not say he *was* taken there. He may have been released after promising subjection to his conqueror." (Knapp)

b. **The king of Egypt did not come out of his land anymore**: In the geopolitical struggle between Egypt and Babylon, Nebuchadnezzar defeated Egypt. They were then the dominant power in that part of the world.

i. "About three years later, in 601 B.C., Egypt tried one more time to return to power by attacking Babylon's army… It was after this brief Egyptian victory that Jehoiakim, hoping to renew his alliance with the Pharaoh against Babylon, rebelled against Nebuchadnezzar (2 Kings 24:3), an action Jeremiah sharply condemned." (Dilday)

B. The reign of Jehoiachin.

1. (8-9) Jehoiachin, another evil king over Judah.

Jehoiachin *was* **eighteen years old when he became king, and he reigned in Jerusalem three months. His mother's name** *was* **Nehushta the daughter of Elnathan of Jerusalem. And he did evil in the sight of the Lord, according to all that his father had done.**

> a. **Jehoiachin was eighteen years old when he became king**: 2 Chronicles 36:9 says that *Jehoiachin was eight years old when he became king*. The difference between these two accounts is probably due to the error of a copyist in Chronicles.
>
>> i. "2 Chronicles 36:9 makes him eight years old at the beginning of his reign… But some Hebrew MSS., Syriac, and Arabic, read 'eighteen' in Chronicles' so 'eight' must be an error of transcription." (Knapp)
>>
>> ii. Jehoiachin "was probably the throne-name of Jeconiah, abbreviated also to Coniah." (Wiseman)
>
> b. **And he did evil in the sight of the Lord**: He carried on in the tradition of the wicked kings of Judah.
>
>> i. "That he was a grievous offender against God, we learn from Jeremiah 22:24, which the reader may consult; and in the man's punishment, see his crimes." (Clarke)

2. (10-12) Jehoiachin surrenders to Nebuchadnezzar.

At that time the servants of Nebuchadnezzar king of Babylon came up against Jerusalem, and the city was besieged. And Nebuchadnezzar king of Babylon came against the city, as his servants were besieging it. Then Jehoiachin king of Judah, his mother, his servants, his princes, and his officers went out to the king of Babylon; and the king of Babylon, in the eighth year of his reign, took him prisoner.

> a. **Then Jehoiachin… went out to the king of Babylon**: The previous king of Judah (Jehoiakim) led a rebellion against Nebuchadnezzar. Now **the king of Babylon** came with his armies against Jerusalem, and Jehoiachin hoped to appease Nebuchadnezzar by submitting himself, his family, and his leaders to the Babylonian king.
>
> b. **Took him prisoner**: Like his rebellious father, God allowed Jehoiachin to be taken as a bound captive back to Babylon.
>
>> i. "His presence in Babylon is attested by tablets listing oil and barley supplies to him, his family and five sons in 592-569 B.C. and naming him as 'Yaukin king of the Judeans.'" (Wiseman)

3. (13-16) Jerusalem is impoverished and taken captive.

And he carried out from there all the treasures of the house of the Lord and the treasures of the king's house, and he cut in pieces all the articles

of gold which Solomon king of Israel had made in the temple of the LORD, as the LORD had said. Also he carried into captivity all Jerusalem: all the captains and all the mighty men of valor, ten thousand captives, and all the craftsmen and smiths. None remained except the poorest people of the land. And he carried Jehoiachin captive to Babylon. The king's mother, the king's wives, his officers, and the mighty of the land he carried into captivity from Jerusalem to Babylon. All the valiant men, seven thousand, and craftsmen and smiths, one thousand, all *who were* strong *and* fit for war, these the king of Babylon brought captive to Babylon.

a. **And he carried out from there all the treasures of the house of the LORD and the treasures of the king's house**: On this second attack against Jerusalem, Nebuchadnezzar took whatever valuables remained in the temple or in the royal palaces of Jerusalem.

i. "The fall of Jerusalem didn't come about in one cataclysmic battle; it occurred in stages." (Dilday)

- Nebuchadnezzar initially subjugated the city about 605 B.C.
- Destruction from Nebuchadnezzar's marauding bands followed from 601 to 598 B.C.
- The siege and fall of Jerusalem occurred under Nebuchadnezzar's main army on 16 March, 597 B.C.
- Nebuchadnezzar returned to completely destroy and depopulate Jerusalem in the summer of 586 B.C.

b. **He cut in pieces all the articles of gold which Solomon king of Israel had made**: This tells us what happened to the furniture and precious things of Solomon's temple. Some ancient traditions tell us that Jeremiah hid the ark of the covenant before this, so that it was not among the things that were cut up and carried back to Babylon.

c. **None remained except the poorest people of the land**: Nebuchadnezzar not only took the *material* treasures of Judah, but also the *human* treasures. Anyone with any skill or ability was taken captive to Babylon.

i. "The like craft useth the devil, when he endeavoureth to take out of the way such as are zealous and active, valiant for God's truth, and violent for his kingdom." (Trapp)

ii. Among these captives was the Prophet Ezekiel, who compiled his book of prophecies while in captivity in Babylon.

iii. "With only the poor and unskilled people of the land remaining, it might be assumed that Jerusalem would cause no further trouble." (Patterson and Austel)

C. The reign of Zedekiah.

1. (17) Nebuchadnezzar makes Zedekiah king of Judah.

Then the king of Babylon made Mattaniah, *Jehoiachin's* uncle, king in his place, and changed his name to Zedekiah.

a. **Then the king of Babylon made Mattaniah, Jehoiachin's uncle, king in his place**: Since Nebuchadnezzar had completely humbled Judah, he put a king on the throne whom he thought would submit to Babylon. He chose an uncle of Jehoiachin, a brother to Jehoiakim.

i. "This king (597-587 B.C.) inherited a much reduced Judah, for the Negeb was lost (Jeremiah 13:18-19) and the land weakened by the loss of its experienced personnel. There were both a pro-Egyptian element and false prophets among the survivors (Jeremiah 28-29; 38:5)." (Wiseman)

b. **Changed his name to Zedekiah**: The name **Zedekiah** means, *The Lord is Righteous*. The righteous judgment of God would soon be seen against Judah.

2. (18-20) The evil reign and rebellion of Zedekiah.

Zedekiah *was* twenty-one years old when he became king, and he reigned eleven years in Jerusalem. His mother's name *was* Hamutal the daughter of Jeremiah of Libnah. He also did evil in the sight of the LORD, according to all that Jehoiakim had done. For because of the anger of the LORD *this* happened in Jerusalem and Judah, that He finally cast them out from His presence. Then Zedekiah rebelled against the king of Babylon.

a. **He also did evil in the sight of the LORD**: 2 Chronicles 36:11-20 tells us more of the evil of Zedekiah, specifically that he did not listen to Jeremiah or other messengers of God. Instead, they mocked and disregarded the message.

i. "Zedekiah's *evil* (v. 19) is fully explained in 2 Chronicles 36:12-14. (i) He was not willing to listen to God's word through Jeremiah; (ii) he broke an oath made in Yahweh's name as a vassal of Babylon; (iii) he was unrepentant and failed to restrain leaders and priests from defiling the temple with the reintroduction of idolatrous practices." (Wiseman)

b. He finally cast them out from His presence: God's patience and longsuffering had finally run its course and He allowed – even instigated – the conquering of the kingdom of Judah.

i. Ultimately, there were many reasons for the exile. One mentioned by 2 Chronicles 36:21 is that Judah was depopulated in exile *to fulfill the word of the* L<small>ORD</small> *by the mouth of Jeremiah, until the land had enjoyed her Sabbaths. As long as she lay desolate she kept Sabbath, to fulfill seventy years.*

c. Zedekiah rebelled against the king of Babylon: Jeremiah tells us that there were many false prophets in those days who preached a message of victory and triumph to Zedekiah, and he believed them instead of Jeremiah and other godly prophets like him. Therefore, he **rebelled against the king of Babylon.**

i. For example, Jeremiah 32:1-5 tells us that Jeremiah clearly told Zedekiah that he would not succeed in his rebellion against Babylon. Zedekiah arrested Jeremiah and imprisoned him for this, but the prophet steadfastly stayed faithful to the message God gave him.

ii. "He had no real faith in Jehovah, Israel's covenant-keeping God, and therefore did not scruple to break his covenant with Nebuchadnezzar. But how dearly he paid for this violation of his oath!" (Knapp)

2 Kings 25 – The Fall of Jerusalem and the Captivity of Judah

A. Jerusalem is conquered.

1. (1-3) Jerusalem under siege.

Now it came to pass in the ninth year of his reign, in the tenth month, on the tenth *day* of the month, *that* Nebuchadnezzar king of Babylon and all his army came against Jerusalem and encamped against it; and they built a siege wall against it all around. So the city was besieged until the eleventh year of King Zedekiah. By the ninth *day* of the *fourth* month the famine had become so severe in the city that there was no food for the people of the land.

a. **They built a siege wall against it all around**: Nebuchadnezzar used the common method of attack in those days of securely walled cities – a **siege wall**. A siege was intended to surround a city, prevent all business and trade from entering or leaving the city, and to eventually starve the population into surrender.

i. "The Babylonians relied initially on tight control using 'watch towers' rather than *siege works*, allowing those who wished to leave to do so (*cf.* 2 Kings 25:11; Jeremiah 38:19; 39:9), but starving out the city (Jeremiah 38:2-9)." (Wiseman)

ii. **In the ninth year of his reign**: "This is the first time in Kings that an event in the history of Israel is dated by a foreign era." (Dilday)

b. **The famine had become so severe in the city**: This was the intended goal of a siege. This indicates that Nebuchadnezzar and the Babylonians were at the point of victory over Jerusalem.

i. "The one-and-a-half-year siege may be due to (i) Nebuchadnezzar's absence at Riblah and concern with containing the Phoenician seaports, and (ii) his watchfulness against Egypt's potential intervention on behalf of Zedekiah (Jeremiah 37:5, 11)." (Wiseman)

2. (4-7) Zedekiah is captured and executed.

Then the city wall was broken through, and all the men of war *fled* at night by way of the gate between two walls, which was by the king's garden, even though the Chaldeans *were* still encamped all around against the city. And *the king* went by way of the plain. But the army of the Chaldeans pursued the king, and they overtook him in the plains of Jericho. All his army was scattered from him. So they took the king and brought him up to the king of Babylon at Riblah, and they pronounced judgment on him. Then they killed the sons of Zedekiah before his eyes, put out the eyes of Zedekiah, bound him with bronze fetters, and took him to Babylon.

a. **Then the city wall was broken through**: At this desperate point for Judah during the siege of Jerusalem, Zedekiah made a last-chance effort to escape the grip of the nearly-completely successful siege. They planned a secret break through the city walls and the siege lines of the Babylonians, using a diversionary tactic.

i. "It seems that the army scattered to avoid capture; some link the prophecy of Obadiah 2-14 about Edom to this time." (Wiseman)

b. **The army of the Chaldeans pursued the king, and they overtook him in the plains of Jericho**: This was a considerable distance from Jerusalem. Zedekiah probably thought that his strategy was successful, and that he had escaped the judgment that prophets such as Jeremiah had promised. Yet God's word was demonstrated to be true, and he was captured **in the plains of Jericho**.

i. "It seems ironic that here, at the very spot where Israel first set foot on the Promised Land, the last of the Davidic kings was captured and his monarchy shattered. Here, where Israel experienced her first victory as the walls of Jericho fell before unarmed men who trusted God, was the scene of her last defeat." (Dilday)

c. **Then they killed the sons of Zedekiah before his eyes, put out the eyes of Zedekiah**: The Babylonians were not known to be as cruel as the Assyrians who conquered the Northern Kingdom of Israel some 150 years earlier, but they were still experts in cruelty in their own right. They made certain that the last sight King Zedekiah saw was the murder of his own sons, and then he spent the rest of his life in darkness.

i. This fulfilled the mysterious promise God made through Ezekiel regarding Zedekiah shortly before the fall of Jerusalem: *I will also spread My net over him, and he shall be caught in My snare. I will bring him to Babylon, to the land of the Chaldeans; yet he shall not see it, though he shall die there.* (Ezekiel 12:13)

ii. "This also fulfilled Ezekiel's prophecy that Zedekiah would be taken to Babylon but not see it (Ezekiel 12:13). Blinding prisoners was a rare occurrence (*cf.* Judges 16:21), for most were put to work. If Zedekiah had heeded the prophet's word, he would have saved both Jerusalem and himself (Jeremiah 38:14-28), for he was to die in Babylon (Ezekiel 12:14)." (Wiseman)

iii. "With his eyes put out, and bound in fetters, he was carried to the court of the conqueror, the symbol of the people who had rebelled against God, and had been broken in pieces." (Morgan)

iv. "The eyes of whose mind had been put out long before; else he might have foreseen and prevented this evil – as prevision is the best means of prevention, – had he taken warning by what was foretold." (Trapp)

v. "Josephus (*Antiquities* x.8.8) says Nebuchadnezzar 'kept Zedekiah in prison until he died; and then buried him magnificently.' This agrees with Jeremiah 34:5." (Knapp)

3. (8-10) The destruction of Jerusalem.

And in the fifth month, on the seventh *day* **of the month (which** *was* **the nineteenth year of King Nebuchadnezzar king of Babylon), Nebuzaradan the captain of the guard, a servant of the king of Babylon, came to Jerusalem. He burned the house of the L**ORD **and the king's house; all the houses of Jerusalem, that is, all the houses of the great, he burned with fire. And all the army of the Chaldeans who** *were with* **the captain of the guard broke down the walls of Jerusalem all around.**

a. **He burned the house of the L**ORD: Solomon's great temple was now a ruin. It would stay a ruin for many years, until it was humbly rebuilt by the returning exiles in the days of Ezra.

i. "The Talmud declares that when the Babylonians entered the temple, they held a two-day feast there to desecrate it; then, on the third day, they set fire to the building. The Talmud adds that the fire burned throughout that day and the next." (Dilday)

ii. "Thus the temple was destroyed in the *eleventh* year of Zedekiah, the *nineteenth* of Nebuchadnezzar, the *first* of the XLVIIIth Olympiad, in the *one hundred and sixtieth* current year of the era of Nabonassar, *four hundred and twenty-four* years *three* months and *eight* days from the time in which Solomon laid its foundation stone." (Clarke)

b. **Broke down the walls of Jerusalem all around**: The walls of Jerusalem – the physical security of the city – were now destroyed. Jerusalem was no longer a place of safety and security. The walls would remain a ruin until they were rebuilt by the returning exiles in the days of Nehemiah.

> i. On **Nebuzaradan the captain of the guard**: "That title in Hebrew is literally, 'the chief executioner' or 'the slaughterer.' Methodically, he set about to demolish the beautiful city, burning the palace and the chief buildings, breaking down the walls, and wrecking the temple." (Dilday)

4. (11-17) The remainder is taken captive and plundered.

Then Nebuzaradan the captain of the guard carried away captive the rest of the people *who* remained in the city and the defectors who had deserted to the king of Babylon, with the rest of the multitude. But the captain of the guard left *some* of the poor of the land as vinedressers and farmers. The bronze pillars that *were* in the house of the LORD, and the carts and the bronze Sea that *were* in the house of the LORD, the Chaldeans broke in pieces, and carried their bronze to Babylon. They also took away the pots, the shovels, the trimmers, the spoons, and all the bronze utensils with which the priests ministered. The firepans and the basins, the things of solid gold and solid silver, the captain of the guard took away. The two pillars, one Sea, and the carts, which Solomon had made for the house of the LORD, the bronze of all these articles was beyond measure. The height of one pillar *was* eighteen cubits, and the capital on it *was* of bronze. The height of the capital was three cubits, and the network and pomegranates all around the capital were all of bronze. The second pillar was the same, with a network.

> a. **Carried away captive the rest of the people who remained in the city**: This was the third major wave of captivity, taking the remaining people all except for the **poor of the land**.
>
> > i. "Of the prominent men of Jerusalem, only Jeremiah and Gedaliah were left behind (2 Kings 25:22; cf. Jeremiah 39:11-14). Jeremiah's stand on the Babylonian issue was doubtless well-known." (Dilday)
> >
> > ii. "In Hebrew, the first twelve verses of the chapter are one long sentence, each verse beginning with 'and.' Clause is heaped upon clause in a kind of cadence, as if each one were another tick of the clock counting down Jerusalem's final hours." (Dilday)
>
> b. **And carried their bronze to Babylon… the things of solid gold and solid silver, the captain of the guard took away**: As the remaining people were taken captive to Babylon, so also the remaining valuables from the

temple were taken. Jerusalem was left desolate, completely plundered under the judgment of God.

> i. Jeremiah 52:17-23 is a detailed inventory of all that the Babylonians looted from the temple.

5. (18-21) The authority of Nebuchadnezzar over Jerusalem and Judah.

And the captain of the guard took Seraiah the chief priest, Zephaniah the second priest, and the three doorkeepers. He also took out of the city an officer who had charge of the men of war, five men of the king's close associates who were found in the city, the chief recruiting officer of the army, who mustered the people of the land, and sixty men of the people of the land *who were* found in the city. So Nebuzaradan, captain of the guard, took these and brought them to the king of Babylon at Riblah. Then the king of Babylon struck them and put them to death at Riblah in the land of Hamath. Thus Judah was carried away captive from its own land.

> a. **The king of Babylon struck them and put them to death**: These last leaders of Jerusalem and Judah were also captured and put to death. The **king of Babylon** had what seemed to be complete rule over the former kingdom of Judah.

> b. **Thus Judah was carried away captive from its own land**: This was the land God gave to His people, the tribes of Israel. They had possessed this land for some 860 years; they took it by faith and obedience but they lost it through idolatry and sin.

>> i. "The reader cannot help but be struck by the passionless tone of the narrative in this chapter. Not once does the author show his feelings, even though he is describing the tragic downfall of his country. We have to turn to the Book of Lamentations for weeping and groaning." (Dilday)

>> ii. "Thus the nation called to peculiar position of honor, became a people scattered and peeled, losing all their privileges because of their failure to fulfill responsibility." (Morgan)

>> iii. "Israel wanted to be as the other nations around her, imitating their organization, and allying herself now with one, and then with another; in consequence she was swept into captivity to the very nation whose fashions she most affected (Isaiah 39)." (Meyer)

>> iv. "And thus was Judah carried away out of her own land *four hundred and sixty-eight* years after David began to reign over it; from the division of the ten tribes *three hundred and eighty-eight* years; and from

the destruction of the kingdom of Israel, *one hundred and thirty-four years… and before Christ five hundred and ninety.*" (Clarke)

B. Judah and Jerusalem under the Babylonians.

1. (22-24) Gedaliah is made the governor.

Then he made Gedaliah the son of Ahikam, the son of Shaphan, governor over the people who remained in the land of Judah, whom Nebuchadnezzar king of Babylon had left. Now when all the captains of the armies, they and *their* men, heard that the king of Babylon had made Gedaliah governor, they came to Gedaliah at Mizpah—Ishmael the son of Nethaniah, Johanan the son of Careah, Seraiah the son of Tanhumeth the Netophathite, and Jaazaniah the son of a Maachathite, they and their men. And Gedaliah took an oath before them and their men, and said to them, "Do not be afraid of the servants of the Chaldeans. Dwell in the land and serve the king of Babylon, and it shall be well with you."

> a. **The king of Babylon had made Gedaliah governor**: It seems that Gedaliah was a good and godly man, who was a friend of the prophet Jeremiah (Jeremiah 26:24 and 39:14).
>
>> i. "Gedaliah had the reputation of being gentle and generous (Josephus, *Antiquities* x.9.1) and his enemies played on this." (Wiseman)
>
> b. **Dwell in the land and serve the king of Babylon, and it shall be well with you**: It seemed unpatriotic and perhaps ungodly to do this, but it was the right thing to do. The best they could do under this situation of deserved and unstoppable judgment was to simply accept it from the hand of God and do the right thing under the Babylonians.
>
>> i. It was the right thing to do because although it was hard to accept, it was true that the Babylonians were doing the work of God in bringing this judgment upon the deserving kingdom of Judah. In this situation, to resist the Babylonians was to resist God. It was better to humble oneself and to submit to the judgment of God brought through the Babylonians.
>>
>> ii. This was the question that bothered the prophet Habakkuk so much: Even though Judah was wicked and deserved judgment, how could God use an even more wicked kingdom like Babylon to bring judgment? Habakkuk dealt with these difficult questions in Habakkuk 1:5-2:8.

2. (25-26) The assassination of Gedaliah.

But it happened in the seventh month that Ishmael the son of Nethaniah, the son of Elishama, of the royal family, came with ten men and struck and killed Gedaliah, the Jews, as well as the Chaldeans who were with him at Mizpah. And all the people, small and great, and the captains of the armies, arose and went to Egypt; for they were afraid of the Chaldeans.

- a. **Came with ten men and struck and killed Gedaliah**: Because Gedaliah led the remaining people of Judah to submit to the Babylonians (also here called **the Chaldeans**), he was assassinated as a traitor to the resistance movement against the Babylonians.

- b. **All the people… arose and went to Egypt**: They did this because they were afraid of what the Babylonians would do to them in light of the assassination of Gedaliah the governor. In this case, going **to Egypt** was worse than submitting to the judgment of God brought through the Babylonians.

    - i. "The existence of the Jews in Egypt in the fifth century is now illustrated by the Elephantine Papyri." (Dilday)

3. (27-30) Jehoiachin's situation in Babylon improves.

Now it came to pass in the thirty-seventh year of the captivity of Jehoiachin king of Judah, in the twelfth month, on the twenty-seventh *day* **of the month,** *that* **Evil-Merodach king of Babylon, in the year that he began to reign, released Jehoiachin king of Judah from prison. He spoke kindly to him, and gave him a more prominent seat than those of the kings who** *were* **with him in Babylon. So Jehoiachin changed from his prison garments, and he ate bread regularly before the king all the days of his life. And as for his provisions,** *there was* **a regular ration given him by the king, a portion for each day, all the days of his life.**

- a. **In the thirty-seventh year of the captivity of Jehoiachin king of Judah**: This King **Jehoiachin** was not the last king of Judah; Zedekiah came after him. But he was taken away to Babylon in bronze fetters (2 Kings 24:10-12). These last events of 2 Kings came when Jehoiachin had been a captive for many years.

    - i. "Since he was seemingly considered by the Judeans the last legitimate king, news of his later condition would be of great significance." (Dilday)

- b. **Released Jehoiachin king of Judah from prison… spoke kindly to him, and gave him a more prominent seat**: The final words of the Book of 2 Kings describe small kindnesses and blessings given in the worst circumstances. Judah was still depopulated; the people of God were still exiled; and the king of Judah was still a prisoner in Babylon. Yet, looking for even small notes of grace and mercy as evidences of the returning favor of God, the divine historian noted that King Jehoiachin began to receive better treatment in Babylon.

i. "This resulted from an agreement (MT, 'spoke good (things) with him') rather than just generally *spoke kindly to him*." (Wiseman)

ii. "The Rabbins tell us that, his father returning to his right mind, after that he had for seven years' space been turned a-grazing among the beasts of the field, cast Evil-merodach into the same prison with Jehoiachin, who told him his case, and thereby found this favour with him." (Trapp)

iii. "This second appendix is added to remind the reader that while Jehoiachin was still in Babylon as the representative of David's dynasty God still preserved his people. Some see this as intended to end the history on a hopeful note, perhaps even of 'Messianic revival'." (Wiseman)

iv. This was small, but evidence nonetheless that God was not done blessing and restoring His people, foreshadowing even greater blessing and restoration to come.

v. "Is it to be supposed that the king of Babylon took more care of Jehoiachin than God will take care of us?" (Meyer)

2 Kings – Bibliography

Clarke, Adam *The Holy Bible, Containing the Old and New Testaments, with A Commentary and Critical Notes, Volume II – Joshua to Esther* (New York: Eaton and Mains, 1827?)

Cook, F.C. (Editor) *The Bible Commentary, 1 Samuel – Esther* (Grand Rapids, Michigan: Baker Book House, 1974)

Dilday, Russell *Mastering the Old Testament Volume 9: 1, 2 Kings* (Dallas: Word Publishing, 1987)

Ginzberg, Louis *The Legends of the Jews, Volumes 1-7* (Philadelphia: The Jewish Publication Society of America, 1968)

Knapp, Christopher *The Kings of Judah and Israel* (New York: Loizeaux Brothers, 1956)

Maclaren, Alexander *Expositions of Holy Scripture, Volume 2* (Grand Rapids, Michigan: Baker Book House, 1984)

Meyer, F.B. *Our Daily Homily* (Westwood, New Jersey: Revell, 1966)

Meyer, F.B. *Elijah: And the Secret of His Power* (Fort Washington, Pennsylvania: Christian Literature Crusade, 1978)

Morgan, G. Campbell *Searchlights from the Word* (New York: Revell, 1926)

Patterson, Richard D. and Austel, Hermann J. "1, 2 Kings" *The Expositor's Bible Commentary, Volume 4* (Grand Rapids, Michigan: Zondervan, 1992)

Payne, David F. *Kingdoms of the Lord* (Grand Rapids, Michigan: Eerdmans, 1981)

Poole, Matthew *A Commentary on the Holy Bible, Volume 1* (London, Banner of Truth Trust, 1968)

Spurgeon, Charles Haddon *The New Park Street Pulpit, Volumes 1-6* and *The Metropolitan Tabernacle Pulpit, Volumes 7-63* (Pasadena, Texas: Pilgrim Publications, 1990)

Trapp, John *A Commentary on the Old and New Testaments, Volume 1 – Genesis to Second Chronicles* (Eureka, California: Tanski Publications, 1997)

Wiseman, Donald J. *1 and 2 Kings, An Introduction and Commentary* (Leicester, England: Inter-Varsity Press, 1993)

As the years pass I love the work of studying, learning, and teaching the Bible more than ever. I'm so grateful that God is faithful to meet me in His Word.

This print edition of 2 Kings welcomes a new proofreader to my work. Thank you, Mary Osgood! The time and skill you gave to this book made it better. I so appreciate your support and eye for detail.

Thanks to Brian Procedo for the cover design and all the graphics work.

Most especially, thanks to my wife Inga-Lill. She is my loved and valued partner in life and service to God and His people.

David Guzik's Bible commentary is regularly used and trusted by many thousands who want to know the Bible better. Pastors, teachers, class leaders, and everyday Christians find his commentary helpful for their own understanding and explanation of the Bible. David and his wife Inga-Lill live in Santa Barbara, California.

You can email David at
david@enduringword.com

For more resources by David Guzik,
go to www.enduringword.com

www.ingramcontent.com/pod-product-compliance
Lightning Source LLC
Chambersburg PA
CBHW032110090426
42743CB00007B/302